FINGER LAKES WINERIES
A PICTORIAL HISTORY

Emerson Klees

Emerson Klees

Cameo Press Imprint

Friends of the Finger Lakes Publishing
Rochester, New York

Friends of the Finger Lakes Publishing
P. O. Box 18131
Rochester, New York 14618

Library of Congress Control Number 2013951719

ISBN 978-1-891046-22-3

Printed in the United States of America
9 8 7 6 5 4 3 2 1

ACKNOWLEDGMENTS

The author is indebted to the following for the contribution of photographs: Greyton H. Taylor Wine Museum for photographs of Taylor Wine Company, Walter S. Taylor, and Paul Garrett; Dr. Frank Vinifera Wine Cellars; Naples Public Library for the Widmer photographs; Glenn H. Curtiss Museum; Hammondsport Public Library; Steuben County Historical Museum; Yates County Historical Museum; and Martin Schlaubach of Cornell University. Jerry Guarino of Patrick Printing provided invaluable assistance in preparing the photographs for publication.

Other Books by Emerson Klees

The Human Values Series

Role Models of Human Values

One Plus One Equals Three—Pairing Man / Woman Strengths:
  Role Models of Teamwork
Entrepreneurs in History—Success vs. Failure:
  Entrepreneurial Role Models
Staying With It: Role Models of Perseverance
The Drive to Succeed: Role Models of Motivation
The Will to Stay With It: Role Models of Determination
Emotional Intelligence: People Smart Role Models
Emotional Intelligence II: People Smart Role Models
Emotional Intelligence III: People Smart Role Models
A Song of the Vine: A Reflection on Life

The Moral Navigator

Inspiring Legends and Tales With a Moral I: Stories From
  Around the World
Inspiring Legends and Tales With a Moral II: Stories From
  Around the World
Inspiring Legends and Tales With a Moral III: Stories From
  Around the World

Books about New York State and the Finger Lakes Region

People of the Finger Lakes Region
Legends and Stories of the Finger Lakes Region
The Erie Canal in the Finger Lakes Region
Underground Railroad Tales With Routes Through the
  Finger Lakes Region
More Legends and Stories of the Finger Lakes Region
The Women's Rights Movement and the Finger Lakes Region
Persons, Places, and Things In the Finger Lakes Region (2000)
The Crucible of Ferment: New York's Psychic Highway
The Iroquois Confederacy: History and Legends
Rochester Lives
Wineries of the Finger Lakes Region—100 Wineries
Persons, Places, and Things Of the Finger Lakes Region (2008)
Paul Garrett: Dean of American Winemakers

PREFACE

Finger Lakes Wineries, A Pictorial History is a collection of photographs of grape growing and winemaking in New York's Finger Lakes Region. This heart-shaped area is bounded the Route 390 Expressway in the west, the New York State Thruway in the north, Route 81 Expressway and Route 13 in the east, and the Southern Tier Expressway (Route 17 / I-86) in the south.

The Finger Lakes Region, an area of scenic lake-country beauty, provides diverse vacation opportunities in a region comprised of 14 counties, 264 municipalities, and over 9,000 square miles. Sites and activities in the region include parks, forests, and trails; shows and festivals; lake cruises and boating; waterfalls; museums; historic sites; and fishing and water sports, in addition to wineries.

The number of wineries in the Finger Lakes Region has grown from 19 in 1975 to over 120 in 2013. Wineries have become the top-ranked tourist destination in the region.

This book provides a history of the early wineries, such as Taylor Wine Company, Pleasant Valley Wine Company, and Urbana / Gold Seal wineries in Hammondsport and Widmer Wine Cellars in Naples. The many wineries that went out of business during Prohibition are discussed as well as Paul Garrett's Garrett & Company, which moved north to Penn Yan. Walter S. Taylor of Bully Hill Vineyards, promoter of French-American hybrid varieties of grapes, and Dr. Konstantin Frank, cool-climate pioneer and driver of the renaissance with European varieties, are highlighted.

The many wineries that were the result of the 1976 Farm Winery Act as well as wineries founded by entrepreneurs and vintners from outside the region are discussed. The Epilogue addresses the recent changes and future trends in the region. The Appendix provides a description of grape varieties and a glossary of grape and wine terms.

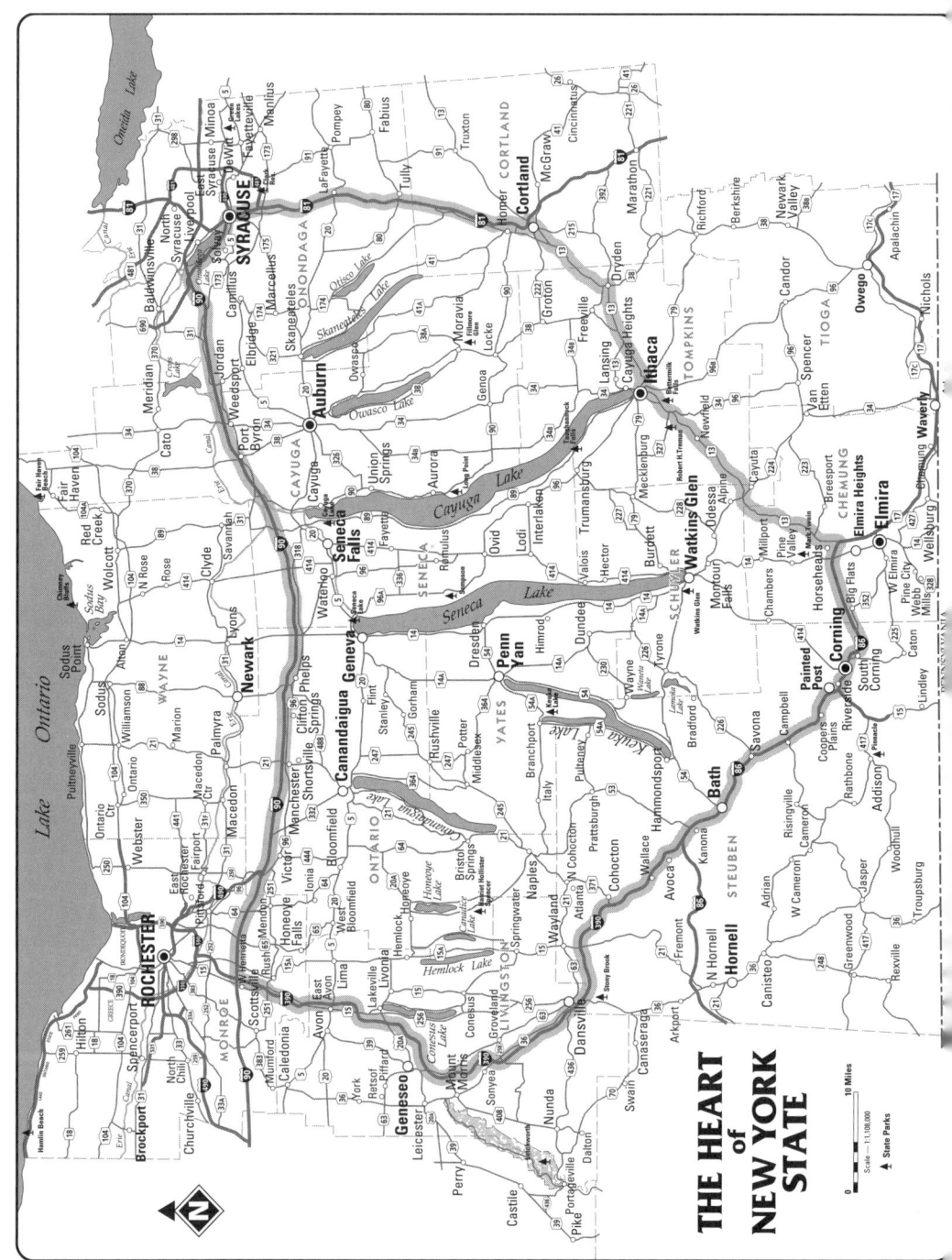

THE HEART
of
NEW YORK STATE

FINGER LAKES WINERIES, A PICTORIAL HISTORY

TABLE OF CONTENTS

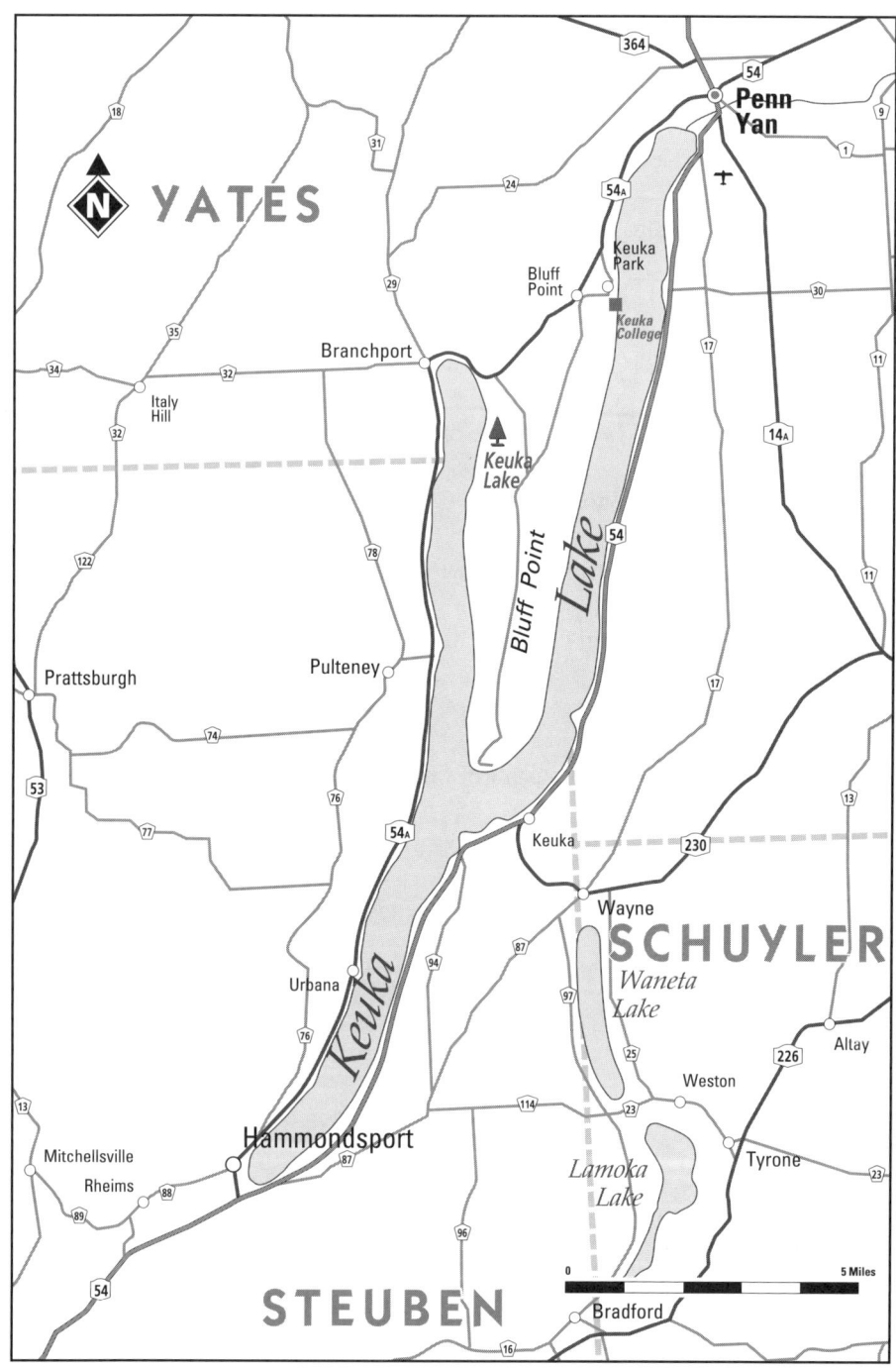

INTRODUCTION

In 1829 in the rectory garden of St. James Episcopal Church in Hammondsport, New York, Reverend William Bostwick introduced the first grapevines to the Finger Lakes Region. He planted Catawba and Isabella vines from the Hudson Valley. In 1853, Andrew Reisinger, a German vineyardist, planted two acres of Catawba and Isabella in Pulteney, north of Hammondsport. The first to do so in the area, Reisinger plowed his vineyard soil, erected trellises, and pruned his vines. He became a pioneer in training grapevines. Other vineyardists, observing his success, followed his example.

The first Finger Lakes Region bonded winery was the Pleasant Valley Wine Company, producer of Great Western Champagne, which began commercial production of wine in 1860 in Pleasant Valley, south of Hammondsport. Charles Champlin, the French winemaker who founded Pleasant Valley Wine Company, was granted U. S. Winery License No. 1. In *Wines of America,* Leon Adams described the origin of the name, "Great Western":

> In 1870, the Masson brothers, Joseph and Jules, served a new sparkling blend of Delaware and Catawba to a meeting of the Pleasant Valley Grape Growers Association. Presiding at the meeting was the famed horticulturalist Colonel Marshall Wilder of Boston, who, on tasting the wine, exclaimed: "Truly, this will be the great champagne of the West!" By West, Wilder explained that he meant "our entire continent," the New World. His remark gave Great Western its name, strange though it seems for a product of New York State. In 1873 at the Vienna Exposition, Great Western became the first American champagne to win a gold medal in Europe, and it later gathered prizes at Brussels, Philadelphia, and at the Exposition Universale in Paris.

The Urbana Wine Company, renamed Gold Seal Winery in 1887, was founded in Pleasant Valley, Hammondsport, in 1865 by Guy McMaster and Clark Bell. In 1880, Walter Taylor and his wife, Addie, founded Taylor Wine Company on Bully Hill, north of Hammondsport, and began to produce wine.

In 1846, Edward McKay planted 150 Isabella vines at Naples, at the southern end of Canandaigua Lake. The vines prospered and an industry grew.

John Jacob Widmer and his wife, Lisette, founders of Widmers Wine Cellars, emigrated from the Swiss village of Scherz in 1882. They planted vineyards immediately upon their arrival in Naples and began making wine when their vines matured. They applied for a loan to expand their winery from the local banker, Hiram Maxfield. Maxfield, owner of a local winery, denied their request for a loan. The Widmers obtained a loan from another bank.

In 1910, the Widmers' son, Will, attended the Royal Wine School at Geisenheim, Germany. Widmer was one of the first wineries in the United States to offer "varietal" wine of one grape variety, as opposed to blended wine, and also was one of the first to offer vintage dated wine. During Prohibition (1919-1933), many wineries went out of business. Taylor and Widmer survived by making and selling grape juice and sacramental wine. In 1920, the sons of Walter and Addie Taylor purchased the Columbia Wine Company in Pleasant Valley and moved the Taylor operation to Columbia's stately, stone headquarters building.

In 1934, president E. S. Underhill of Gold Seal Winery brought Charles Fournier, who had trained in the cellars of Veuve Cliquot Ponsardin in Rheims, France, to become production manager to restore its pre-Prohibition reputation. Fournier, educated at the University of Paris and at schools of enology in France and Switzerland, brought French-American hybrid grapes, initially Ravat 6 (Ravat Blanc) and Seibel 1000 (Rosette) to area vineyards.

In 1943, Fournier successfully introduced his champagne, Charles Fournier Brut, to the U. S. market. In 1950, the California State Fair opened its wine competition to Eastern and foreign wine. The only gold medal awarded was Charles Fournier New York State Champagne. In subsequent years, no non-California wines were allowed to compete at the State Fair in Sacramento.

In 1953, Fournier hired Dr. Konstantin Frank to establish a *Vitis vinifera* (European) grape nursery at Gold Seal. Dr. Frank, who had been working at the New York State Agricultural Experiment Station at Geneva, also served as a consultant. Dr. Frank had seen vinifera grape varieties grow in the Ukraine, where the winters were colder than the Finger Lakes Region.

10

Dr. Frank convinced Fournier that past problems growing European varieties of grapes in the Finger Lakes Region were due to disease, such as mildew and fungus, which could be controlled. Winter temperatures were not the principal problem. In addition, Dr. Frank recommended grafting vinifera vines onto hardy rootstock that would allow the canes of the vines to ripen before the first winter freeze.

Gold Seal Vineyards began to graft vinifera vines onto hardy rootstock obtained from a convent in Quebec. The first real test came in February 1957 when the temperature plunged to 25 degrees below zero. Many *Vitis labrusca* (native) varieties, particularly Duchess and Isabella, had 100% bud damage. The grafted vinifera vines experienced only 10% bud damage. Fournier and Frank knew that their experiment had been successful.

In 1976, the New York State Legislature passed the Farm Winery Act. Removing the requirement for wineries to be bonded, which was expensive, stimulated the Finger Lakes wine industry. Many vineyardists began to make wine instead of selling all of their grapes to wineries. By the early 21st century, over 120 wineries flourished in the Finger Lakes Region.

Riesling has become the signature grape variety of the Finger Lakes Region. The region is recognized as one of the top three regions in the world for growing this variety. Cabernet Franc has become one of the more popular Finger Lakes red wines. Although the variety does not rank in the top tier with Cabernet Sauvignon and Pinot Noir, Cabernet Franc, along with varieties such as Merlot and Malbec, is one of the varieties blended with Cabernet Sauvignon to make Bordeau wine.

Hammondsport and Keuka Lake are discussed in Chapter 1 because they are the cradle of the wine industry in the Finger lakes Region. It all began there. Highlights of the Finger Lakes Region are also provided in Chapter 1 for readers unfamiliar with the area.

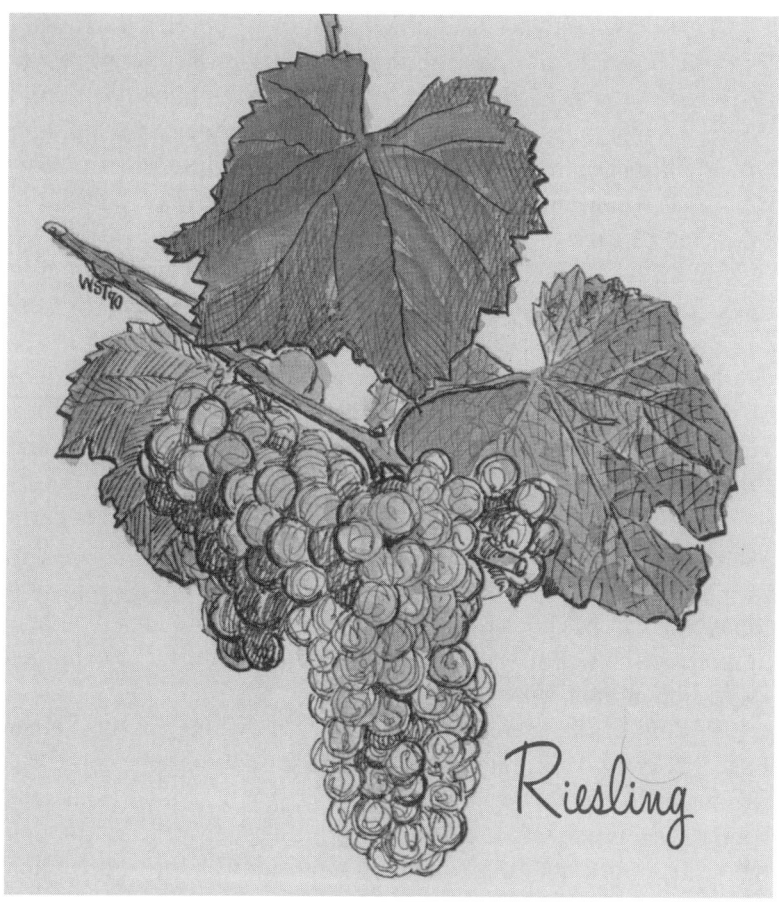

Riesling is one of the world's most popular grape varieties because of its ability to age and to retain its style wherever it is grown. Riesling wine, which has a desirable level of acidity, is made with a wide range of sweetness. Riesling made with higher levels of sweetness has probably diminished the variety's reputation in comparison to other varieties, such as Chardonnay. The taste of Riesling is sometimes described as steely with an aroma of flowers, honey, or tropical fruit. Riesling is also used in making ice wine from frozen grapes. Riesling from Keuka Lake vineyards is crisp and lean, whereas Riesling made from grapes from Seneca Lake tends to be more fruit forward.

CHAPTER 1 KEUKA LAKE AND AREA HIGHLIGHTS

> To one who would make this spot his home,
> He would live in paradise.
> Indians say that God's own Hand
> Planted His fingerprints here
> To bless the land for His children
> To show them His garden rare,
> And as I gaze at its beauty
> I cannot help but feel awed
> To think that this marvel of nature
> Was blessed by the Hand of God.
>   From *Inspiration* by A. Glenn Rogers

According to Iroquois legend, the Finger Lakes were created by the hand of the Great Spirit reaching down from above. Supposedly, the Great Spirit made six major lakes, not five, because his hand slipped. The Finger Lakes were formed by glacial activity during the Pleistocene Epoch (Ice Age), which lasted over a million years and ended 4,000 to 8,000 years ago. The first major advance remolded the land; the second glacier spread rock debris, blocked the southern ends of the lakes, and made major alterations.

Formation of the Finger Lakes was a topological event created by the enormous force of the ice advance opposed by a surface configuration unique to central New York State. The result is a land formation with unparalleled features. The legacy is a scenic and multi-faceted tourist destination.

The six major lakes, west to east, are Canandaigua, Keuka, Seneca, Cayuga, Owasco, and Skaneateles; the five minor lakes are Conesus, Hemlock, Canadice, and Honeoye in the west, and Otisco in the east. Rochester is the western gateway to the region, Syracuse is the eastern gateway, and Corning and Elmira are the southern gateways. The Finger Lakes Region is within an eight-hour drive of over 100 million people in the Northeast, including those in the southeastern cities of Canada.

The region is rich in history. During the 1800s, the region was very active in the temperance movement, the antislavery movement with accompanying Underground Railroad activity, and the founding of the national women's rights movement. In addition, Mormonism was founded in the region, and it was the home of the Fox sisters, proponents of Spiritualism.

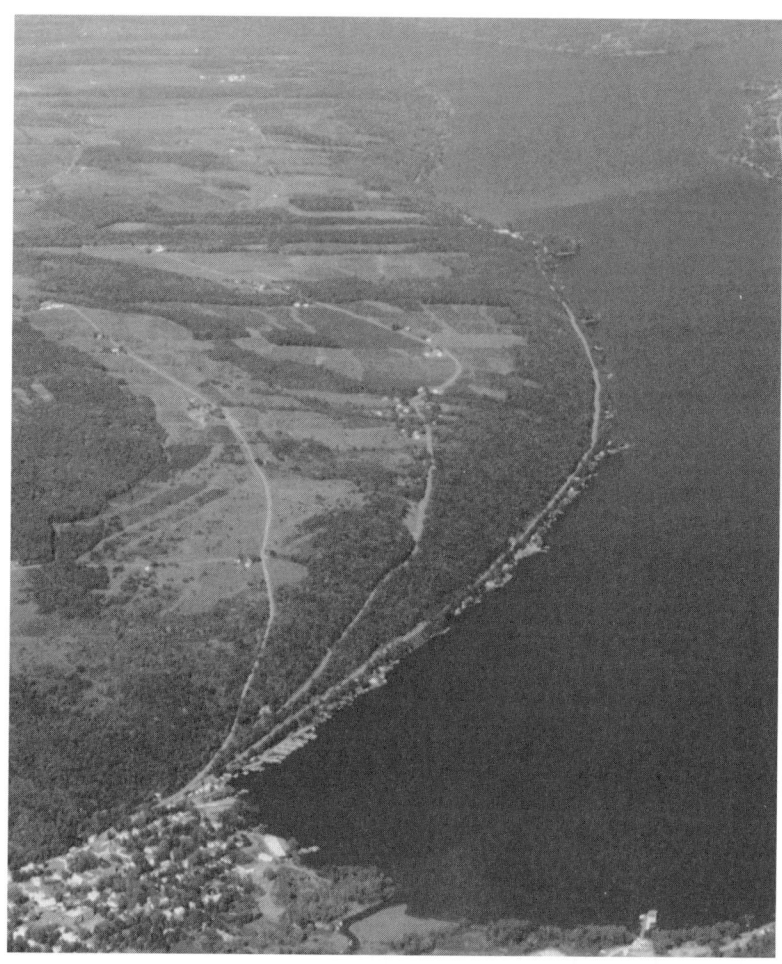

The Village of Hammondsport occupies a scenic location at the southern end of Keuka Lake. The head of the western branch of the Y-shaped lake is Branchport, 16 miles north of Hammondsport; the head of the eastern branch is Penn Yan, 20 miles north of Hammondsport. The Bluff of Keuka Lake rises over 800 feet above the west branch and the east branch of the Y. Keuka Lake is called "the lady of the lakes" because of its natural beauty. It was called "crooked lake" by early settlers and "Keuka" by the Iroquois, which meant "canoe landing place." In 1857, it was named Keuka Lake by New York State to conform with the Iroquois names of the other Finger Lakes.

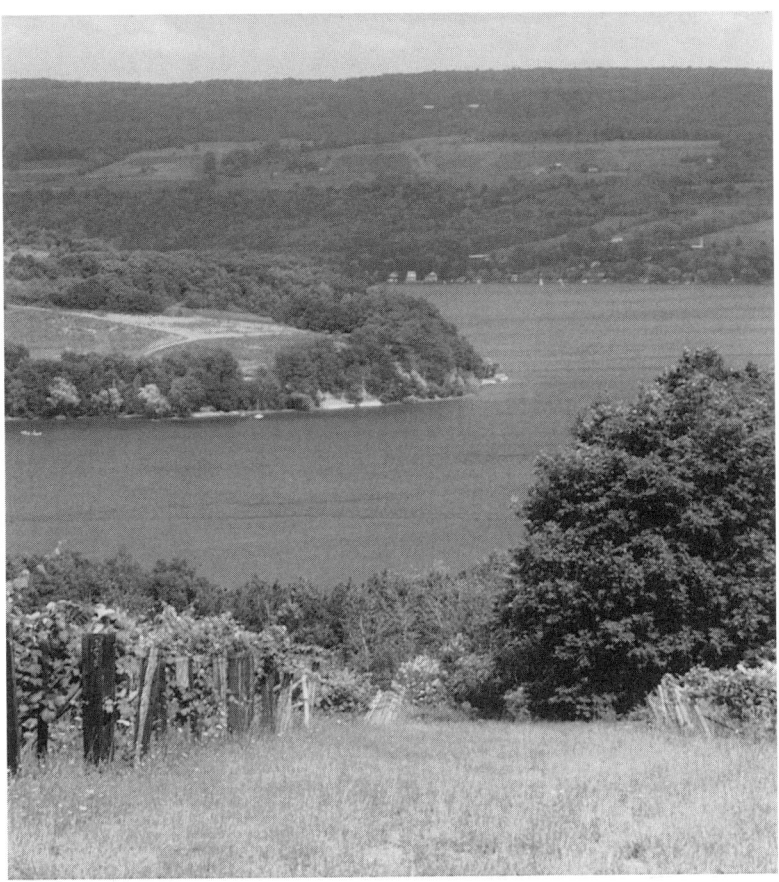

The deepest point in Keuka Lake, 187 feet, is in the west branch. The lake's average width is three-quarters of a mile, and it is two miles wide at its widest point, the wide waters area south of the Bluff. Until the 1880s, the Bluff was the site of a smaller version of Stonehenge with large, flat stones varying in width from three to eight feet that were configured in lines up to 300 feet in length. Unfortunately, it was not preserved. The shoreline of the lake is almost 60 miles long. Keuka Lake is one of the cleanest of the major Finger Lakes and is rated as an excellent fishing lake.

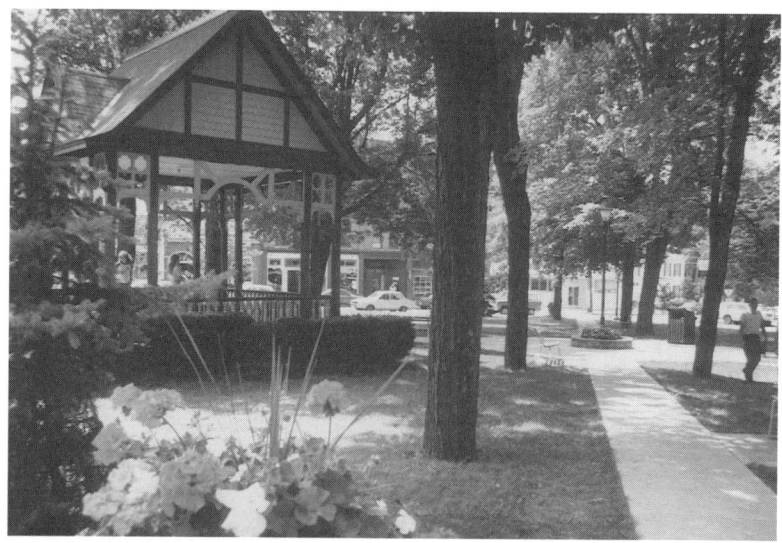

Pulteney Square, the village square in Hammondsport, was named for Sir William Pulteney, the early owner of land in the region. His agent, Charles Williamson, established the first newspaper, theater, and county fair in the region and developed roads in the area.

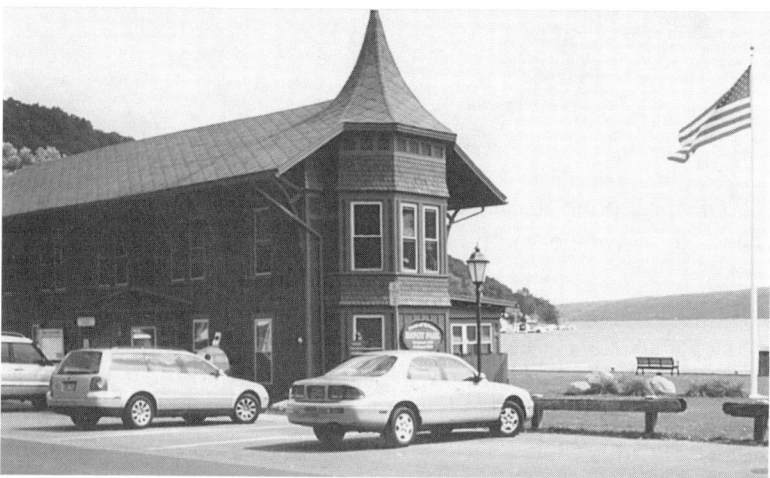

The Bath & Hammondsport Railroad is nine miles long. It was used to haul grapes from Keuka Lake vineyards to canal boats at Bath for transporting to markets in Philadelphia and Baltimore on Southern Tier rivers. Keuka Lake is in the background.

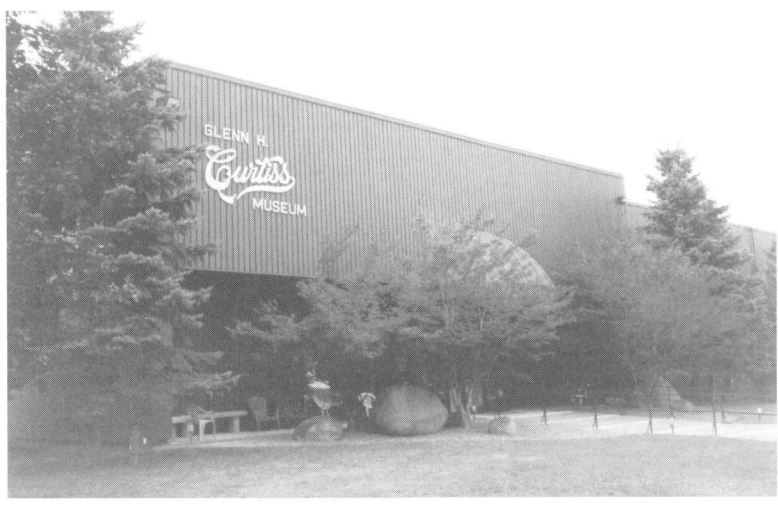

The Glenn H. Curtiss Museum in Hammondsport is principally an aircraft museum that showcases the contributions of native son Glenn Curtiss to the field of aviation. The 56,000 square-foot museum provides exhibits that tell the story of Curtiss's lifetime.

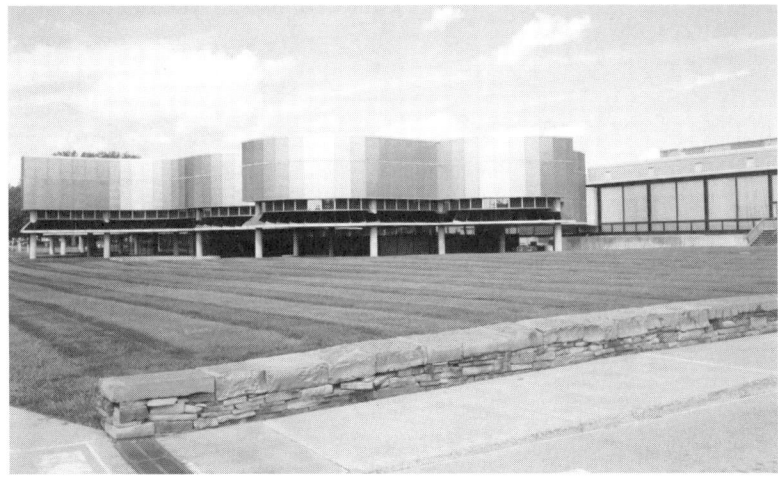

The Corning Museum of Glass includes the Steuben Factory with live, narrated glassmaking demonstrations and the Hall of Science and Technology. The museum, which contains the world's largest collection of glass, provides displays of the 3,500-year-old glass-making craft. Historic videos and interactive exhibits are offered.

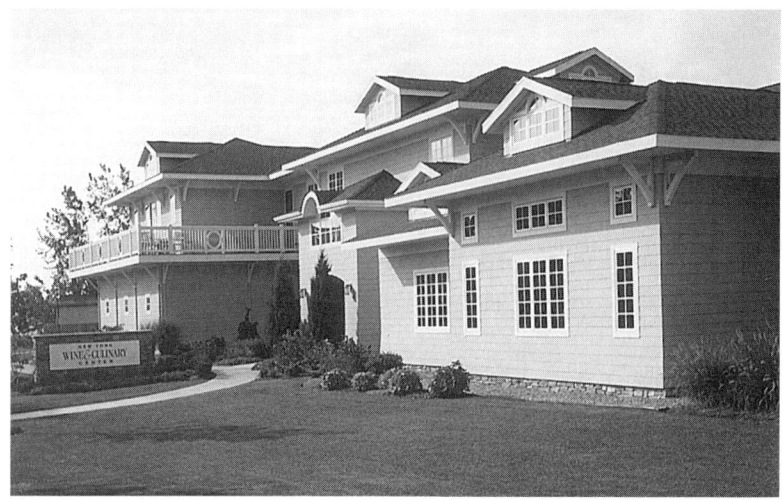

The 18,000-square-foot New York Wine & Culinary Center in Canandaigua is a joint, nonprofit venture of Rochester Institute of Technology, New York Wine & Grape Foundation, Constellation Brands, Inc., and Wegmans Food Markets. The center marries the two top industries in the State, agriculture and tourism.

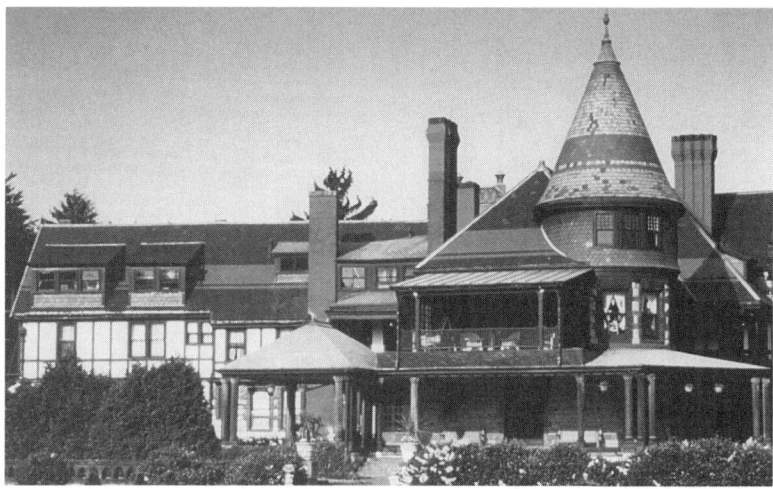

Sonnenberg Gardens and Estate in Canandaigua is a 50-acre site with ten gardens, greenhouses, ponds, statuary, and a 49-room mansion built in 1887. Ernest Bowditch, highly regarded horticulturist / landscape gardener, oversaw construction of the gardens.

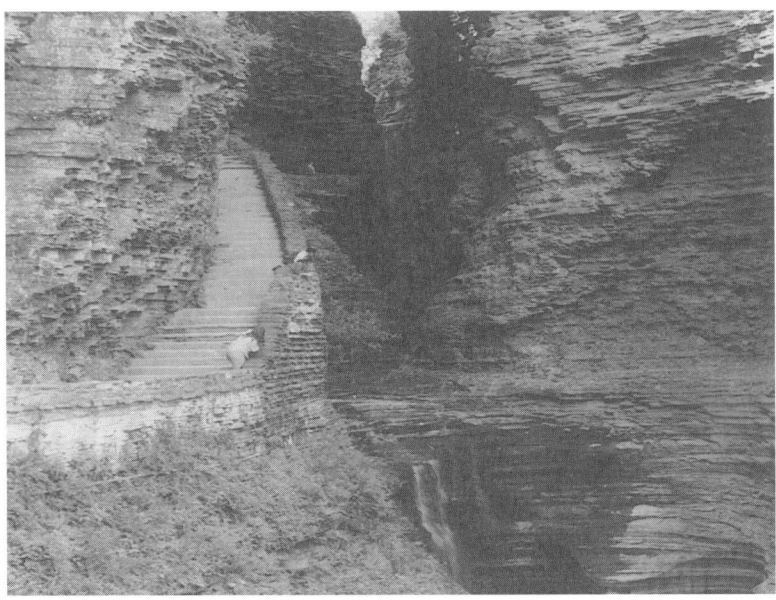

Watkins Glen State Park, a spectacular 776-acre park, has an erosion-sculpted chasm, craggy rock formations, and 19 cascading waterfalls. Visitors see grottoes and rock caverns and walk behind two waterfalls as they climb up or down 600 feet of elevation.

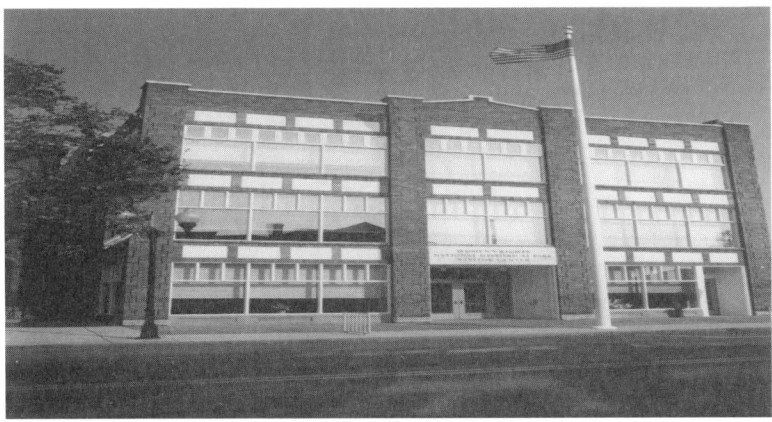

Women's Rights National Historic Park in Seneca Falls honors the organizers of the first National Women's Rights Conference in Seneca Falls in 1848. Lucretia Mott and Elizabeth Cady Stanton were the principal organizers, and Stanton was the author of the *Declaration of Sentiments*, with a plea for women's right to vote.

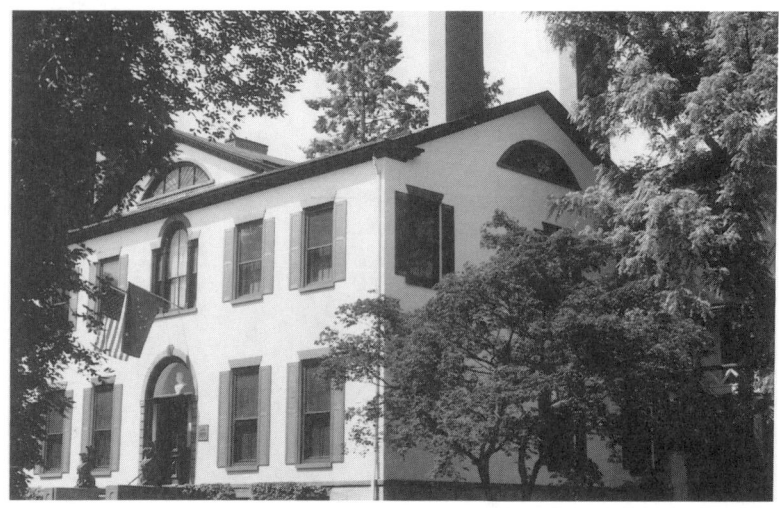

Seward House in Auburn was built in 1816-17 by Judge Elijah Miller, father-in-law of William H. Seward, Secretary of State for Abraham Lincoln and Andrew Johnson. Half of the 30 rooms in the National Historic Landmark are open to the public and are furnished with original family pieces, gifts, and other memorabilia.

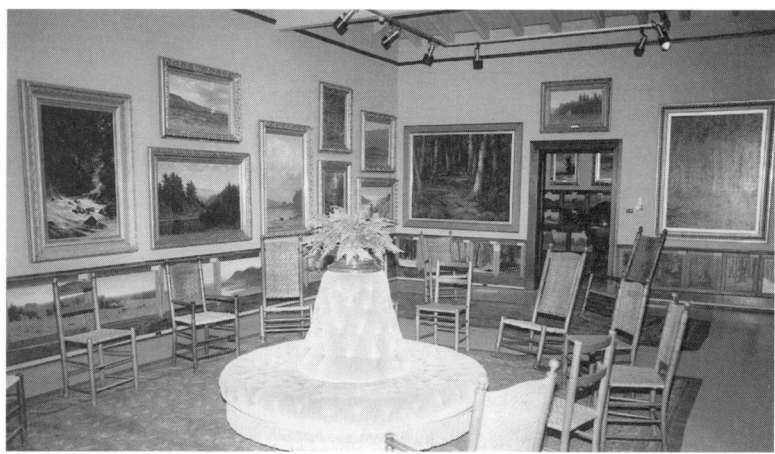

The John D. Barrow Art Gallery adjoins the Skaneateles Public Library. Barrow was a member of the Hudson River School of artists. Most of his paintings were landscapes, including many of the Finger Lakes Region. The gallery's two exhibition rooms display most of Barrow's lifetime output, over 300 paintings.

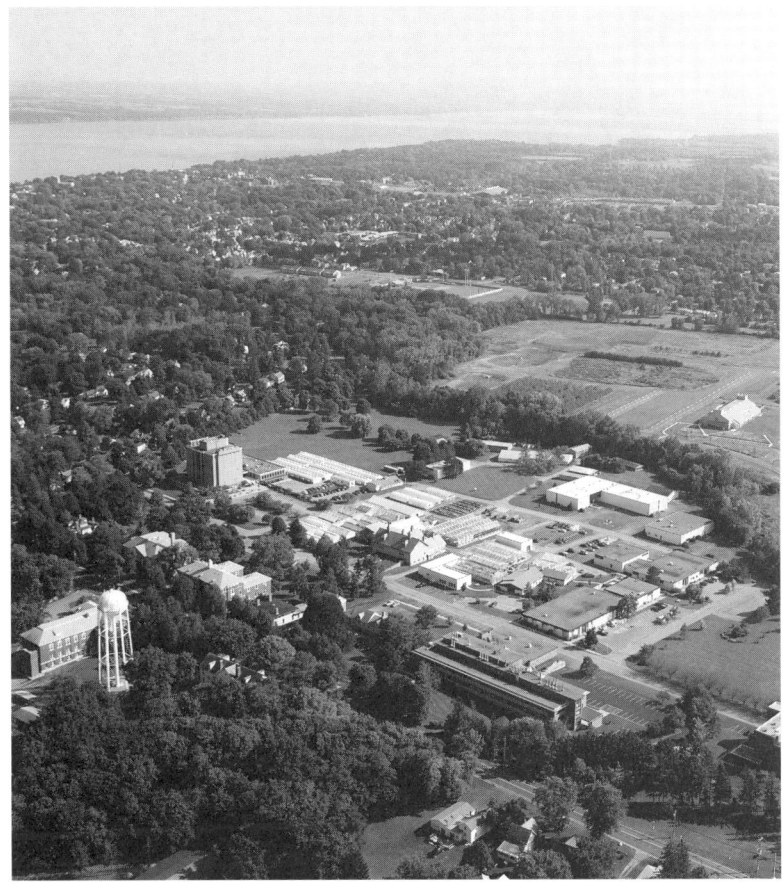

The New York State Agricultural Experiment Station at Geneva is a unit of the College of Agriculture and Life Sciences of Cornell University. The Experiment Station, established in 1880, has a 914-acre campus, including 864 acres of farmland for research. It is four academic units divided into: Entomology, Food Science & Technology, Horticultural Sciences, and Plant Pathology. The Experiment Station introductory brochure notes that "Enology and viticultural programs at Geneva helped grow New York's wine and grape industry by providing research-based technology and education. . . New York State's wineries and vineyards positively impact rural economic development and contribute over $3.4 billion in gross sales per year to the State's economy."

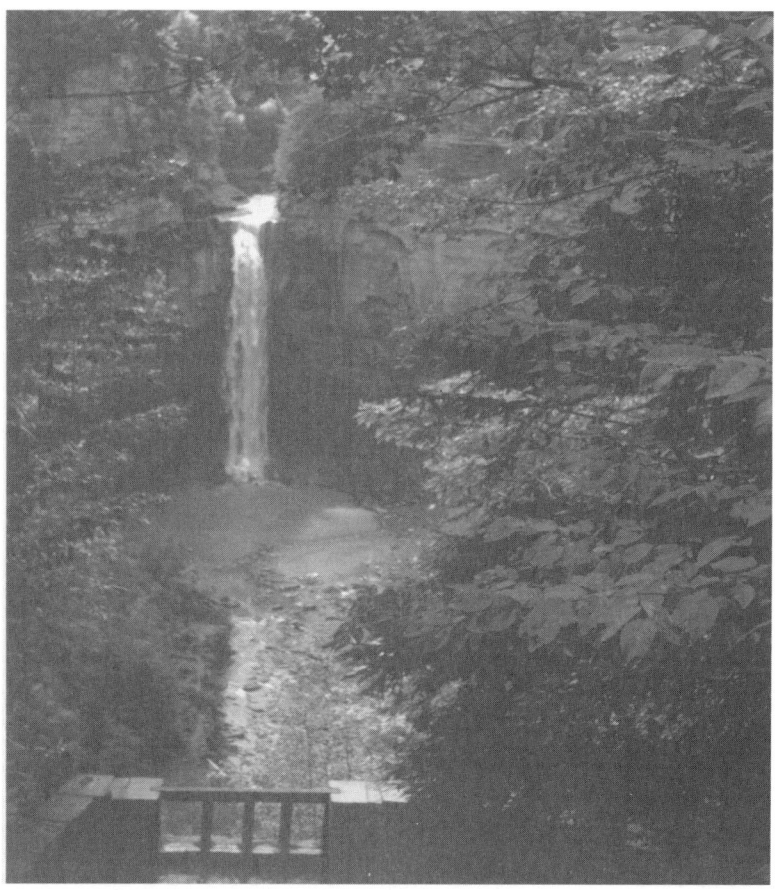

Taughannock Falls State Park is on the west side of Cayuga Lake north of Ithaca. The most notable attraction is 215-foot-high Taughannock Falls, the highest straight falls in the Northeast—50 feet higher than Niagara Falls. Visitors can envision the outline of a door high on the wall to the right of the waterfall. The Iroquois created a legend to explain it. A Delaware brave fell in love with a Cayuga maiden, but the Cayuga chief would not allow their union. The couple leapt off the top of the falls to what they thought was certain death. The Great Spirit sympathized with them; he opened a door high in the ravine that led to a domain where the couple could live in happiness forever. The State Park has two lookout areas, one at the end of a three-quarter-mile trail at the base of the falls and one in a panoramic overlook that can be reached by car.

> Keuka . . . exudes the spirit of peace. She is the lady of the
> lakes. She is lovely in any season but most enchanting
> when the smoky haze of autumn hovers over Bluff Point,
> the promontory that divides the lake into two [branches]
> . . . Like a giant mastiff, Bluff Point watches over the
> waters of the lake it splits into two arms. From that head-
> land, one can see on a clear day, it is said, seven counties
> and a dozen lakes.   Arch Merrill, *Slim Fingers Beckon*

Hammondsport on Keuka Lake was the cradle of the wine industry
in the region. Hammondsport was originally settled in 1792. The
village was named for Lazarus Hammond, who laid out its streets
and village square in 1807.

Hammondsport prospered throughout the steamboat age in the
1830s. The local economy boomed with the entry of railroads to the
region during the last half of the nineteenth century.

One of Hammondsport's favorite sons was Glenn H. Curtiss,
who began his career making bicycles and motorcycles and pro-
gressed to making aircraft for the Navy and the Army Air Corps.
More of his "Jenny" aircraft were produced during World War I
than any other aircraft in the world.

Charles Champlin, who was born and raised in Hammondsport,
was a writer for *Life* and *Time* magazines and then columnist and
principal film critic for the Los Angeles *Times*. He described his
hometown in the book, *Back There Where the Past Was:*

> Hammondsport was rural, I suppose, more so then than
> now, but the wine and the flying gave it, in this [20th] cen-
> tury certainly, a cosmopolitan flavor that not many outly-
> ing towns its size have had. Alexander Graham Bell, one of
> the attendants of the birth of [naval] flight, was a frequent
> visitor in the early years of the [20th] century when Glenn
> Hammond Curtiss was trying to perfect a flying machine.
> Hammondsport may have been remote, but it was never
> isolated. It is a lake town, literally a port town in its early
> days and even to the first two decades of this [20th] centu-
> ry, and there have always been summer cottagers to enrich
> the life of Hammondsport in every sense.

In 2012, Hammondsport was chosen the "coolest small town in
America" in a Budget Travel Organization poll.

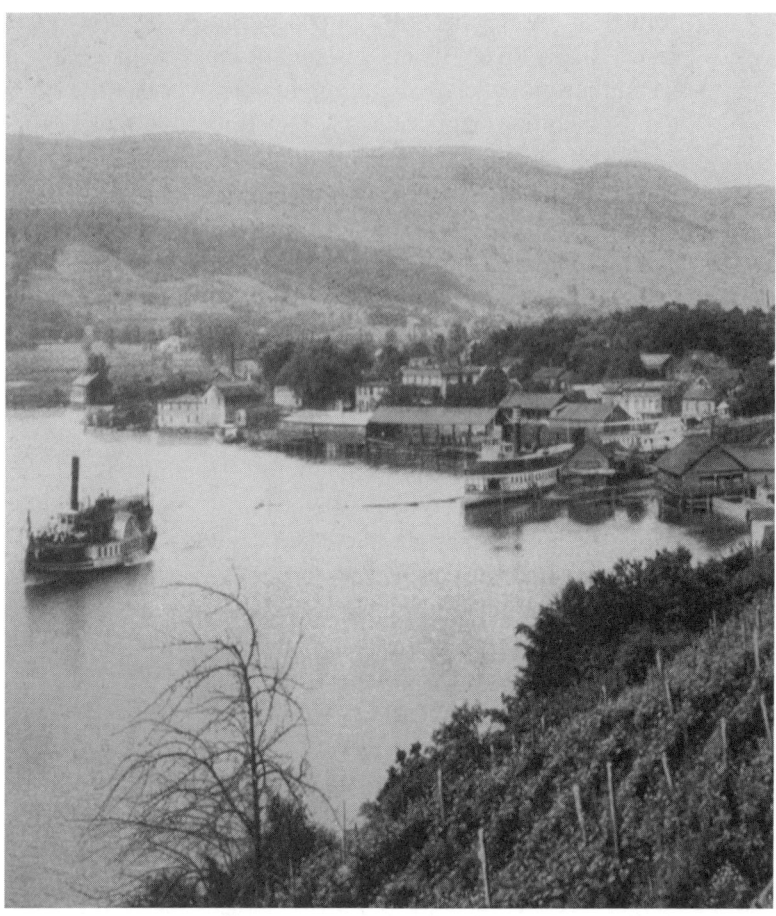

The first settlers in Hammondsport, William Aulls and his son, Tom, arrived in 1792. In 1796, John Shether built a store and mill on several acres of lakefront land. Local historian Laura Swartout observed of early Hammondsport: "Warehouses and dry docks lined the lake edge. Stores, small factories, mills, and cafes clustered around Water Street." The first steamboat on the lake, the *Keuka,* was built in Hammondsport and launched in 1835. Another first was the first trans-Atlantic crossing by air, made by a Curtiss flying boat. After the World War I armistice, the Navy commissioned Commander John Towers to cross the ocean from America to Europe. Towers started with three flying boats, N-C 1, 3, and 4. Only N-C 4 made it from the Azores to Spain.

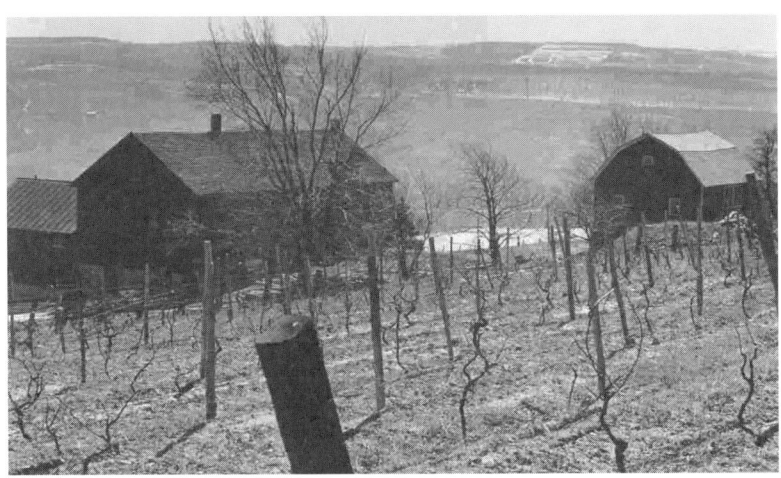

When Walter and Addie Taylor moved to the region in 1878, they settled on Bully Hill, north of Hammondsport. They began growing grapes in a seven-acre vineyard and planted additional acres as their business expanded. In 1880, the Taylors went into making and selling wine as the Taylor Wine Company.

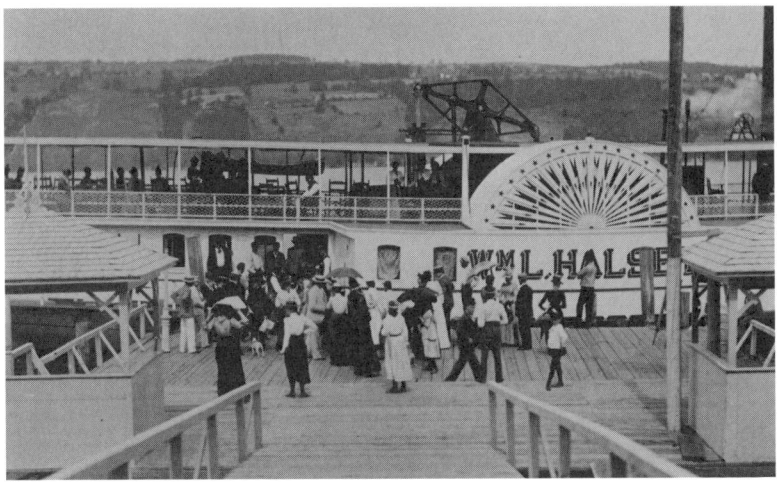

The *William L. Halsey* steamboat was launched in 1887. Earlier boats were mainly used to transport grapes to Hammondsport or to Penn Yan for shipment. Later boats were popular with passengers. Over the years, 12 steamboats plied the waters of Keuka Lake. The shoreline had over 60 steamboat landings.

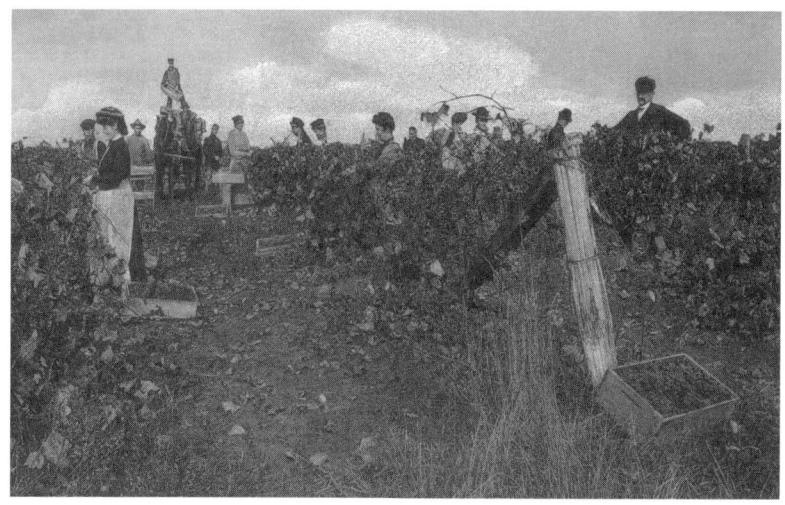

Horse-drawn wagons were used to haul grapes for shipment. In 1856, Mr. Prentice made the first sizable shipment of grapes from Keuka Lake, a ton of Isabella grapes to New York City. By 1860, 200 acres of table grapes had been planted in Pleasant Valley.

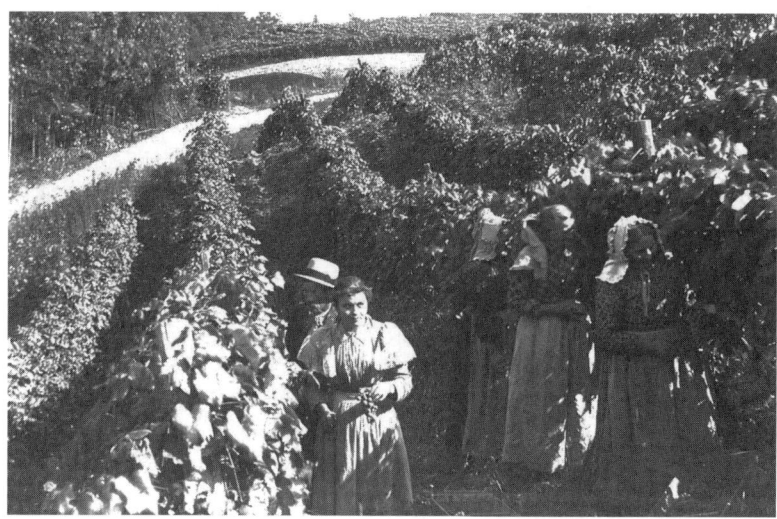

These grape pickers, including foreman Gottlieb Knuckle, were working in Urbana Wine Company vineyards. In 1858, Aaron Baker of Pleasant Valley visited Ohio and brought back 20,000 grapevine cuttings, stimulating the planting of additional vineyards.

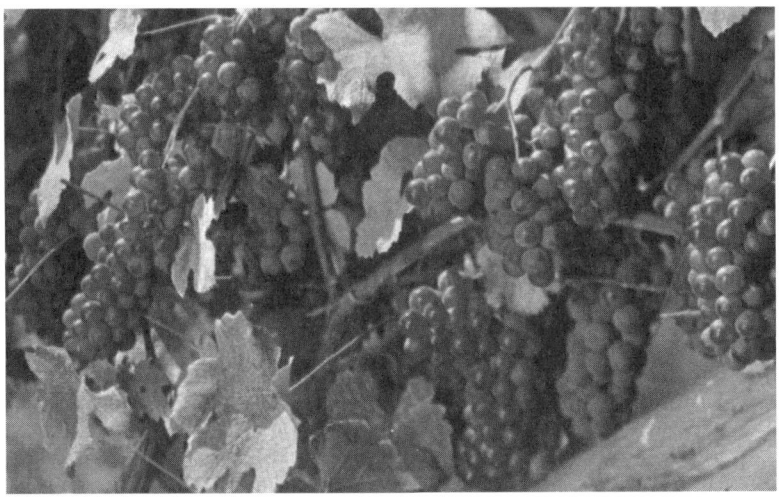

Delaware is a highly regarded Native American white grape variety with high sugar and only a moderate *Vitis labrusca* (foxy) flavor. It yields excellent table grapes that are also very good for wine. The variety produces a light, flowery fruity, dry or semi-dry wine with a delicious aroma. It is used in many champagne blends.

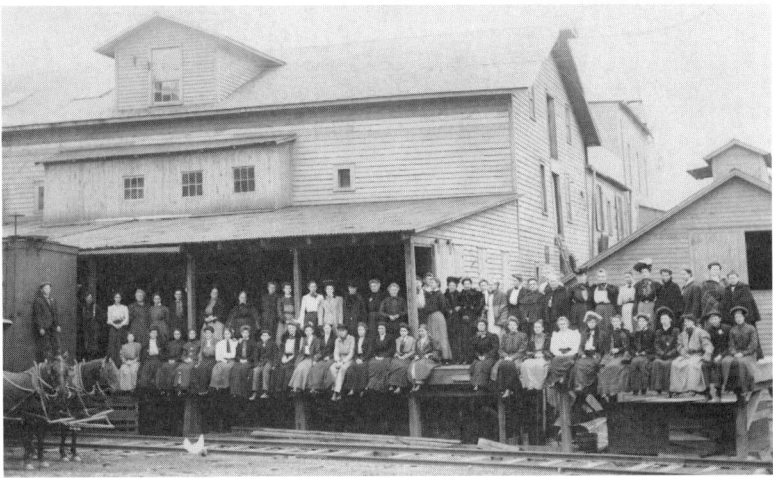

Lyons Packing House workers are gathered at the end of the grape picking season. Many grape pickers and grape packers were housewives earning supplemental income. The Grimly and the Lyons Brothers packing houses were located on Water Street.

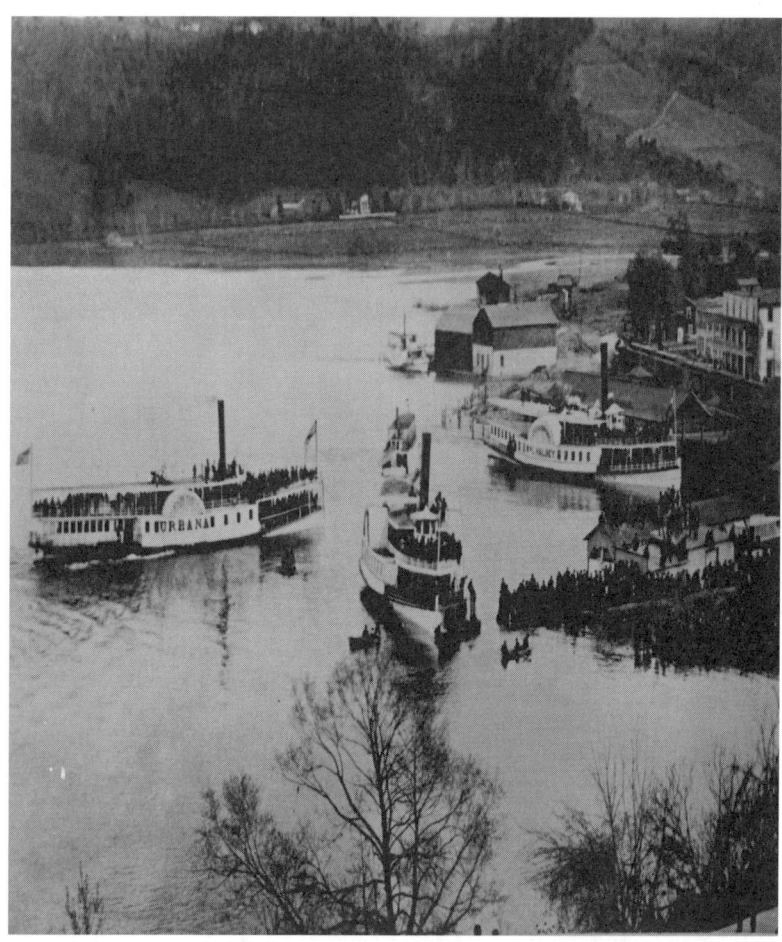

The steamship *Urbana*, entering Hammondsport harbor, was built in Hammondsport in 1880. She operated on Keuka Lake until 1904. The largest of the steamboats, the *Mary Bell*, was 124-feet long with a beam of 24 feet and could accommodate 600 passengers.

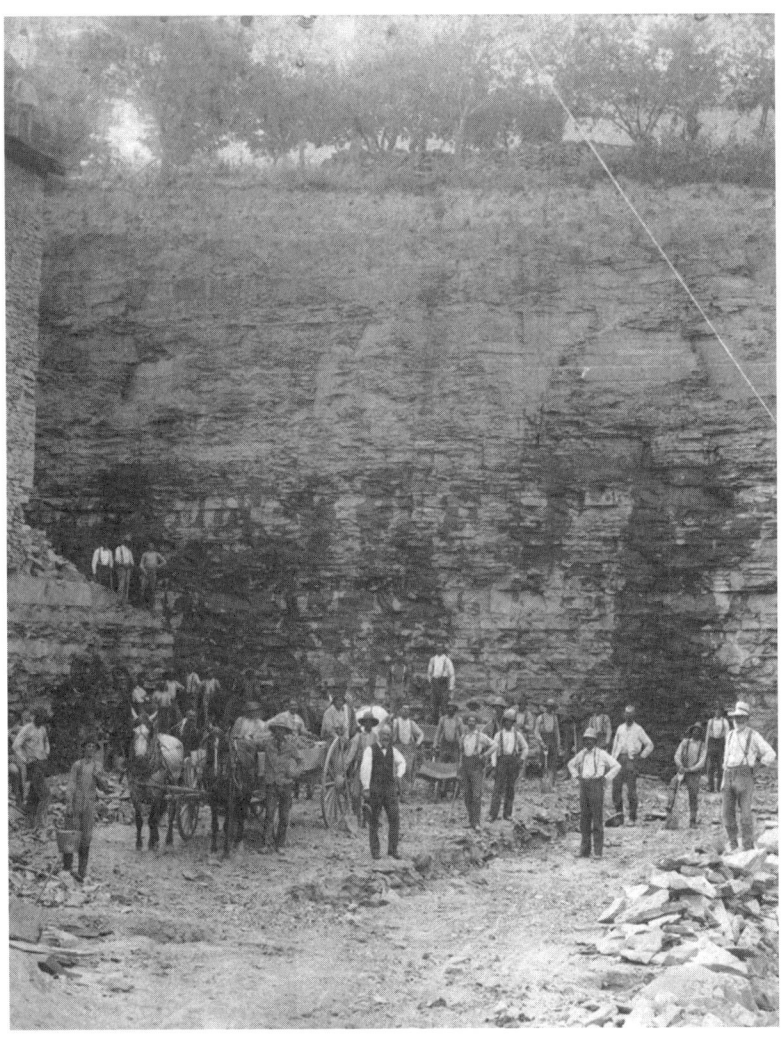

In 1880, the founders of Pleasant Valley Wine Company used manual labor to dig into the Pleasant Valley hillside to create caverns to store wine. The caves were used to keep wine at the desired storage temperature year round, so that refrigeration would not be required.

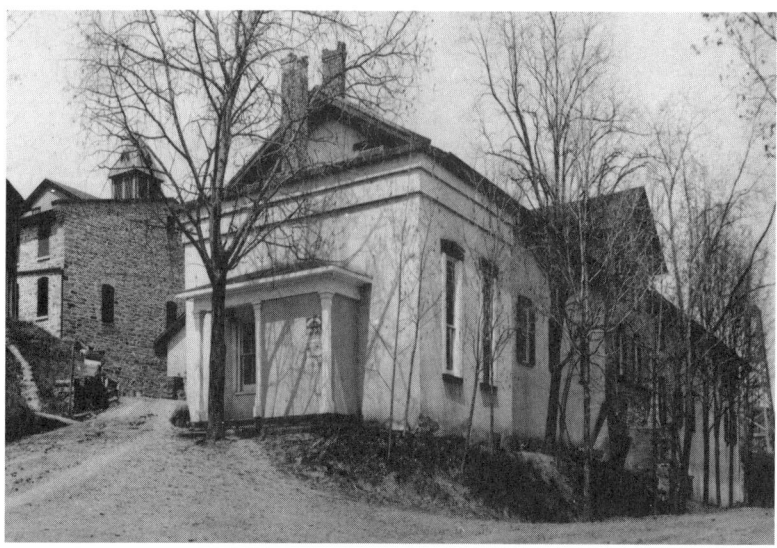

Eight stone buildings of Pleasant Valley Wine Company are listed in the National Register of Historic Places. The visitor center has a museum featuring items used in the 1800s. The company's modern bottling facility is adjacent to the museum.

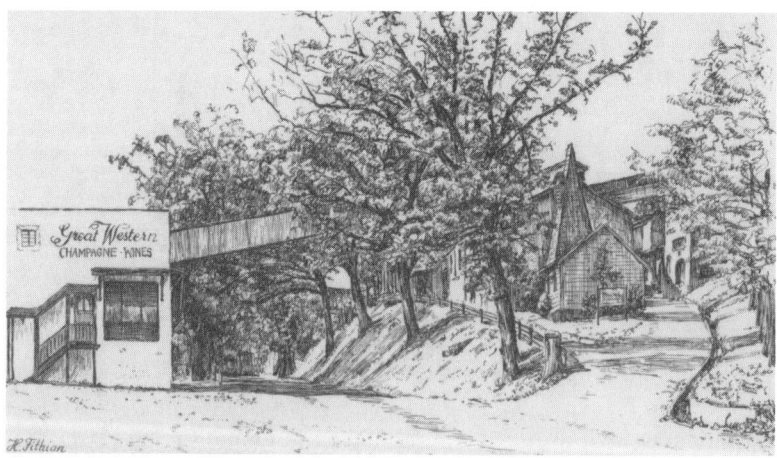

This sketch is of early Pleasant Valley Wine Company buildings. Following its first gold medal in 1867, Great Western Champagne won awards in Vienna in 1873, at the Philadelphia Exhibition in 1876, in Paris in 1889 and 1900, and in Brussels in 1887 and 1910.

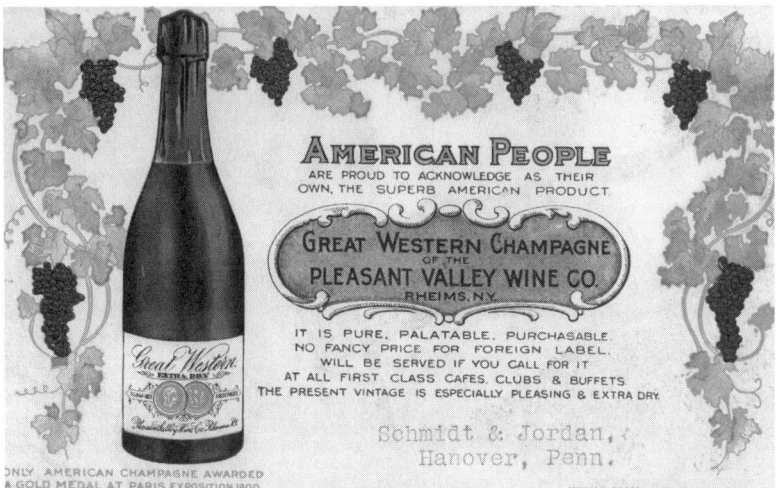

This advertisement is an early example of the promotion of Great Western Champagne. The company made wine for sacramental and medicinal purposes from 1920 to 1925. From 1926 to 1932, it went out of business. In 1933, it was reopened by the Champlin family.

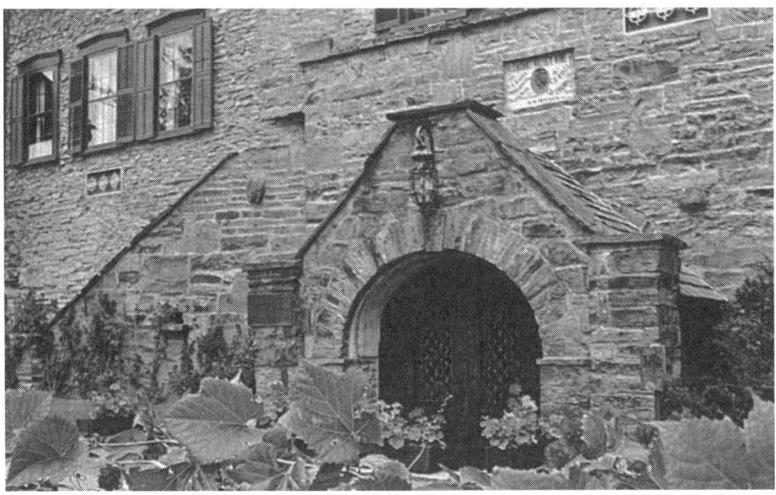

This is the entrance to the Great Western Winery, part of the Pleasant Valley complex. In 1962, it was sold to Taylor, and in the 1980s it was sold to Seagram, then Coca-Cola, and then Canandaigua Wine Company. In 1996, Michael Doyle reopened it.

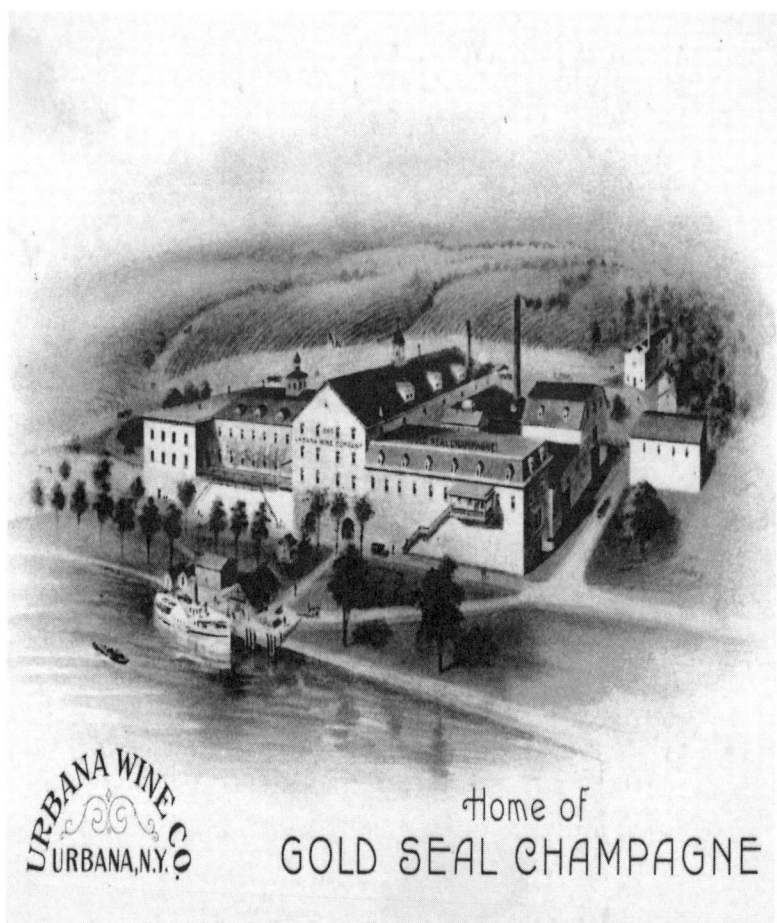

Home of
GOLD SEAL CHAMPAGNE

URBANA WINE CO.
URBANA, N.Y.

Urbana Wine Company, again renamed Gold Seal Winery in 1897, was founded in 1867 by Clark Bell and others. Charles LeBreton of Nantes, France, was the winemaker. In 1881, LeBreton moved to Crooked Lake Wine Cellars and was succeeded by Jules Crance from the champagne region of France, who had worked for Moet et Chandon. From then until the 1960s, four generations of the Crance family worked for Urbana / Gold Seal. In 1919, with the advent of Prohibition, Gold Seal began making sacramental wine and "tonic medicine" wines for the Smith, Kline & French Pharmaceutical Company. When Prohibition was repealed, it resumed the name Urbana Wine Company and began to make wine again.

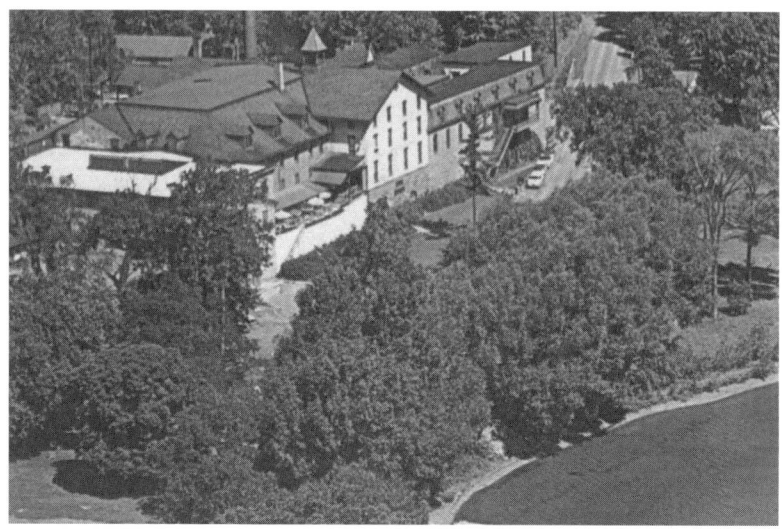

Gold Seal Winery, north of Hammondsport on the west side of Keuka Lake, was a beautiful winery with a winetasting terrace overlooking the lake. In 1979, Seagram bought the winery, and, in 1984, production was moved to Taylor and the winery was closed.

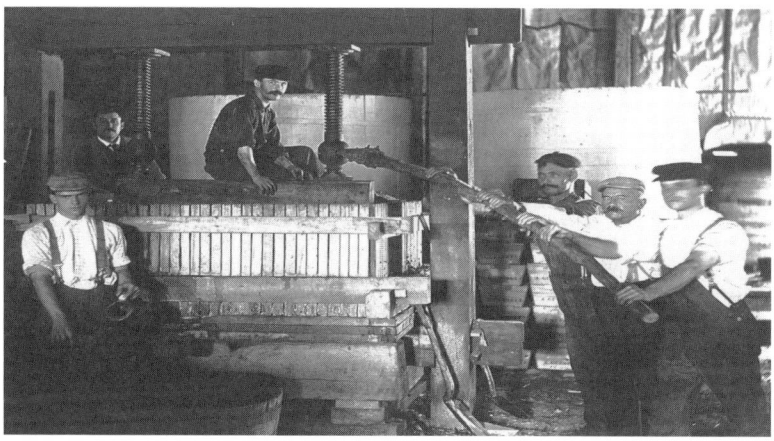

This grape pressing team is straining to force as much juice out of the grapes as they could. The first juice out of the press, the free run juice, is the highest quality. Modern hydraulic presses are much less labor intensive. The residue of skins, pulp, and seeds from the pressing operation is called pomace.

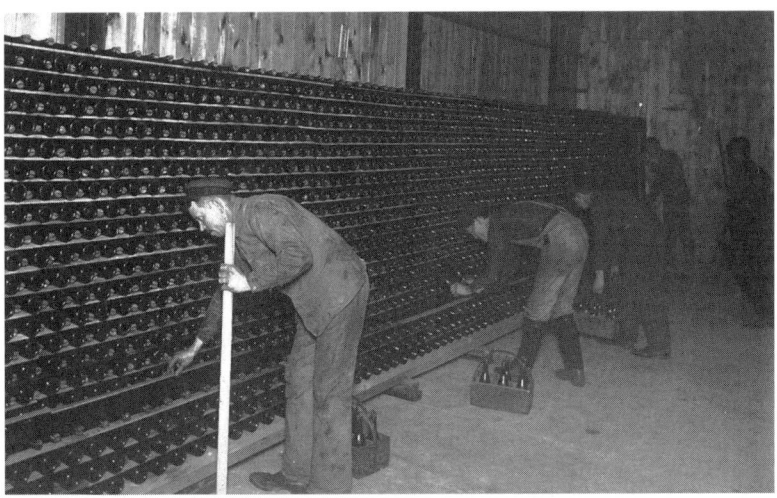

These men are riddling champagne bottles in wine racks. Riddling is the process of rotating bottles of ferment-in-the-bottle champagne a partial turn to move sediment into the neck of the bottle so that it can be disgorged. Prior to capping, the neck of the bottle is frozen so the sediment in an ice plug can be disgorged.

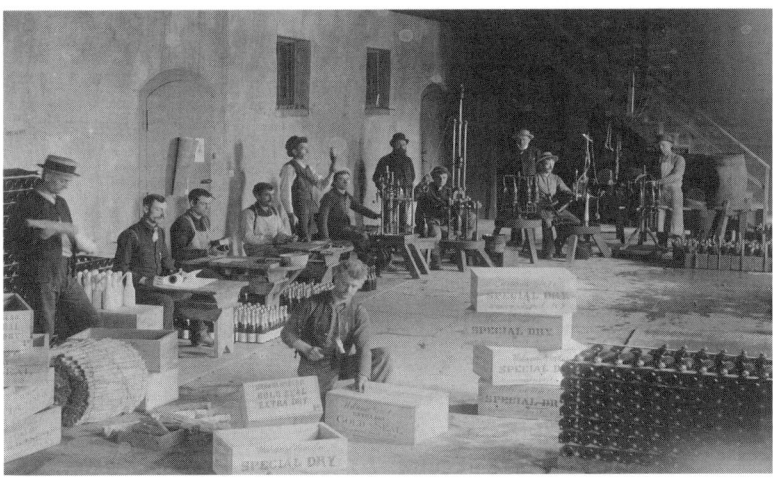

In capping and packing Gold Seal Champagne at Urbana Wine Company, each bottle was wrapped in paper before being packed. Finishing operations were labor intensive until recent years.

CHAPTER 3 TAYLOR WINE COMPANY

Philip Wagner, editor of the Baltimore *Sun,* was a grape grower, a winemaker, and author of *A Wine-Growers Guide*. Of the Taylor Wine Company, he observed:

> They are the pacesetter on wages. They are the pacesetters on prices paid top independent growers, and on premium payment for superior quality. They are the pacesetters on Seaton Mendall's extension service for growers. They are pacesetters in assuming a large share of the chance [risk] of grape growing by buying vineyards and installing the former owners on them as employees on salary, in their own homes. They are pacesetters in applying modern processing techniques to the ancient art of converting grapes into wine.

Taylor Wine Company was a excellent company for employees and contractors to work for.

In 1959, sales of Taylor wine were almost two and a half million gallons, and the winery was in a position to grow even further. By the early 1960s, Taylor had become the largest winery in upstate New York and by a considerable margin the largest winery in the country outside of California.

After buying the Pleasant Valley Wine Company in 1962, Taylor's wine storage capacity reached 17.3 million gallons, including 3.3 million gallons at Pleasant Valley Wine Company. In 1968, Taylor sold 6.6 million gallons of wine; four years later it sold almost 10 million gallons. The company "went public" in 1977.

Unfortunately, Taylor continued to make wine from native grape varieties, such as Catawba, Delaware, Isabella, and Niagara. Other regional wineries began to make wine from French-American hybrid grapes and from vinifera (European) varieties. Taylor made as good a wine as it could from its source material; however, it could not compete with wine made from hybrid and vinifera grapes.

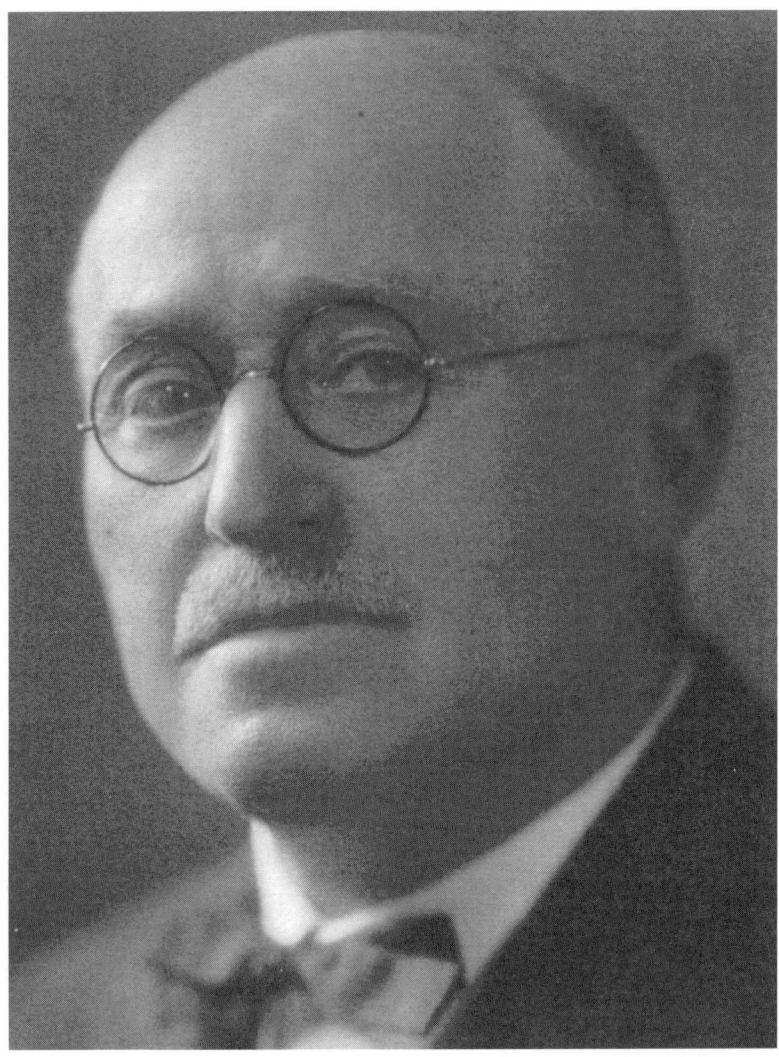

Walter Taylor, Sr., a master cooper, worked with his father, also a master cooper, before moving to Hammondsport to make barrels for the thriving grape industry. The cooperage business prospered and soon they were making barrels for their own grape juice and later, their wine. They made barrels from oak trees on their own property and adjacent properties. Today, high-quality oak used to make barrels and casks is from France and is expensive. Oak from Arkansas and Missouri is less expensive.

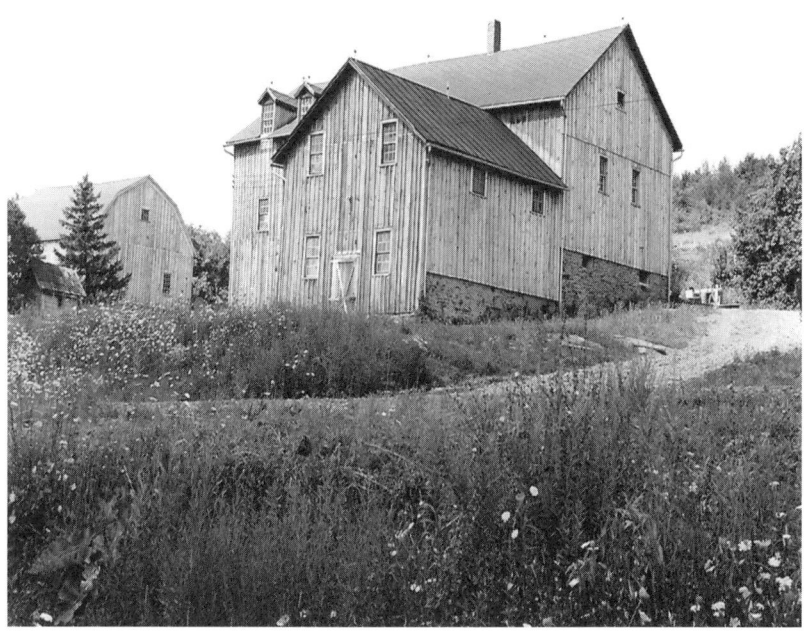

In 1878, Walter Taylor and his young bride, Addie Chapman Taylor, moved to the Hammondsport area and purchased a seven-acre vineyard on Bully Hill. After three years as vineyardists and commercial grape shippers, they purchased a 60-acre farm just north of their original vineyard. The vineyard on the farm had 35 acres planted with native grape varieties, such as Catawba, Delaware, Duchess, Elvira, and Niagara. They planted additional acres of Delaware and Ives.

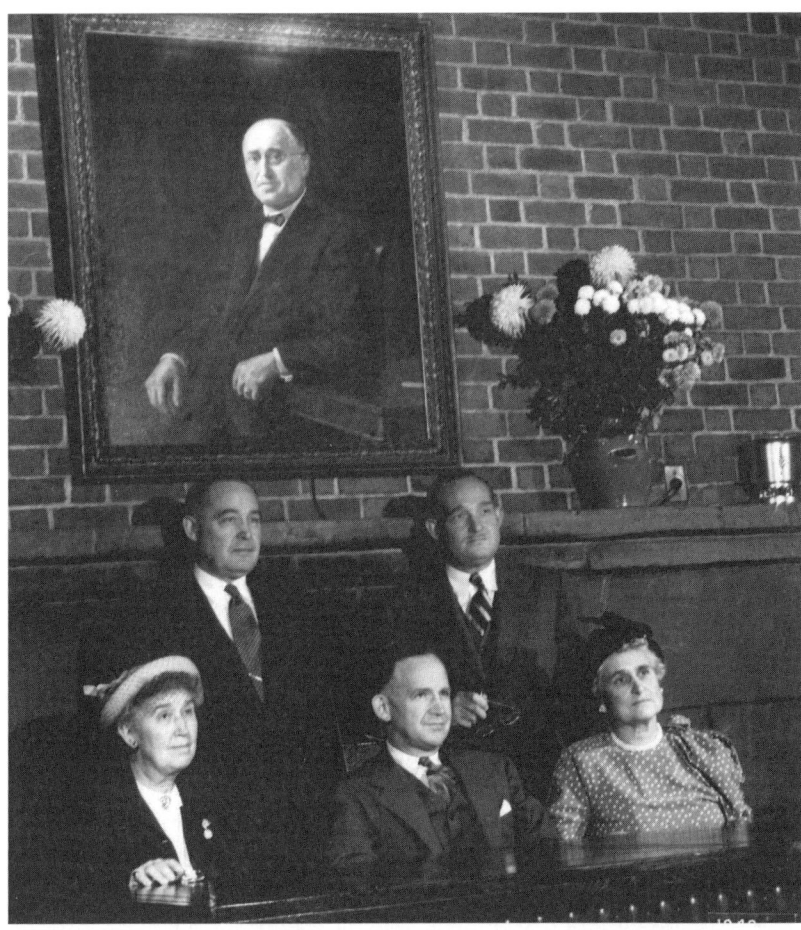

Walter and Addie Taylor had two daughters, Flora and Lucie, and three sons, Fred, Greyton, and Clarence. Left to right, they are Flora, Greyton, Fred, Clarence, and Lucie. For many years, management of the Taylor Wine Company was a family affair. All five children grew up in the business and contributed to its growth until before World War I, when salesmen were hired to sell wine in barrels and bottles in several surrounding States.

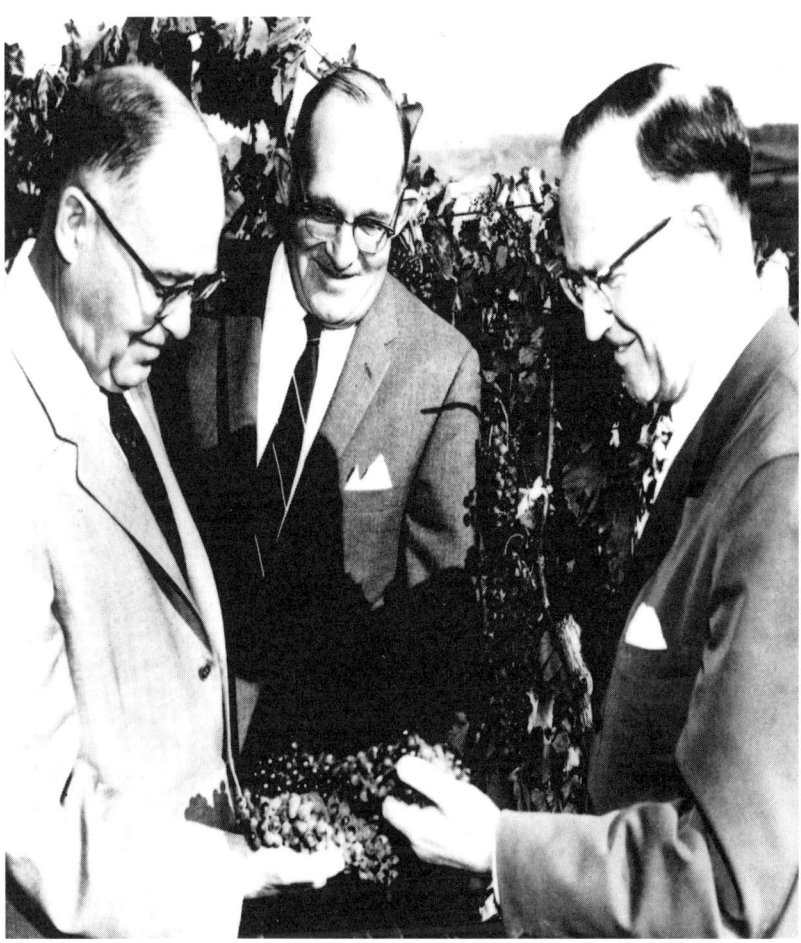

Fred, Greyton, and Clarence Taylor are shown checking the grapes in a Taylor Wine Company vineyard. Fred, the oldest brother, was the president of the company, Greyton was responsible for marketing, and Clarence, whose nickname was "Stubby," was in charge of production. Taylor's first product was dessert wine, which it barreled and shipped to New York City. As the market expanded, the winery made dinner wines.

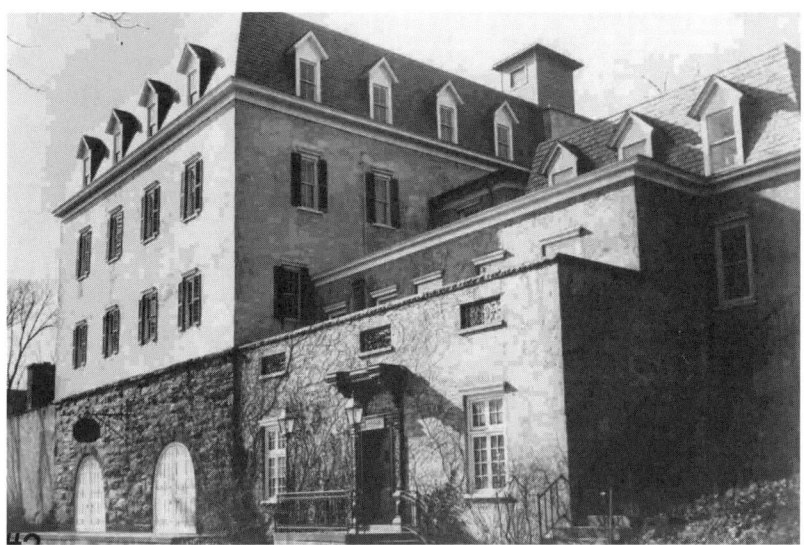

In 1920, when Columbia Wine Company on Pleasant Valley Road went out of business due to Prohibition, Taylor Wine Company purchased it and moved from its winery on Bully Hill. In 1939, construction of an additional building for champagne was completed.

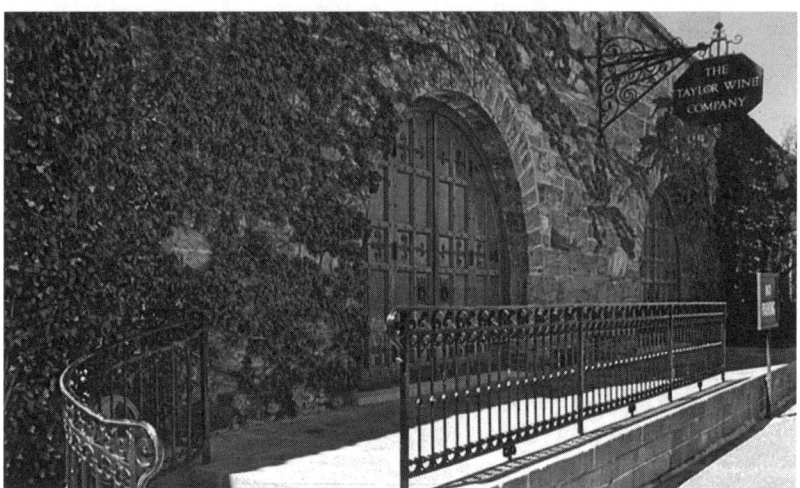

The ornate entrance to Taylor headquarters was widely photographed. With the move to Pleasant Valley, Taylor gained access to the Bath & Hammondsport Railroad. After Prohibition, production increased significantly but did not reach earlier levels until World War II.

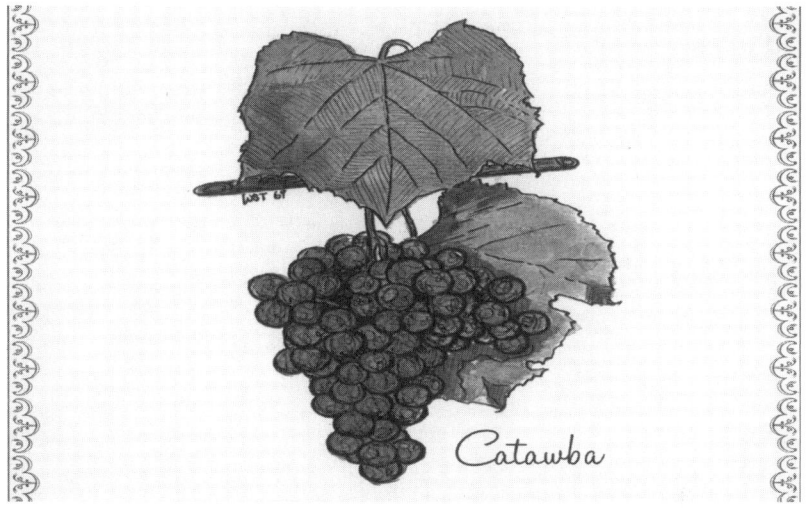

Catawba was the most widely planted grape variety in the U. S. in the 1880s. The variety has a high sugar content and high acidity. Catawba wine is made in a wide variety of styles. It has a clean taste and a spicy aroma. Its slightly tart flavor occurs occasionally as an after-taste. It is used in some sparkling wine blends.

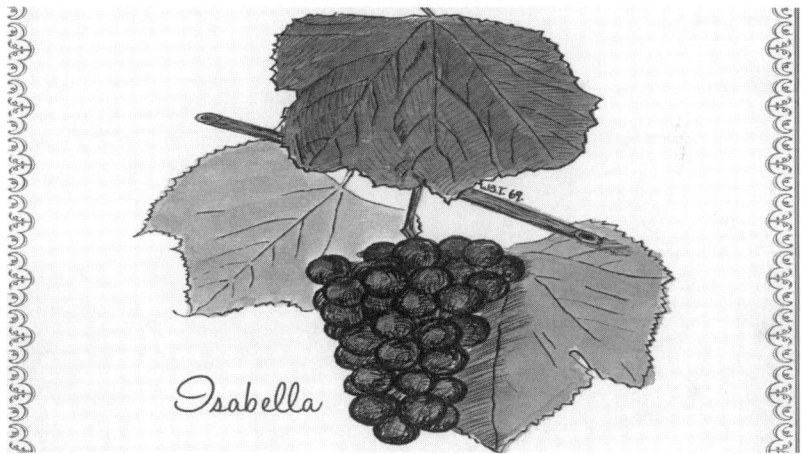

Isabella is rarely made as a varietal wine; it is usually blended. Occasionally, it is fermented on the skins to make pink wine. The wine has a foxy, grapy flavor with a musky aroma. When pressed and fermented in white-wine style, the foxiness is reduced, and the resulting wine is pale and grows paler with age.

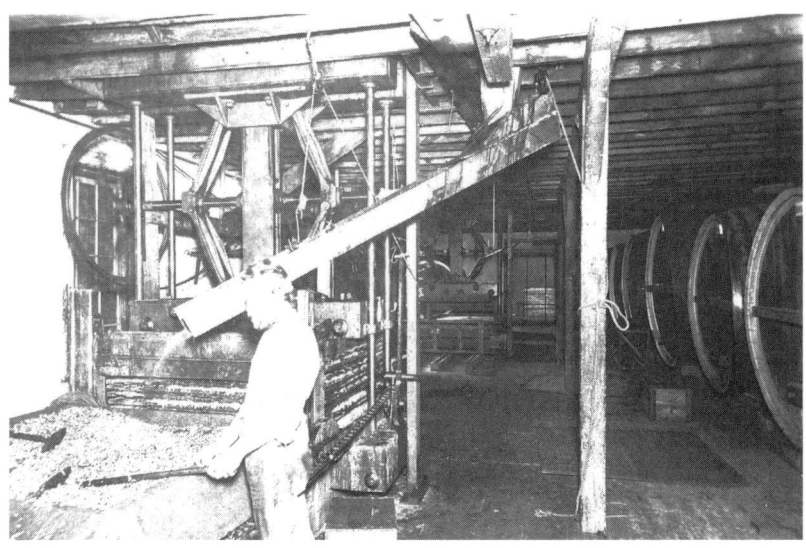

Freshly picked grapes, with the stems removed, in picking boxes were emptied into the grape crusher before going to the grape press. It is important to get picked grapes to the crusher promptly, otherwise natural yeast on the skins will begin an uncontrolled fermentation.

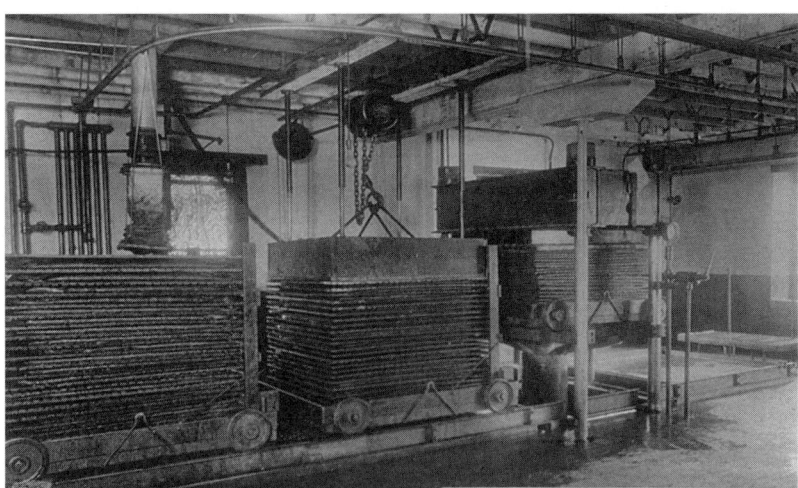

Hydraulic grape presses are very efficient. Grapes are placed in layers separated by crosshatched frames. Even a small hydraulic press used by a home winemaker can apply a pressure of one to two tons.

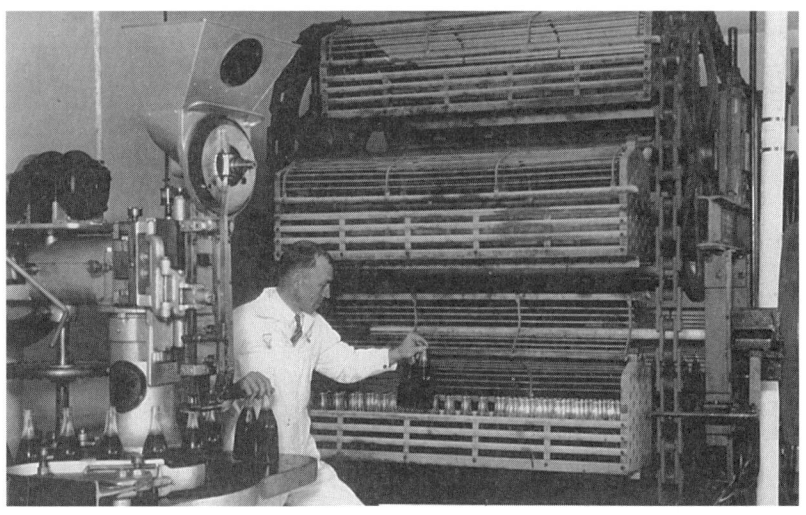

Pasteurization is the process of sterilizing wine and other liquids by heating them (usually to 130-170 degrees) to destroy the microorganisms they contain, thus making them stable. Louis Pasteur discovered pasteurization while experimenting with wine. In his opinion, "Wine is the most hygienic and healthful of beverages."

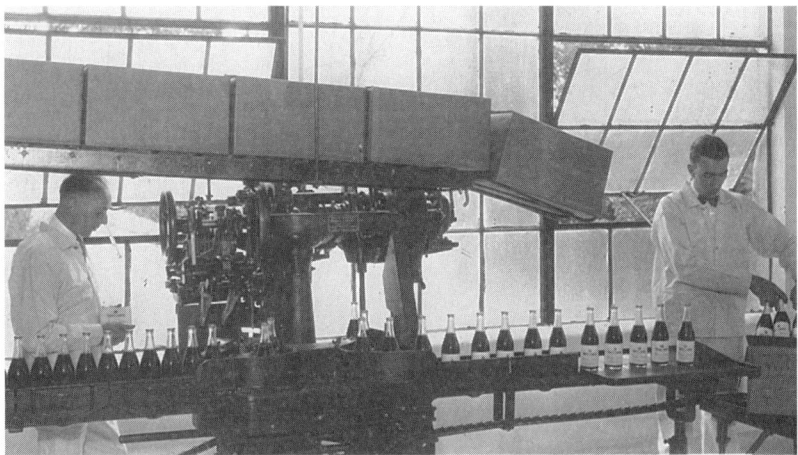

Pasteurization of wine is only done for wine destined for early consumption, such as dessert wine and sweet wines. Fine wines are not pasteurized; it cuts short the development and the possibility of improving the flavor of a superior wine. From the pasteurizer, bottles are labeled and placed in cartons for shipment.

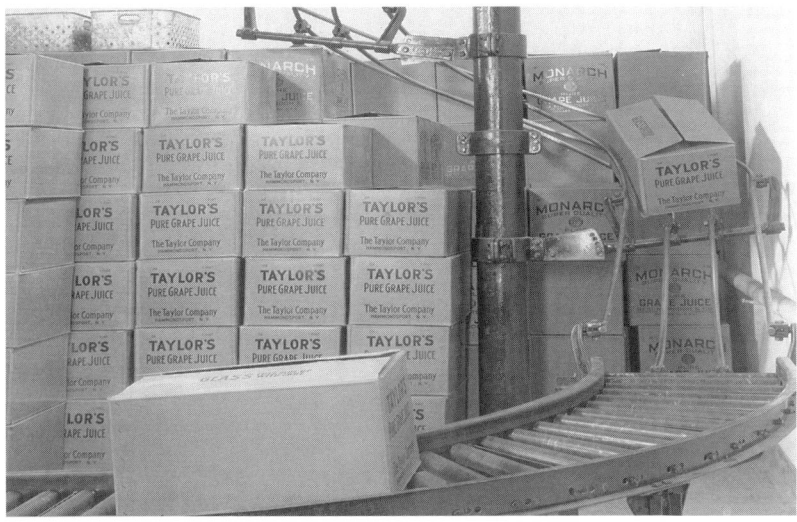

Empty cartons for Taylor grape juice are moving down a conveyor belt to be stacked prior to being filled with bottles. Grape juice was an important product during Prohibition because each head of household was allowed to make 200 gallons of wine in his home for personal consumption each year.

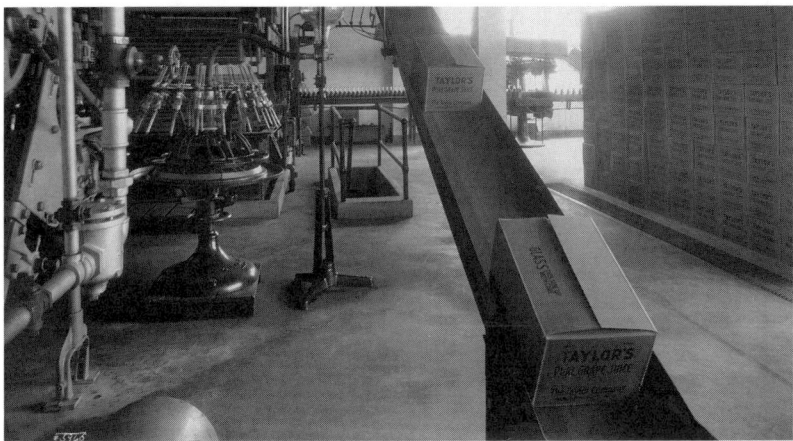

Packed cartons of Taylor grape juice after pasteurization are moving down a conveyor belt to be sealed and shipped. During Prohibition, Taylor offered to deliver juice by company truck, and a company representative would show you "what not to do" or wine would result.

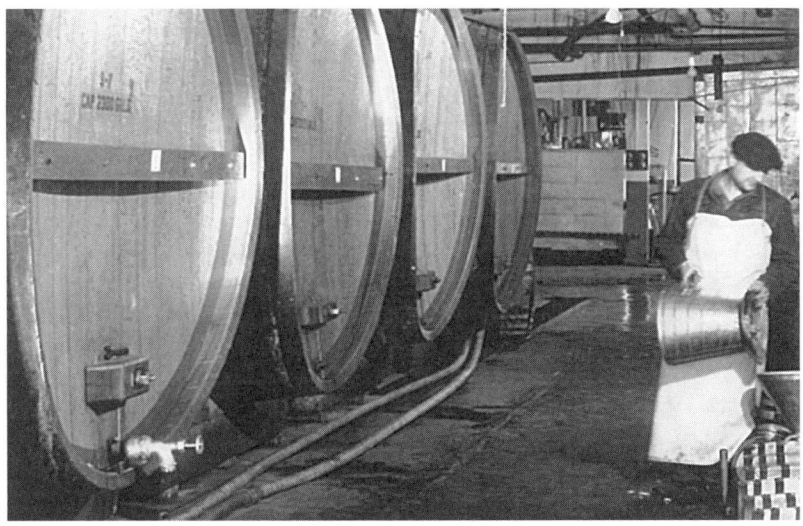

Following crushing and pressing of grapes, yeast is added to the juice and a violent primary fermentation begins. The juice is then placed in large casks where a controlled secondary fermentation occurs. The fermenting juice remains in the casks until it is bottled.

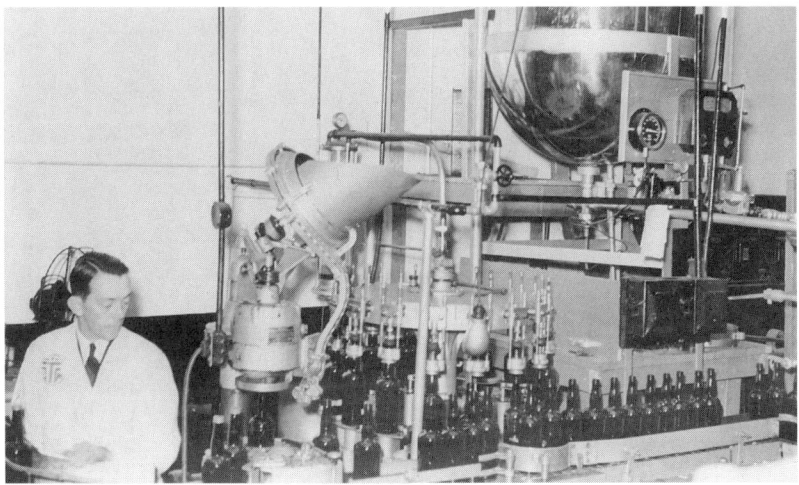

Corks are being placed in bottles in the Taylor bottling line. Corks are from the bark of the cork oak, mainly from Spain and Portugal. Corks are necessary for fine wine capable of aging and improvement in the bottle. They allow the slow evaporation and eventual slight oxidation.

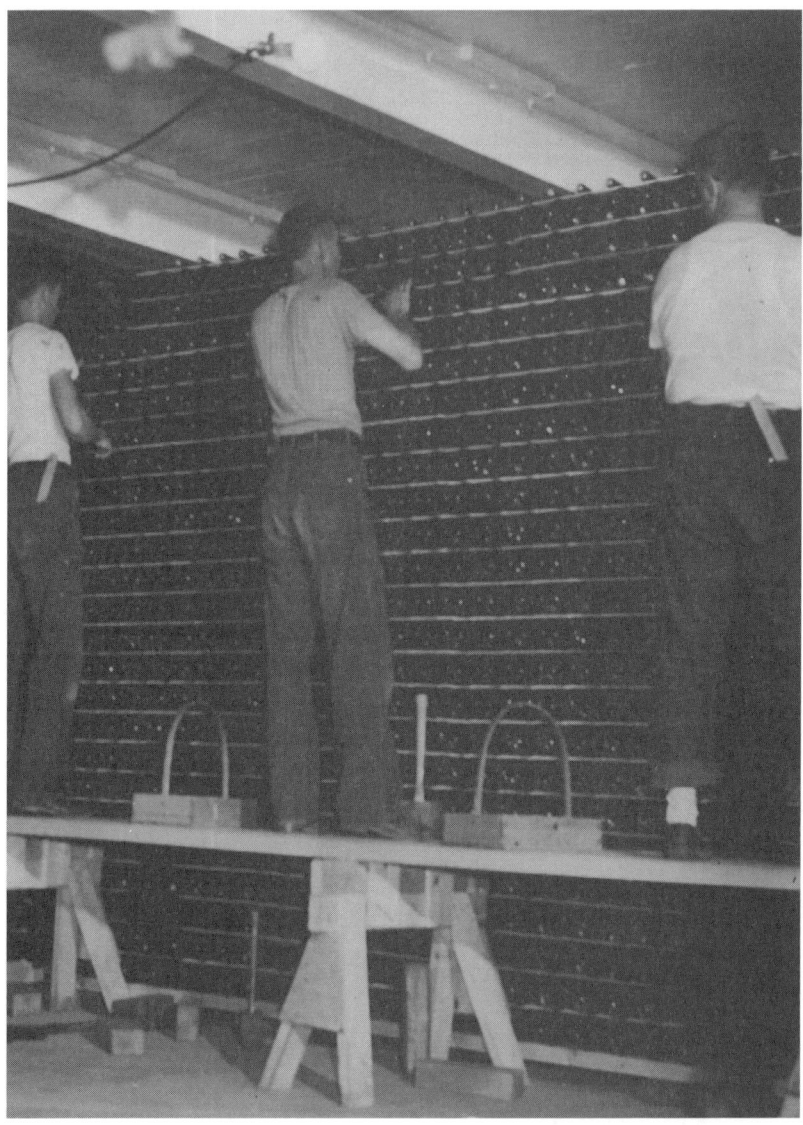

These men are riddling, that is, turning each bottle a partial turn, neck-down in the rack, to move yeast and sediment to the neck of the bottle so that it can be disgorged. Length of time to clarify champagne in the bottle varies widely and can take several weeks.

CHAPTER 4 WIDMER WINE CELLARS

Naples, at the southern end of Canandaigua Lake, the easternmost of the major Finger Lakes, was the home of Widmer Wine Cellars from the time of its first vintage in 1888. Widmer Wine Cellars, which ultimately had a storage capacity of three million gallons, was the only winery in the Naples Valley and was its principal industry and tourist attraction. Early settlers were of English and Scottish origin; however, many settlers in the mid-1800s were from Germany or from Switzerland, as were John Jacob Widmer and his wife, Lisette.

In 1848, local lawyer Edward McKay planted the first grapes in the area, a vineyard of Isabella. However, it was Andrew Reisinger, who moved to the area from Keuka Lake in the 1850s, who is credited with founding the Naples grape industry. Reisinger is known as a pioneer in the cultivation of vineyards and the trellis training of grapevines.

The first winery in Naples was built in 1861 by Hiram Maxfield, the leading banker in the village. Maxfield, the banker-vintner, denied the Widmers' request for a loan to begin their winery because he did not want competition. The Widmers obtained a $1,000 loan from the Granby Bank, a competing bank.

Naples is known for its Grape Festival in September. It became so popular that it had to be cancelled in the 1970s because traffic could not pass through the village on Main Street. The festival was resumed later with improved crowd control.

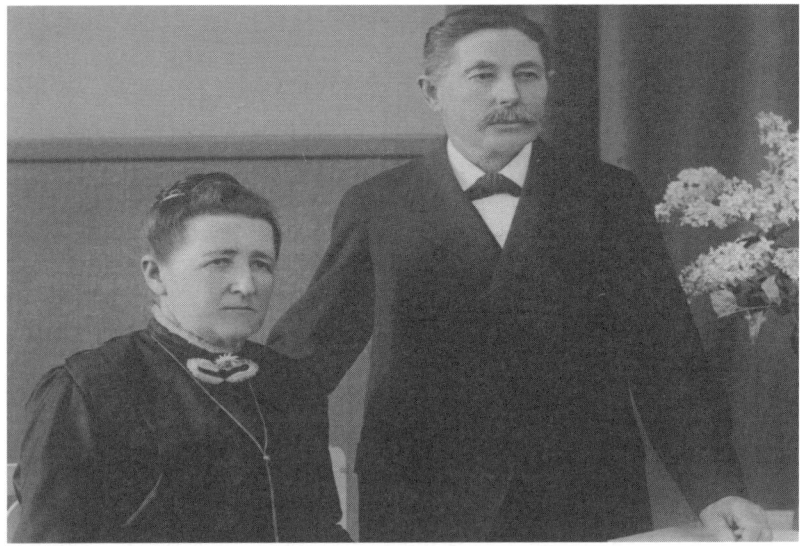

John Jacob Widmer and his wife, Lisette, founders of Widmer Wine Cellars, moved to Naples from the Swiss village of Scherz in 1882. They bought property and planted grapevines. During the day, they worked in the vineyard and, in the evening, built their home.

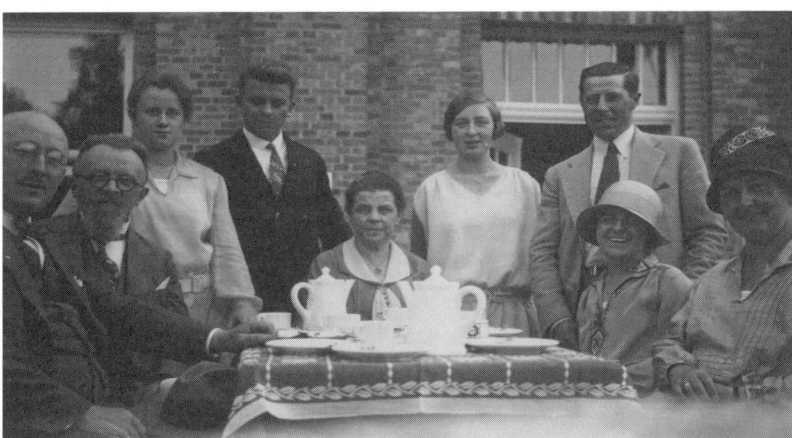

The Widmer family is gathered outside their home in Naples with John Jacob on the left, Lisette in the center, and son, Will, on the right. Widmer was the first New York State winery to offer varietal wine, as opposed to blends. Widmer was also a leader in vintage labeling of wine made from a single year's harvest.

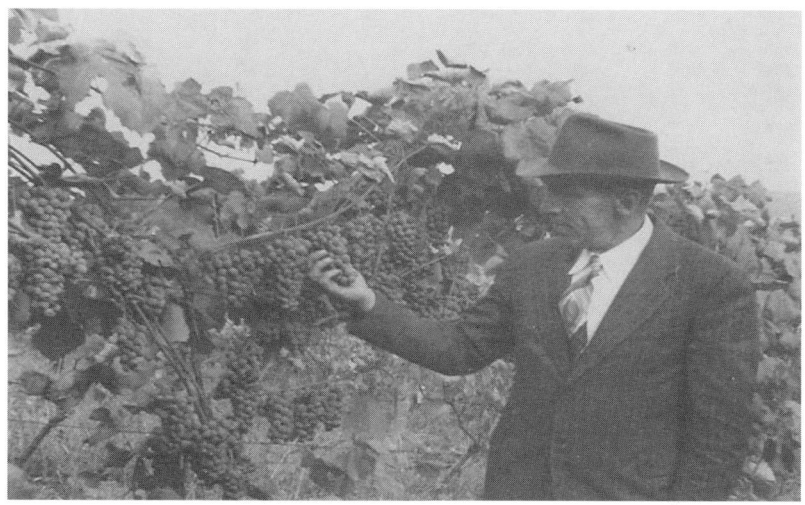

Will Widmer is inspecting grapes in their vineyards in 1947. In 1910, Will attended the Royal Wine School of Germany at Geisenheim, where he was trained in viticulture and enology. He learned about things like "Auglese" (selected picking), "Spatlese" (late picking), and *Botrytis Cinerea* mold (noble rot), which flavors the grapes.

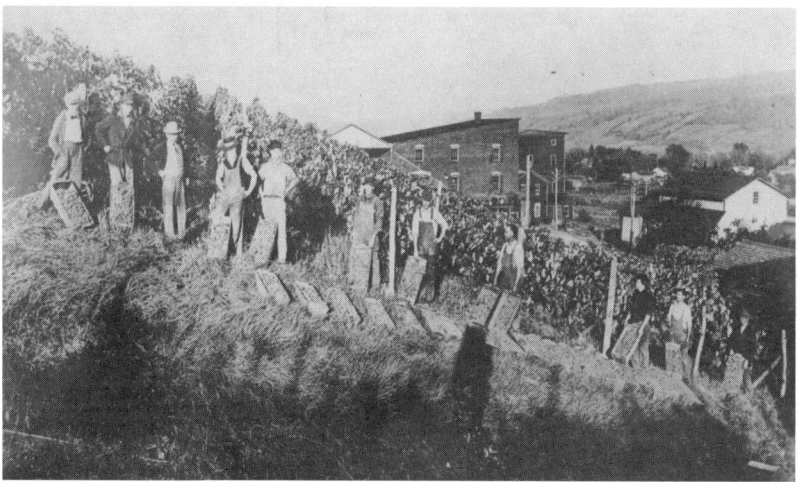

Workers are picking grapes uphill from the Widmer Wine Cellars buildings. The slope is such that the vineyard was hand picked. Even after the availability of automated pickers, they could never be used in this vineyard because the hillside was too steep.

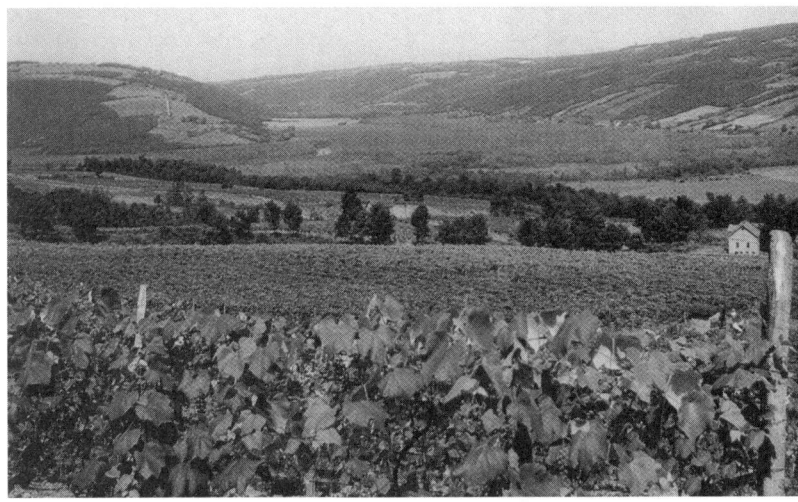

This is a view of the beautiful Naples Valley, home of Widmers. Woodville is at the southern end of Canandaigua Lake; the Village of Naples is five miles south of Woodville. The City of Canandaigua is at the northern end of the lake. Canandaigua Lake is 15 and a half miles long and one and a half mile wide. Its deepest point is 275 feet.

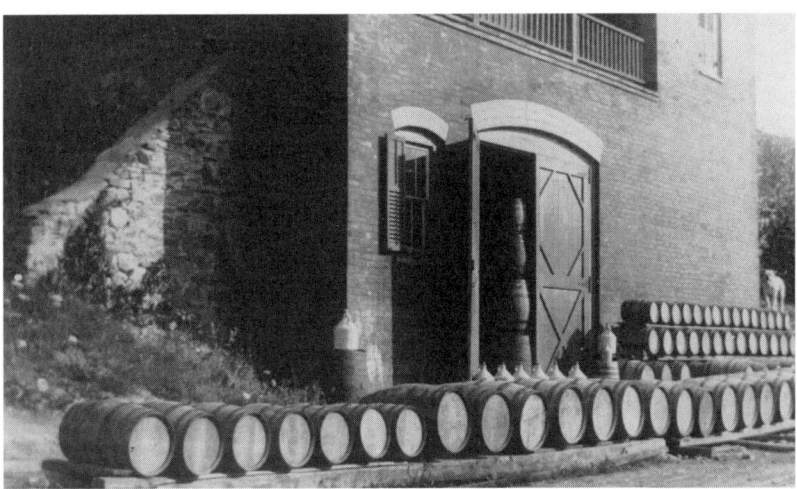

Casks of sherry were stored outside an early Widmer Wine Cellars building to expose them to summer heat and winter snow. Widmer sherry was exposed to the elements for four years before being blended with sherry from other years, using the solera process.

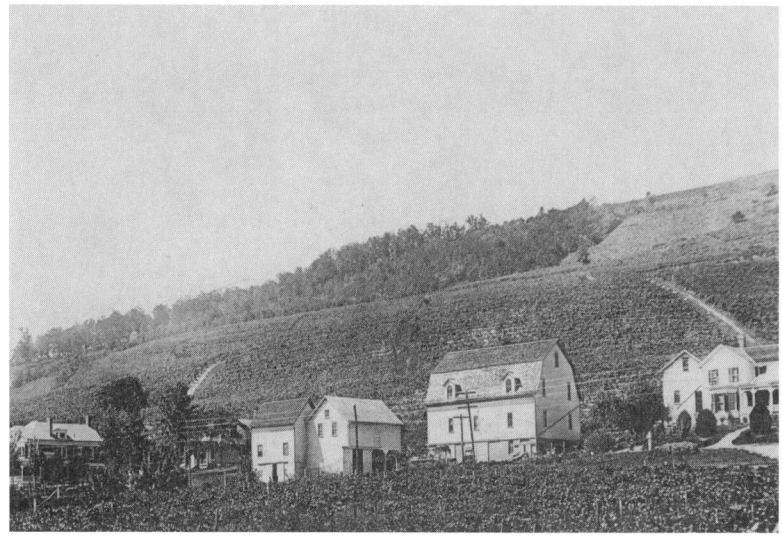

This view is of early Widmer Wine Cellars buildings. The Widmer family built one building at a time as their business expanded. The family homestead is the second white building from the left, partially obscured by trees.

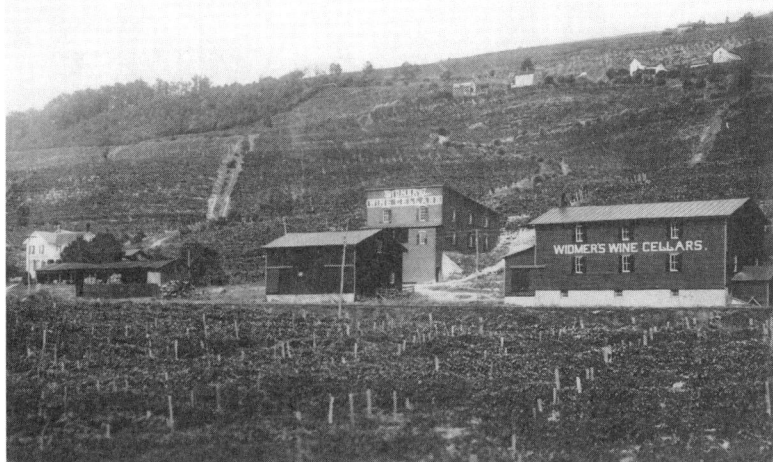

Shown here are early Widmer Wine Cellars buildings. Horse-drawn wagons were used to transport boxes of grapes from the vineyards to the grape crushing facility. Vineyard rows had to be planted far enough apart to allow wagons to travel between the rows of vines.

𝔚𝔦𝔡𝔪𝔢𝔯'𝔰 𝔚𝔦𝔫𝔢 ℭ𝔢𝔩𝔩𝔞𝔯𝔰

NAPLES, N. Y.

JACOB WIDMER,   -   -   -   -   Proprietor

PRODUCERS OF

Widmer's Famous New York State Wines

NOTED FOR THEIR EXCELLENCE AND PURITY

ST. JULIEN   PORT   RIESLING   SHERRY   CLARET   TOKAY
RHINE WINE   SWEET CATAWBA   VINTAGE OF 1902 CLARET
WIDMERHEIMER (ROTH UND WEISS) in bottles only

OWNERS of over 100 acres of best cultivated vineyards in Western Central
New York, located on the western hillsides of beautiful Naples Valley.

This Widmer Wine Cellars advertisement is from the early 1900s.
Tokay is one of the finest dessert wines in the world. It came from
Hungary; it is spelled Tokaj in Hungarian. The main grape variety is
Furmint. It is unlikely that Widmer made their Tokay with Furmint.

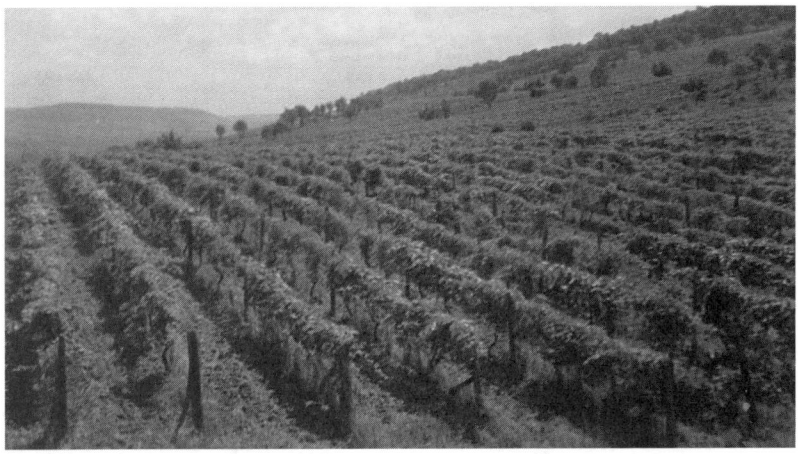

These grapevines are uphill from the Widmer winery, which had 100
acres of vineyards in the early 1900s. Ultimately, Widmer had over
1,000 acres of vineyards. Varieties planted in early Widmer vineyards
were Catawba, Delaware, Elvira, and Isabella. Included in the varieties planted later were Diamond, Duchess, and Niagara.

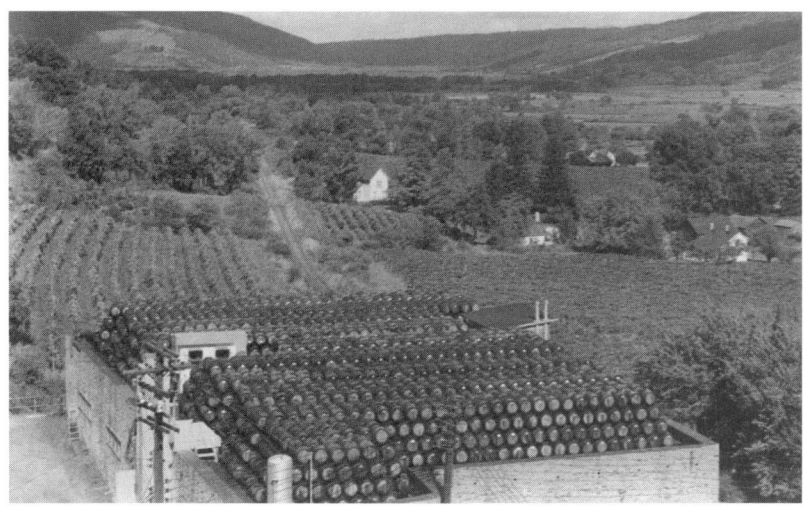

Widmer used the solera process for making sherry, which consists of tiers of sherry of different years. Sherry to be bottled is taken from the bottom tier, which contains the oldest wine. The bottom barrels are left half-full, and are filled with wine from the second tier, and the process is repeated. New sherry is placed on the top tier.

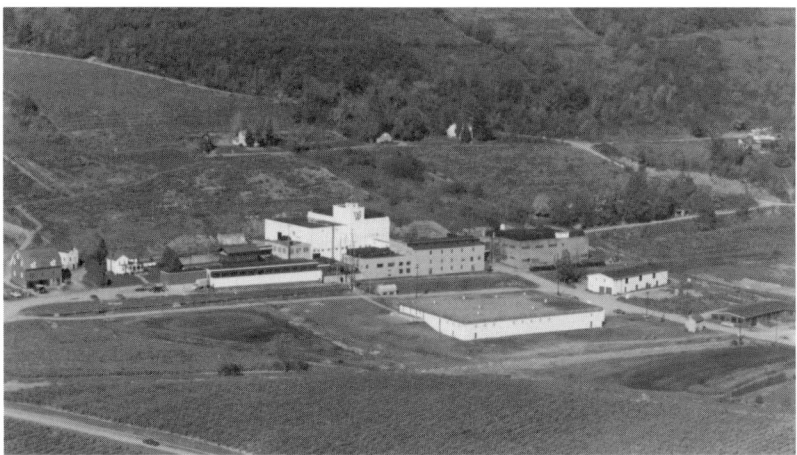

This is an aerial view of Widmer Wine Cellars. In 1961, Widmers was obtained by financiers. In 1970, it was sold to the R. T. French Company and later purchased by Constellation Brands, Inc. In 2011, Constellation Brands moved production of Widmer wine to a Canandaigua facility.

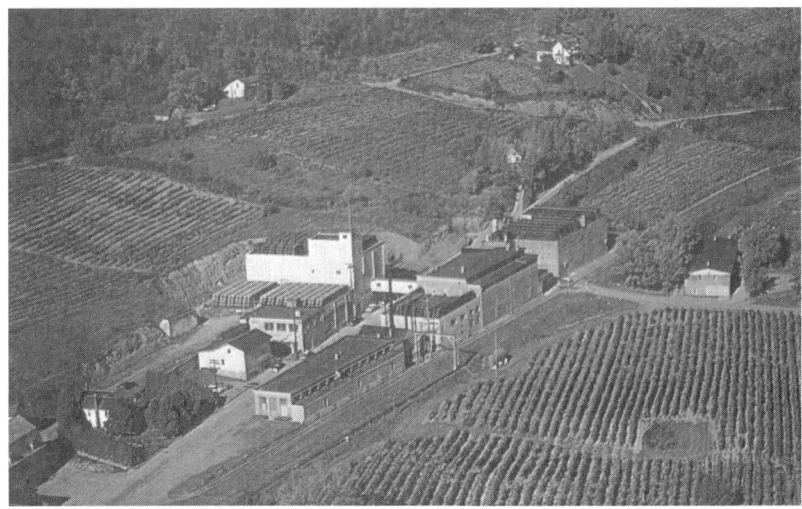

This aerial view of Widmer Wine Cellars is taken from the northeast. In 2011, Widmer Wine Cellars was purchased by Hazlitt 1852 Vineyards on Seneca Lake. Wines produced at Hazlitt Red Cat Cellars, managed by Doug Hazlitt and Leigh Hazlitt Triner, include semi-sweet wines, such as the best-selling Red Cat, a Catawba blend.

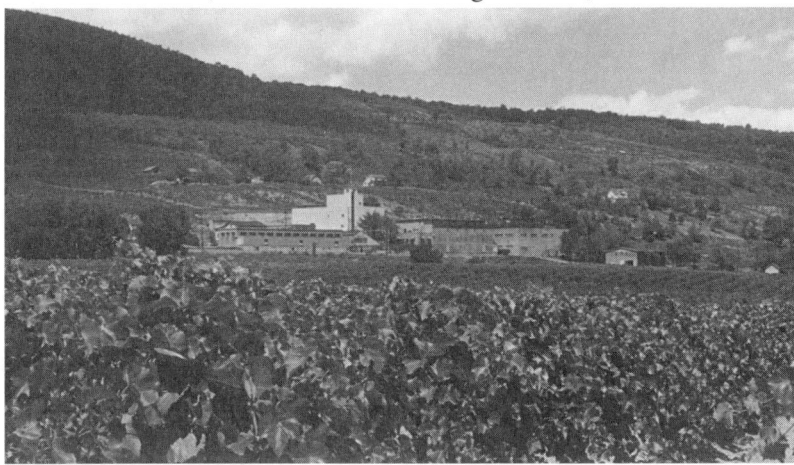

This view of Widmer Wine Cellars, now Hazlitt Red Cat Cellars, is taken from the northeast. In addition to making its own wine, the winery processes products for others in the beverage industry in its three-million-gallon-facility. It also provides contract services, such as grape crushing, pressing, and bottling.

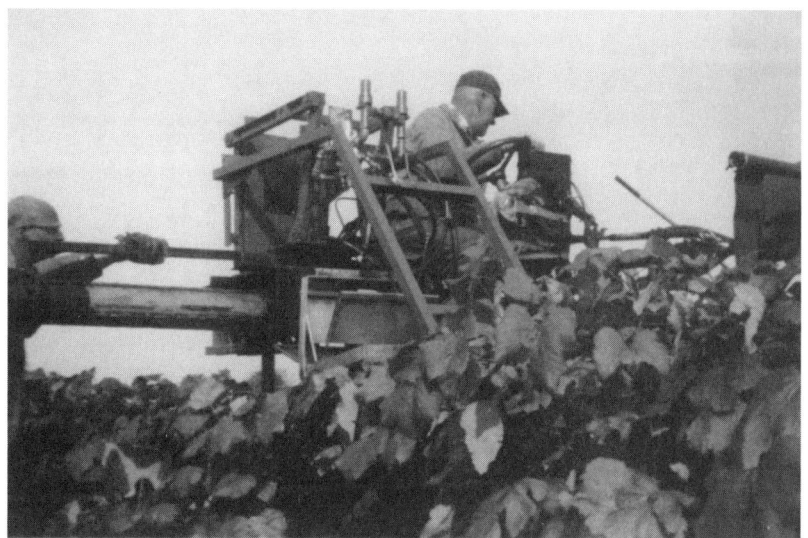

This early automated grape picker was used at Widmer Wine Cellars. Modern pickers have have a conveyor belt on each side of the machine that transports grapes to a bin at the rear of the picker. Automated pickers tend to miss the grapes close to the end posts.

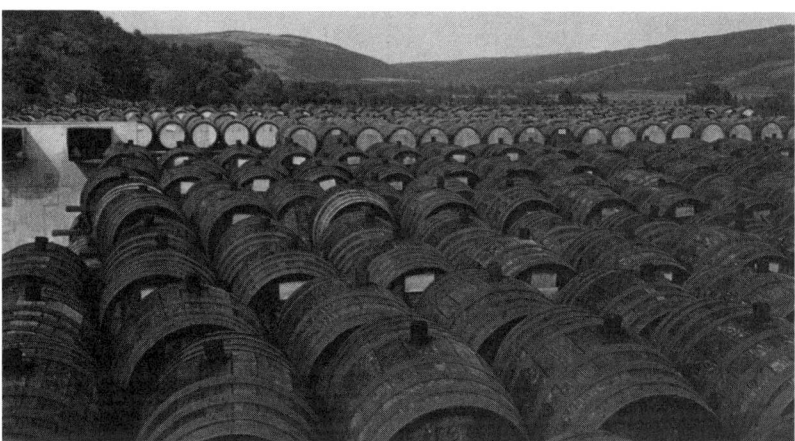

Widmer Wine Cellars had thousands of barrels of sherry in its Solera process. The solera process preserves the quality and character of the sherry over the years by refreshing older wine with younger wine to keep it from losing its freshness. Unlike full-bodied red wine, sherry does not improve with age.

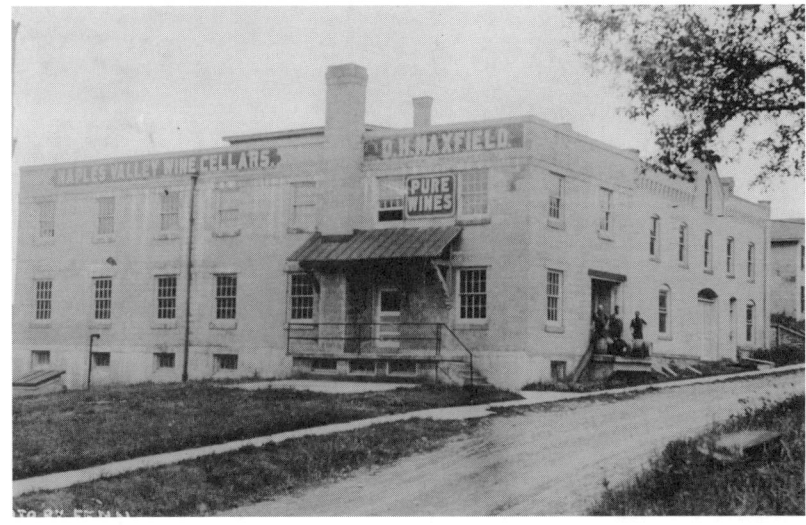

Maxfield Wine Cellars closed during Prohibition. Rival Widmer Wine Cellars stayed in business making grape juice, nonalcoholic wine jellies, and wine sauce. Both Maxfield and Widmer resumed making wine when Prohibition was repealed in 1933. In 1940, Will Widmer bought Maxfield Wine Cellars.

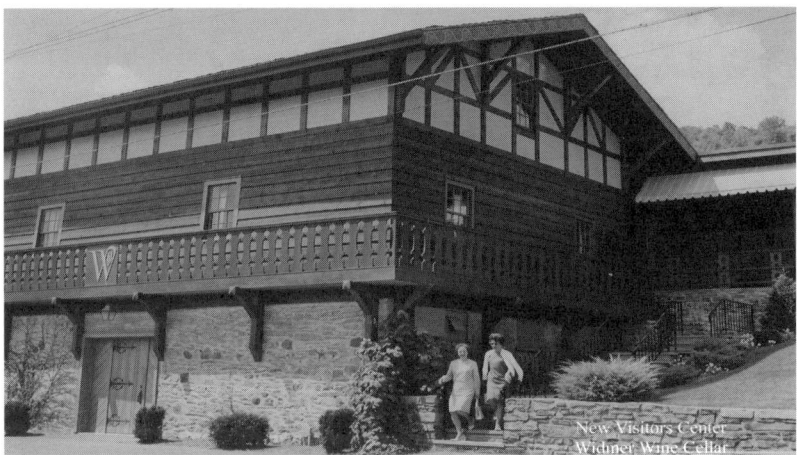

The Niagara Chalet was the visitor center for Widmer Wine Cellars. It was named for Widmer's most popular wine, Lake Niagara, which was recommended to be served very cold. Currently, the Niagara Chalet is used as the visitor center for Hazlitt Red Cat Cellars.

CHAPTER 5 BEFORE TO AFTER PROHIBITION

The temperance movement gained momentum slowly in the U. S., beginning with the 1816 law banning the sale of alcoholic beverages on Sunday. During the 1830s, many towns and counties in the East and Midwest went Dry. Entire States began to go Dry, beginning with Kansas in 1880 and Iowa in 1882. On January 15, 1919, the 18th Amendment to the Constitution was ratified.

Unfortunately, wine was grouped with hard liquor as "intoxicating" by the Volstead Act that became law on October 28, 1919. President Wilson had proposed defining "intoxicating" drinks as those containing more than 10 to 12 percent alcohol. The wine industry would have been saved; however, Wilson's veto was overridden by Congress.

Most wineries went out of business. Some tried to remain profitable by producing medicinal and sacramental wine. Many vineyards in California and New York were ripped out, thus wiping out much of the progress U. S. wineries had made since the mid-1800s. In the early 1920s, a demand existed in the East for grape juice to produce legal wine up to 200 gallons a year per head of household. Eastern vineyards could not supply the demand, so California began to replant vineyards.

Unfortunately, the varieties planted were not the ones that made the best wine, but the varieties that traveled well and did not rot upon shipment to the East. Riesling, Cabernet Sauvignon, and particularly Pinot Noir had thin skins and did not ship well. Course, thick-skinned Alicante Bouschet, a red grape, was one of the varieties that shipped well and sold well.

The once-proud U. S. wine industry, which in the last half of the 1800s had exported wine around the world and won many prizes in international competitions, was in ruins, making inferior wine from a poor choice of grape. On December 5, 1933, the 21st Amendment to the Constitution was ratified, repealing Prohibition. The U. S. wine industry had been set back over three decades in competing with wineries around the world. In the Finger Lakes Region, many wineries had gone out of business, never to reopen.

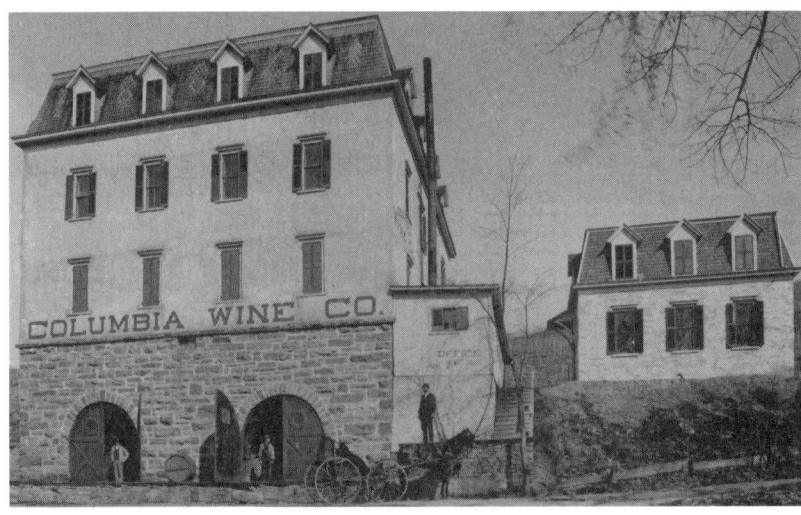

In 1887, Joseph Moosbrugger, the winemaker for the Hammondsport Wine Company, purchased the just completed building of the Columbia Wine Company in Pleasant Valley. The Columbia Wine Company went out of business in 1920, and the facility was purchased by Taylor Wine Company.

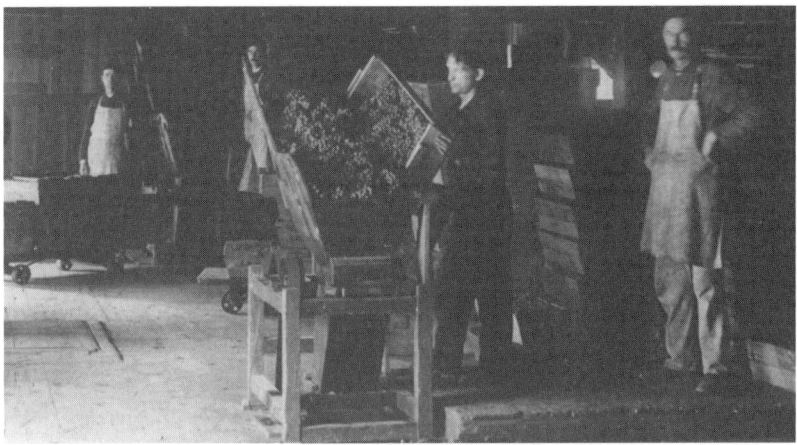

In 1879, Philip Argus established the Western New York Wine Company on the west side of Keuka Lake. In 1929, the winery was destroyed by fire and rebuilt. Following Repeal, the winery was renamed the Rheims Valley Wine Company. The press room of Western New York Wine Company is shown here.

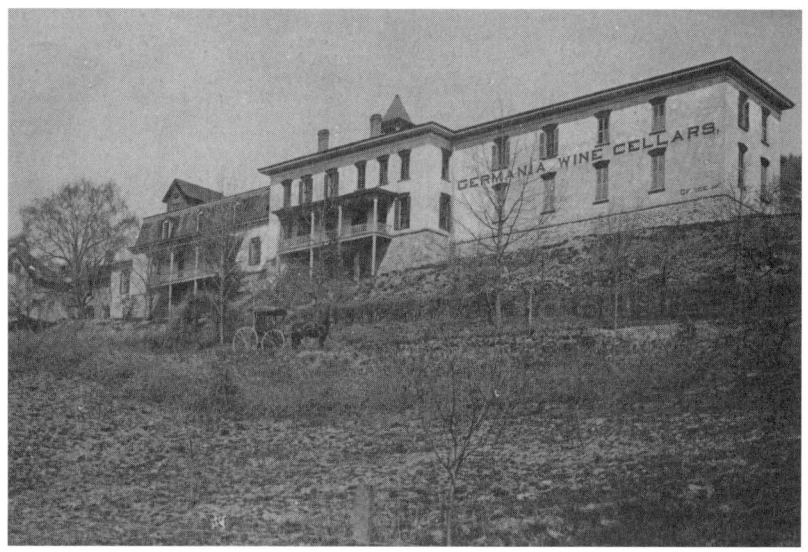

In 1879, Jacob Frey began construction of Germania Wine Cellars in Pleasant Valley. New buildings were added from 1883 until 1889, when the winery doubled its capacity. Another large building was added in 1902. This photograph shows the facility in 1893.

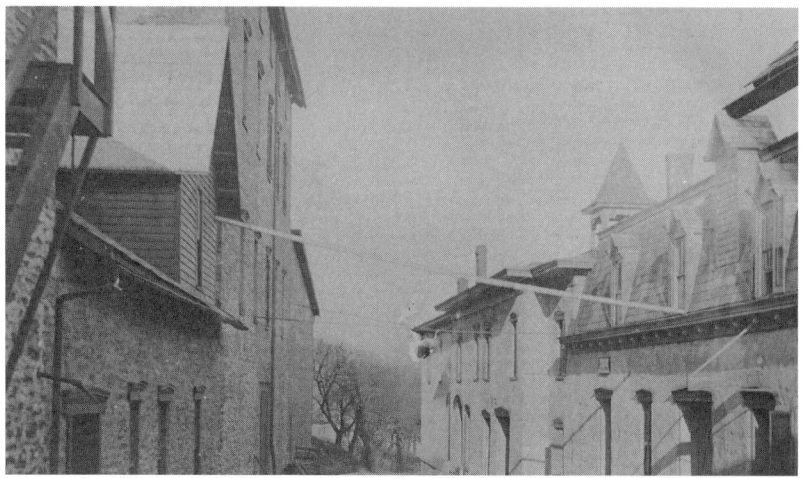

In 1920, Germania Wine Cellars completed another expansion. It was purchased by the Griffenhagen family and renamed Monopole. Over th next 18 years, they used the names Montage Vineyards Company and Jermania Wine Cellars. The winery was closed in the late 1930s.

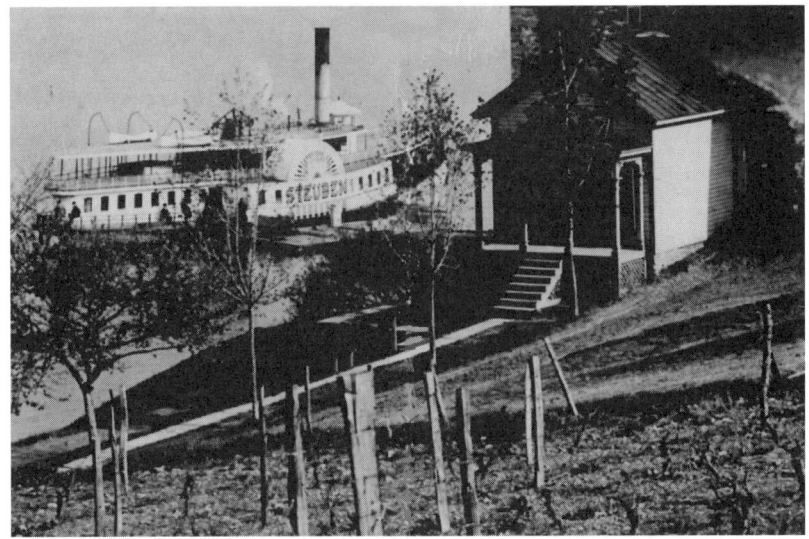

Lake Keuka Wine Cellars was founded as Crooked Lake Wine Cellars. When, in 1878, the State Legislature changed the name of Crooked Lake back to its Iroquois name Keuka Lake, the winery changed its name also. The steamship *Steuben* is shown at the dock.

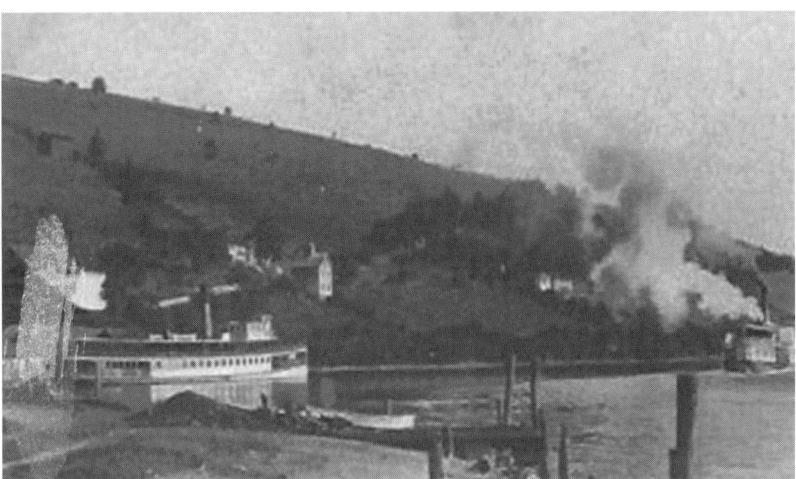

The steamship *Yates* is shown leaving her pier and the steamship *Mary Bell,* the largest of the steamships that plied the waters of Keuka Lake over the years, at her dock in Hammondsport.

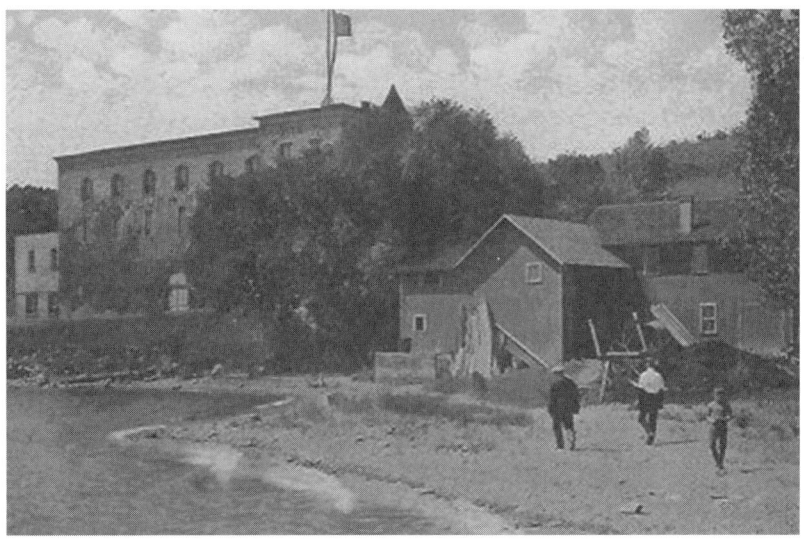

In 1902, the name of Keuka Lake Wine Cellars was changed to White Top Wine Cellars. White Top Wine Cellars was the only Finger Lakes Region winery to be successfully raided by area Prohibition enforcement officers.

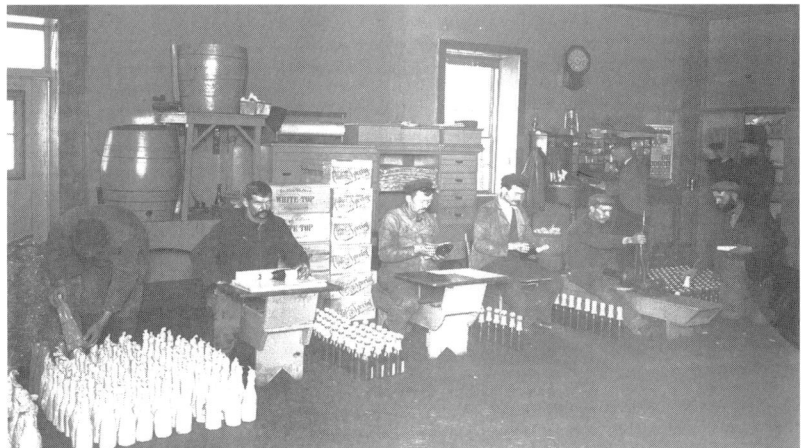

Workers are shown labeling and wrapping champagne bottles. In the 1940s, White Top Wine Cellars, the only "Exclusive Champagne Producer in America," was purchased by Robin Fils Company of Batavia, New York. It was destroyed by fire in the 1950s.

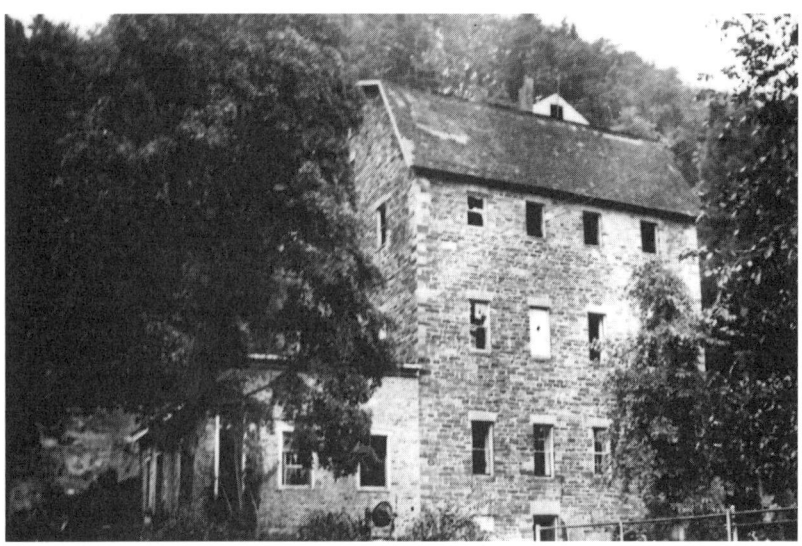

This view of the Glen Winery on Pulteney Street in Hammondsport was taken looking west. It was built in 1835-36 as a mill with three overshot wheels. It was closed in 1840, and the facility was used as a storehouse until 1881, when it became Glen Wine Company.

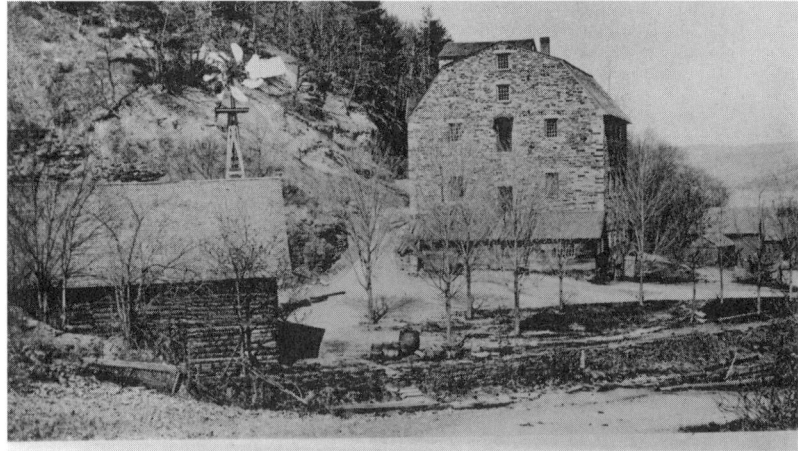

This view of Glen Wine Company is looking northeast towards Keuka Lake. In 1901, the winery was sold and renamed Roualet Wine Company. The winery was severely damaged in the 1935 flood, when barrels of its inventory rolled into the streets of Hammondsport. It never reopened and is now used as a storehouse.

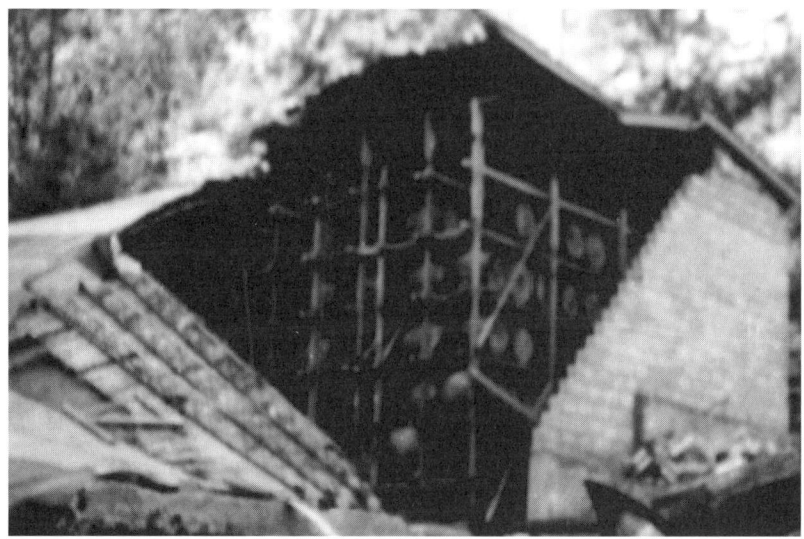

When the Roualet Wine Company was severely damaged in the flood of 1935, 500 barrels of grape brandy rolled into the streets of Hammondsport. Locals tapped the barrels for personal use until officials arrived.

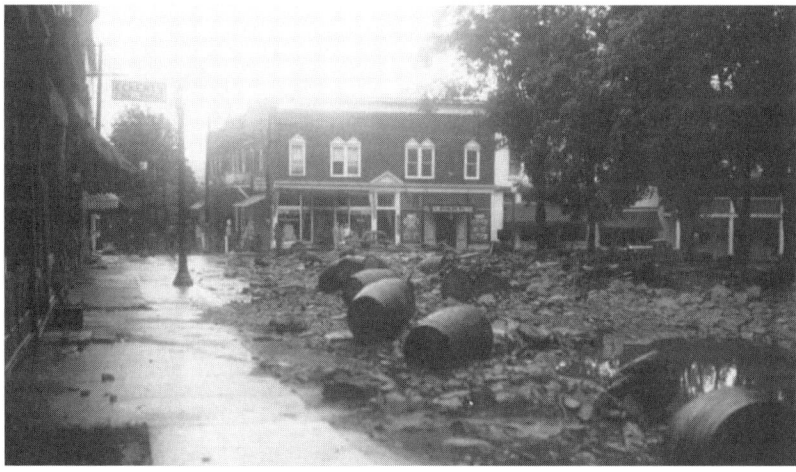

Pulteney Street was "littered" with barrels of grape brandy from the flood. Two men from Penn Yan came to Hammondsport by boat and struggled to load two barrels into their boat. When they arrived home, they discovered that their two barrels were filled with pomace.

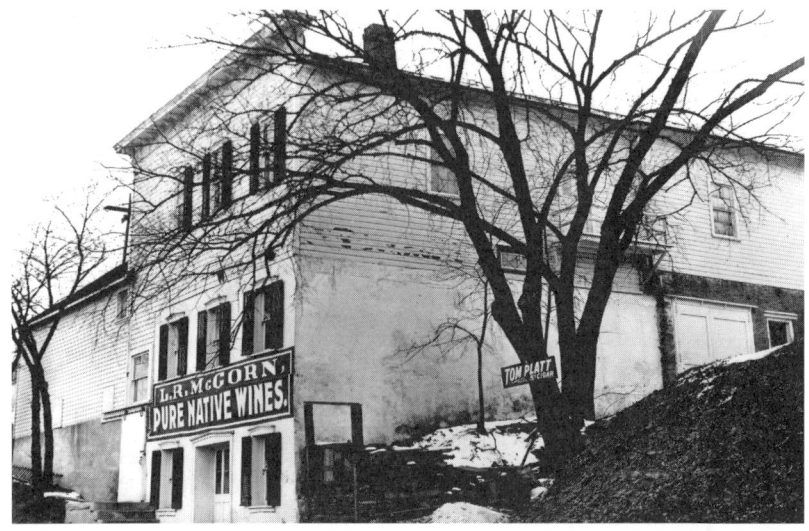

LaRay McCorn erected a winery on Pulteney Road in Hammondsport in 1891, two years after purchasing a vineyard. In 1912, LaRay sold the winery to his brother, VanBuren, who operated it successfully until the beginning of Prohibition, when he went out of business.

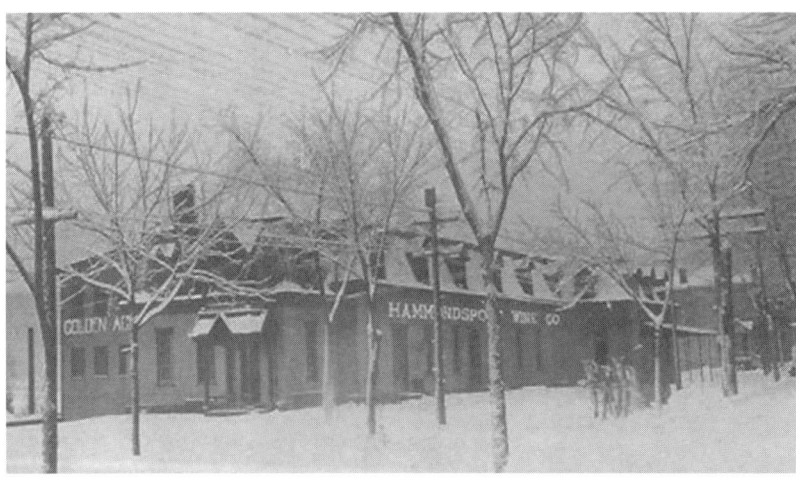

Wheeler Wine Company, predecessor of Hammondsport Wine Company, was founded by Grattan Wheeler in 1858. In 1867, Wheeler purchased property for wine vaults. The buildings burned down in 1867 and were rebuilt. Wheeler sold the winery in 1878.

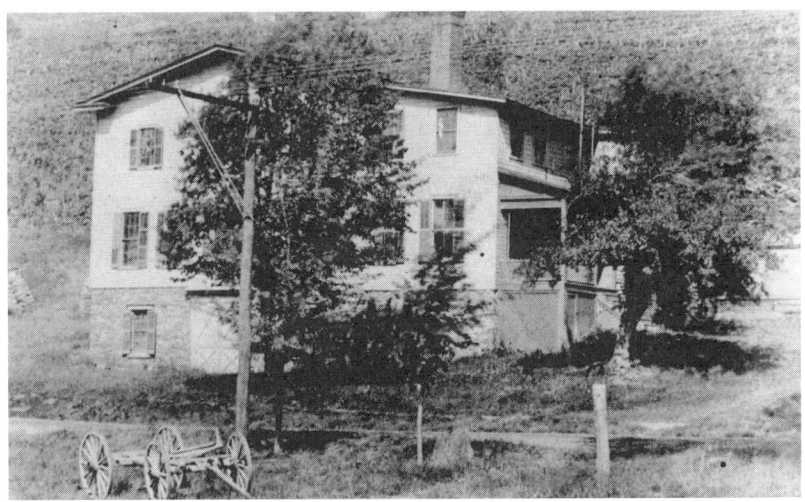

In 1889, O. H. Younglove established the Monarch Wine Company on his vineyard property in Pleasant Valley and added an office building in 1900. In 1906, the winery and 50,000 gallons of wine were destroyed by fire. Younglove rebuilt the winery to collect the insurance money but never reentered the wine business.

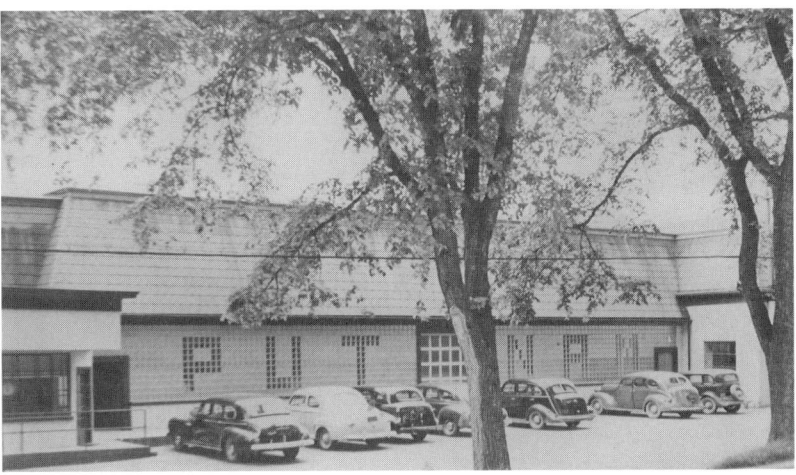

The Putnam Company was founded in 1926 to sell grapes and juice. With the repeal of Prohibition, Putnam resumed producing Golden Age Champagne and wine. In the 1970s, the winery was sold to the Canandaigua Wine Company.

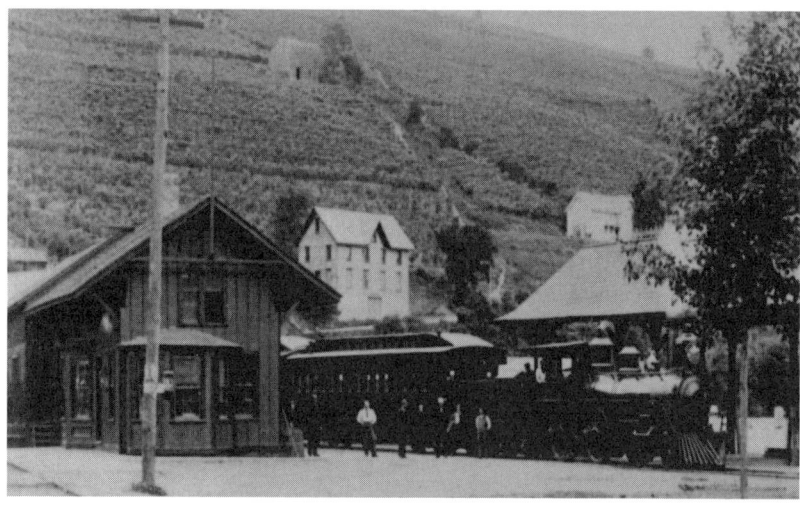

The Bath & Hammondsport Railroad was used to transport grapes from Hammondsport to Bath for loading on canal boats to Philadelphia and Baltimore. Canal boat travel on the Cohocton, Chemung, and Susquehanna Rivers required many portages. Later, the Erie Railroad passed through Bath.

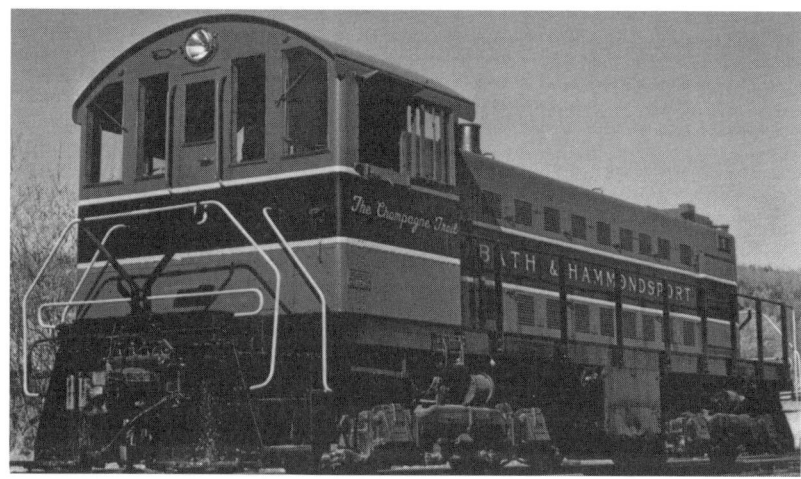

After the nine-mile-long Bath & Hammondsport Railroad began to transport wine and champagne instead of grapes, it became known as the "Champagne Trail." Its slogan was, "Our rails may not be as long as others, but they are just as wide."

CHAPTER 6 PAUL GARRETT / THE PENN YAN AREA

Paul Garrett, dean of American winemakers in the early years of the twentieth century, became a multimillionaire making and selling wine. He was born in North Carolina and by the age of 14 was working for Medoc Vineyard, North Carolina's first winery. It was owned by his father, country doctor Francis Garrett, and his uncle, Charles Garrett, who ran the winery.

Paul Garrett promoted wine made from the Scuppernong grape. He was the father of he Virginia Dare label, the best-selling wine in the United States in the two decades prior to Prohibition. He established his first winery, Garrett & Company, in North Carolina in 1900, and by 1903, he owned five wineries in the State.

The Anti-Saloon League was very active, and the southern States began to go Dry. In 1909, North Carolina law prohibited the manufacture and sale of intoxicating liquor. Garrett moved his wine company, first to Virginia and then to Penn Yan, New York, where he opened his first northern winery in 1910. He was familiar with the Finger Lakes Region from his purchases of Finger Lakes wine for resale and for blending with Garrett & Company wines.

Garrett expanded into other States, and by 1913 he owned vineyards and wineries in Penn Yan, as well as warehouses in Canandaigua and Hammondsport. In 1919, he owned 17 plants for processing grape juice and wine with a total capacity of 10 million gallons in the States of California, Missouri, New York, North Carolina, Ohio, and Virginia.

With the onset of Prohibition, Garrett could have retired a multimillionaire, but he held on to his wine empire, not believing that Prohibition would last. He lost money on de-alcoholized wine, a cola-flavored grape drink, flavoring extracts, and grape concentrates.

In the early 1930s, Garrett moved his headquarters to the Bush Terminal in Brooklyn, where Garrett & Company had substantial blending and bottling facilities. When Prohibition was repealed in 1933, Garrett was the only vintner capable of marketing wine in every Wet State.

Garrett's main theme was "American Wine for Americans." He was in New York City promoting this concept when he contracted pneumonia and died on March 18, 1940.

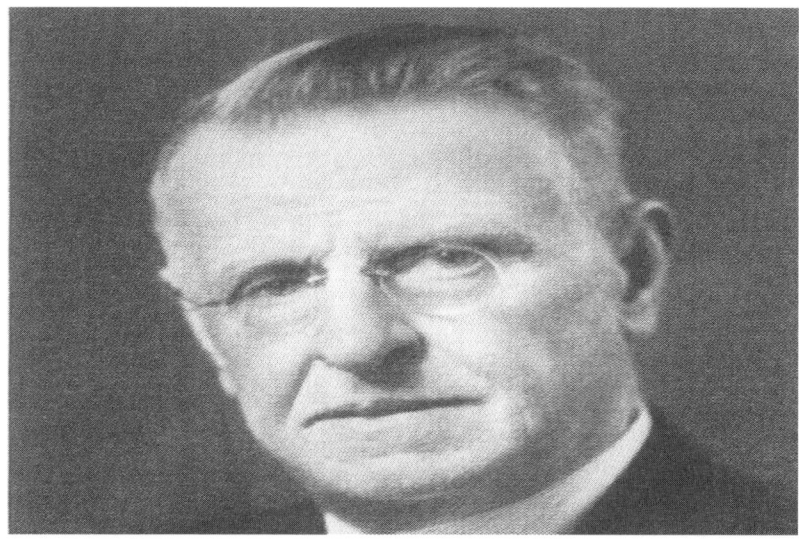

Initially, Paul Garrett made Virginia Dare wine from the Scuppernong grape. Eventually, demand for the variety outstripped the supply, and Garrett made the wine a blend of Concord; Scuppernong, which hid the foxy or grapy flavor of the Concord grape; and California wine.

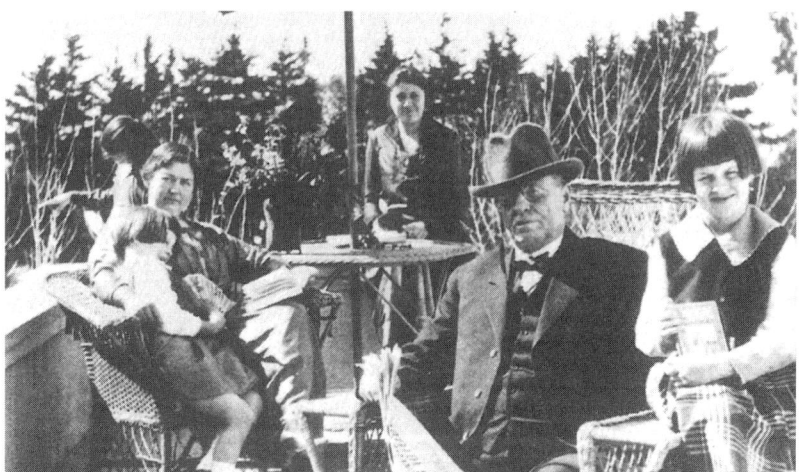

When Paul Garrett died in 1940, he was survived by his wife, Evelyn Edwards Garrett, and daughters, Dorothy, Evelyn, and Emily. He was preceded in death by their son, Charles Williams Garrett, a graduate of Phillips Exeter Academy and Yale University.

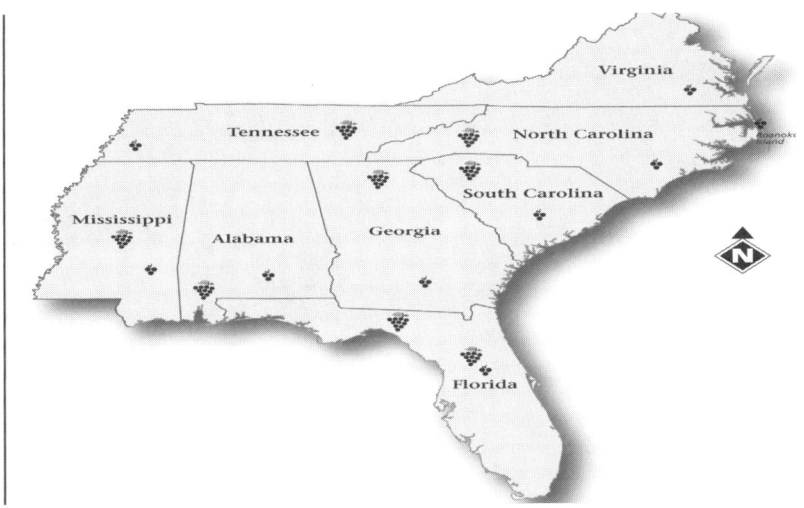

Scuppernong grapes grow wild in the woods from southern Virginia to Florida. The variety is usually shaken from the vine, not picked, and the fruit is not produced from the current year's growth but from spurs that are one or more years old. Scuppernong vines do not need pruning and are not subject to disease or pests.

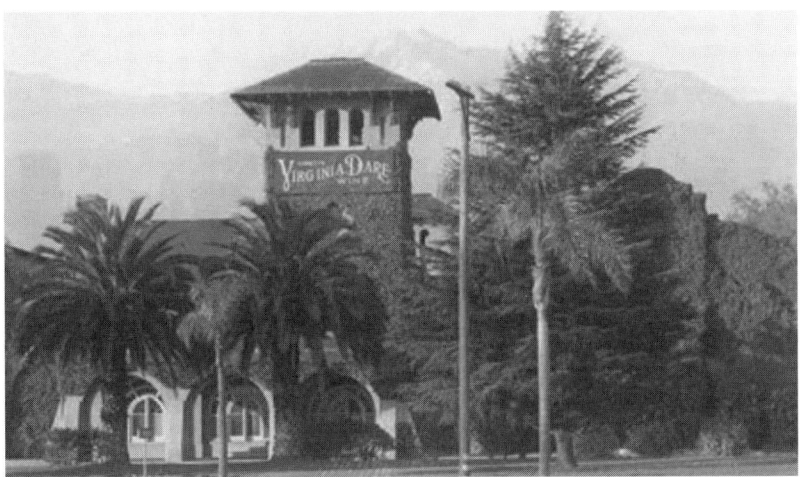

In 1911, Garrett purchased 2,000 acres in San Bernardino County, California, and established Mission Vineyard and Winery in Cucamonga. Garrett used California juice (high sugar, low acid) for blending with eastern juice (low sugar, high acid).

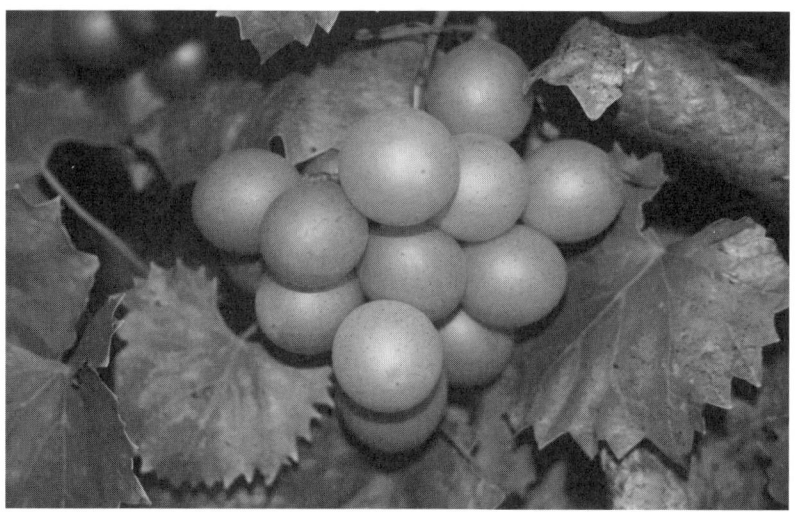

The greenish-bronze Scuppernong grape variety, a member of the Muscadine family, is native only to the southern States, and when fermented dry makes an amber, strong tasting, somewhat bitter wine. When sugar is added, it becomes a wine with the distinct taste of plums with a musky aroma. (Courtesy of Dr. Peter Cousins)

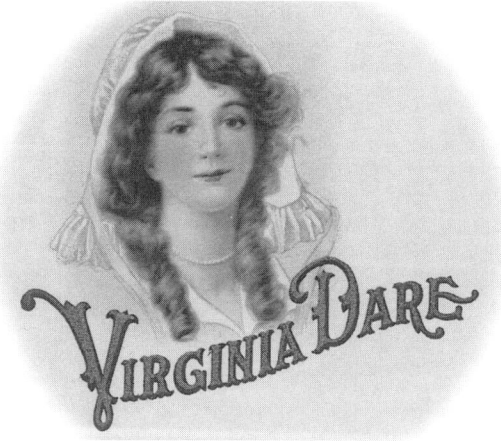

Virginia Dare, the first English child born on American soil, was born August 18, 1587, on Roanoke Island, North Carolina. Because the name Virginia Dare symbolized wholesomeness and purity, as well as new beginnings, promise, and hope, Garrett chose it as the brand name for Garrett & Company's Scuppernong wine.

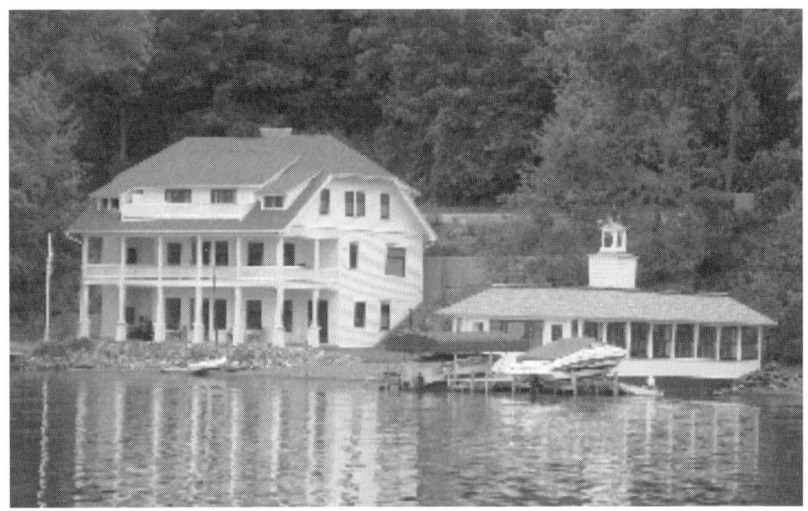

Paul Garrett built this home on the shoreline of Keuka Lake, south of Penn Yan. At one time the Garrett family owned 50 acres of land on the Bluff of Keuka Lake and 1,000 feet of lake frontage. The home is still owned by the Garrett family today. (Courtesy of Richard McAlpine).

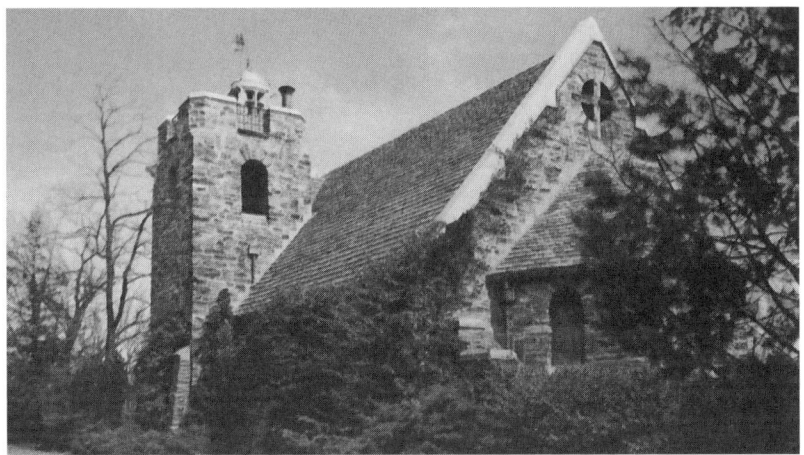

Garrett Memorial Chapel was built in 1931 in memory of the Garrett's son, Charles Garrett, who died of tuberculosis at the age of 26. The "Little Chapel on the Mount" is located near the tip of the Bluff, off Skyline Drive. It is open to the public at scheduled times, including Sundays for worship services during July and August.

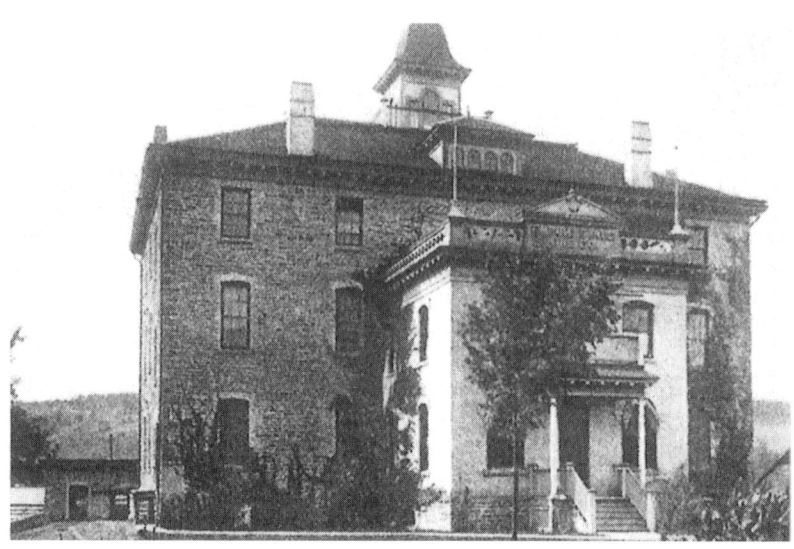

Harriet and Clinton Brooks founded Empire State Winery in Penn Yan in 1896. The winery produced State Seal Champagne and Vineyard Queen and sweet Catawba wines. The winery went out of business in 1944; the building was demolished in 1990.

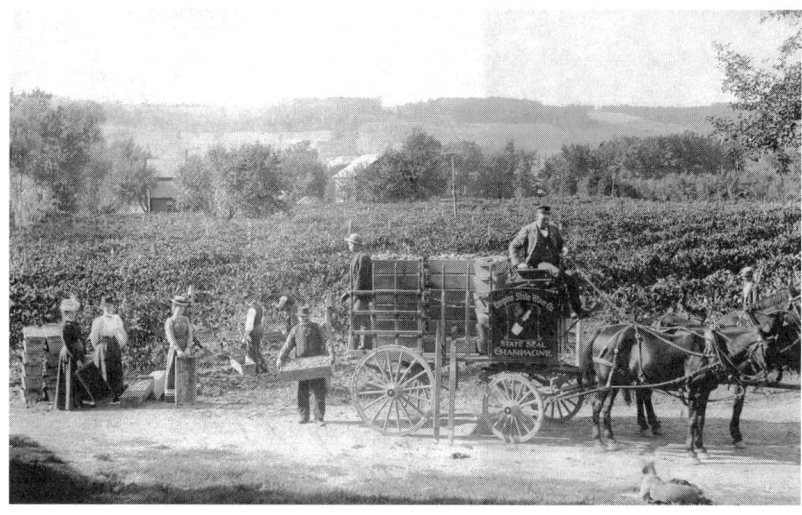

Empire State Winery workers are shown picking grapes in Penn Yan vineyards to make State Seal Champagne. During Prohibition, the winery made grape juice, sacramental wine, and medicinal wine.

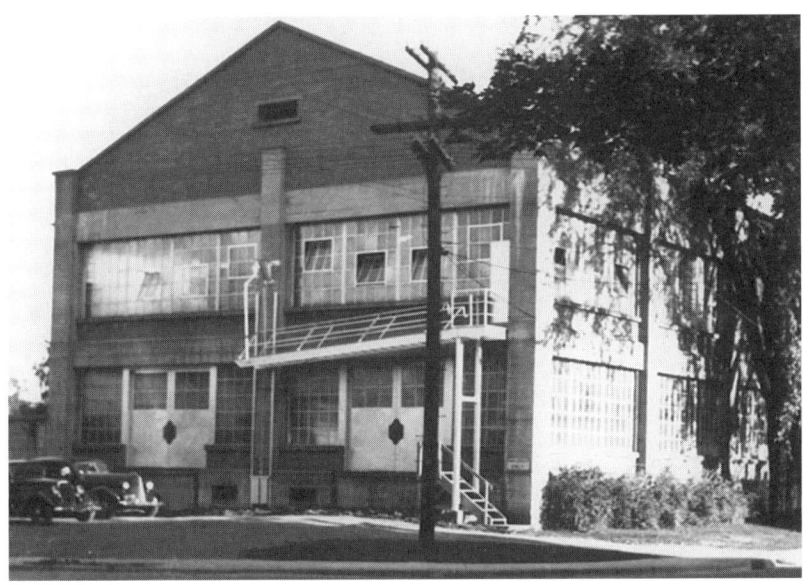

Shown is the Garrett & Company winery headquarters that Paul Garrett used when he moved from North Carolina and Virginia. Later, it was Philip Wagner's Boordy Winery. It is now an office building.

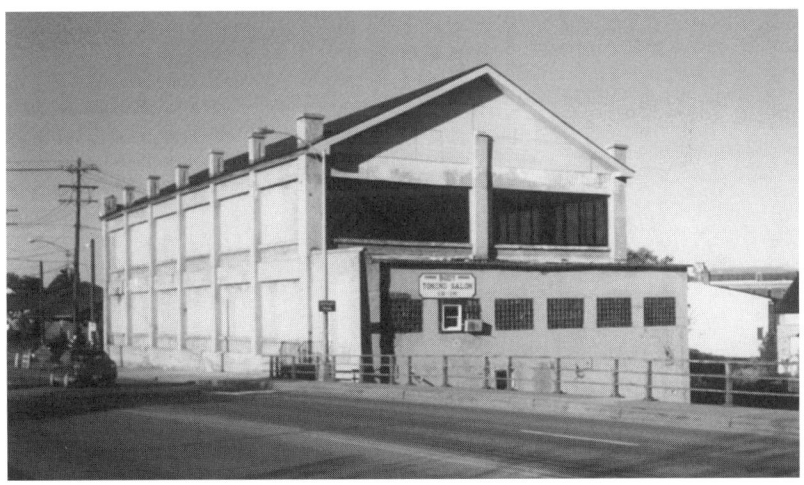

Philip Wagner was a promoter of French-American hybrid grapes, In 1970, He opened Boordy Vineyards winery in Penn Yan in the old Garrett & Company winery. He produced wine made from French-American hybrid grapes.

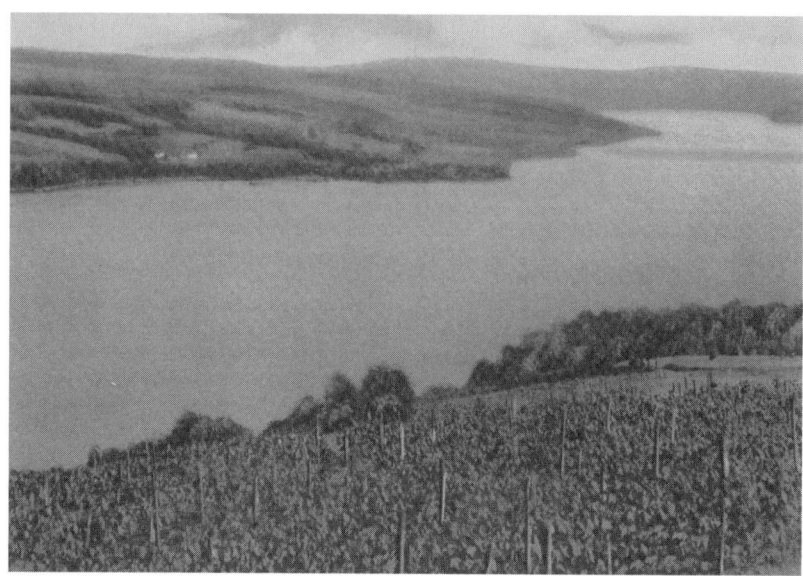

This view shows vineyards along Keuka Lake near Penn Yan, a major grape growing area in the region. The area had many vineyards that provided grapes for the table grape market and for wineries.

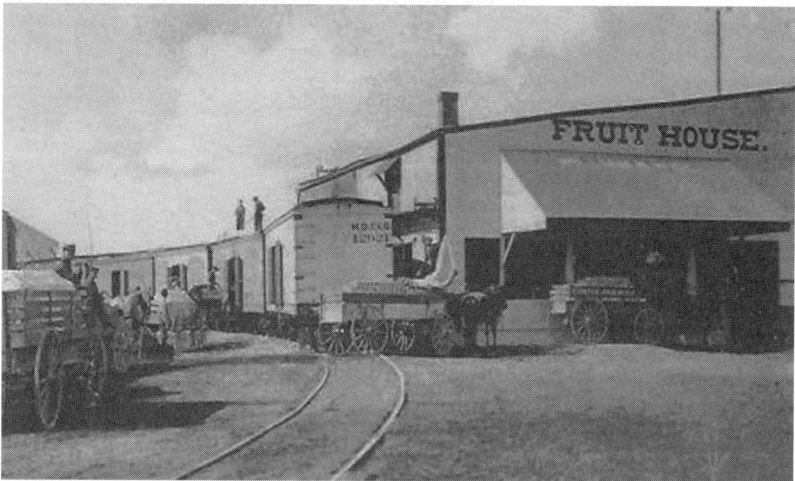

Grapes are shown being off loaded from horse-drawn wagons and loaded into railroad cars for shipment to market. The Penn Yan area supply of grapes was sufficiently large to have warehouses such as the Fruit House to store grapes until shipped.

CHAPTER 7   WALTER S. TAYLOR AND BULLY HILL

Walter S. Taylor was a vice president of Taylor Wine Company until 1970, when he left the company after speaking out against the large New York State wineries for using as much as 25 percent California juice in New York State wines and for ameliorating (adding water to) wine to reduce acid content. His slogan was "Wine without water." Although these practices were legal, Taylor thought the wine-buying public was being misled.

In 1958, Taylor and his father, Greyton, had bought back the original 60-acre Taylor Wine Company property on Bully Hill from the Sprague family to pursue their interests in French-American hybrid grape varieties. Taylor incorporated Bully Hill Vineyards in 1970 and began to make Bully Hill wine. He insisted on listing all ingredients in his Bully Hill wine on his labels.

Also, Taylor pioneered noting, on the back label of the bottle, all growers from whom he had purchased grapes of a particular variety. Finger Lakes Region grape juice tends to be high in acid, which adds crispness in wine. Acid can be reduced in two ways, adding water or adding calcium carbonate.

Taylor made quality wine and was a talented artist and poet. He produced many creative wine labels, motivating him to produce wine with unusual names. His art is displayed at the Greyton H. Taylor Grape and Wine Museum and Art Museum at Bully Hill Vineyards. Walter specialized in French-American hybrid wine, and he had a comprehensive nursery that sold hybrid vines to other vineyardists and wineries. In 1968, Hermann Wiemer emigrated from the Mosel Valley in Germany to be the vineyard manager at Bully Hill and to run the nursery. He left Bully Hill in 1980 to establish his own winery on Seneca Lake.

In 1990, Taylor's van collided with a truck north of Tampa, Florida. His neck was broken, and he became a respirator-dependent quadriplegic. His wife, Lillian, who had been active in running Bully Hill Vineyards, took over its management with the able assistance of Greg Learned, the winemaker.

Taylor passed away in 2001. In addition to being a talented winemaker and artist, he was a very charismatic individual. He contributed in many ways to the lore of the region, as by holding his annual overnight pig roasts that were attended by 1,500 wine lovers.

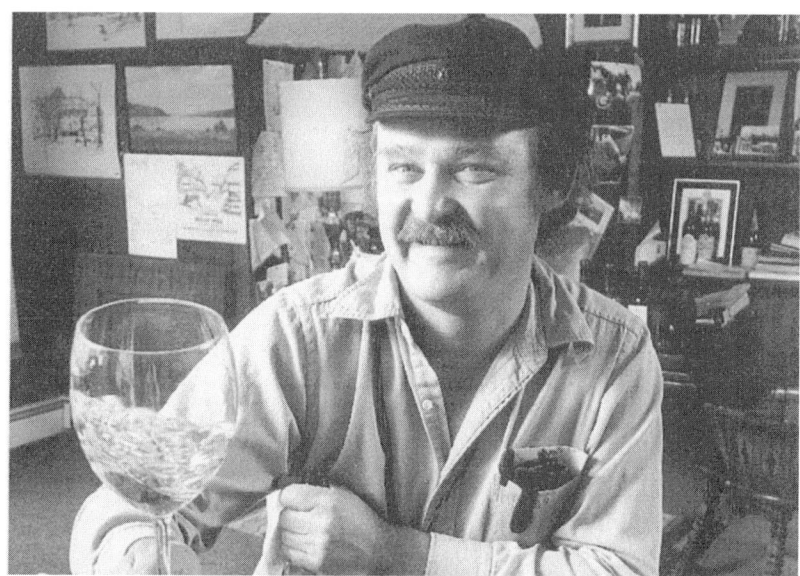

After Walter Taylor (pictured) and his father, Greyton, bought back the Taylor Wine Company property on Bully Hill in 1958, they planted French-American varieties, such as Aurora, Chambourcin, Ravat 51 (Vignoles), Seyval Blanc, Baco Noir, and Marechal Foch.

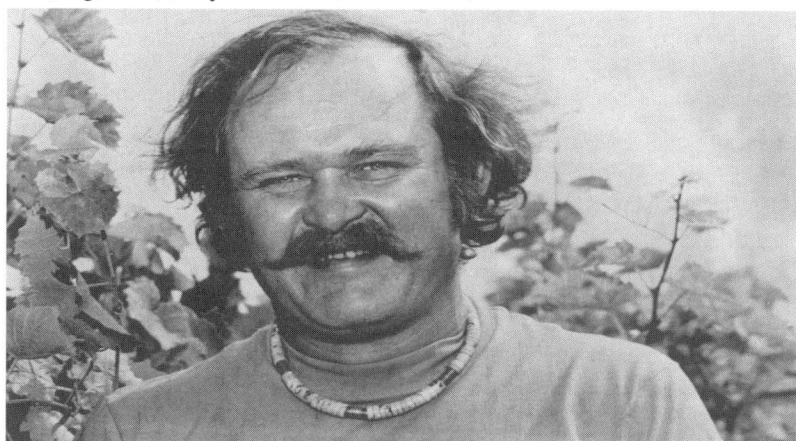

In 1976, Taylor Wine Company and its parent, Coca-Cola, filed a suit against Walter to prevent him from using the name, "Taylor," on his Bully Hill Wine labels. He blackened out Taylor, leaving Walter S. XXXXXX. The classic David versus Goliath confrontation was, in terms of free publicity alone, won by Walter Taylor.

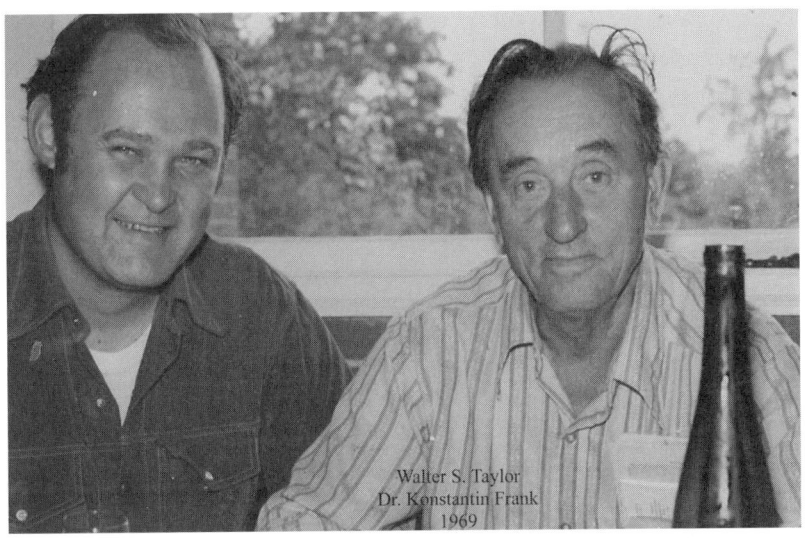

Walter S. Taylor
Dr. Konstantin Frank
1969

Walter Taylor and Dr. Konstantin Frank were pioneers: Walter in pro-moting French-American hybrid varieties and Dr. Frank in introduc-ing vinifera varieties and in promoting cool-climate viticulture. They lived only four miles apart and met at many wine functions.

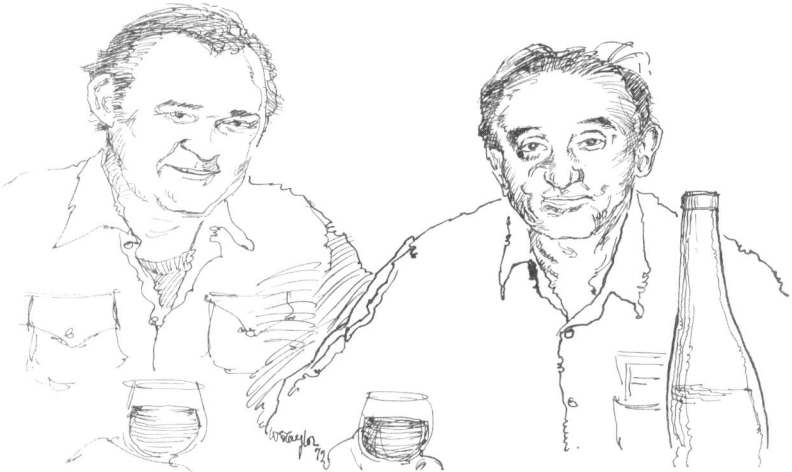

Walter drew this sketch of himself and Dr. Frank. He could produce facial features in such detail in a line drawing that there is no ques-tion who the subjects of the drawing were. Taylor also drew many striking waterfront scenes.

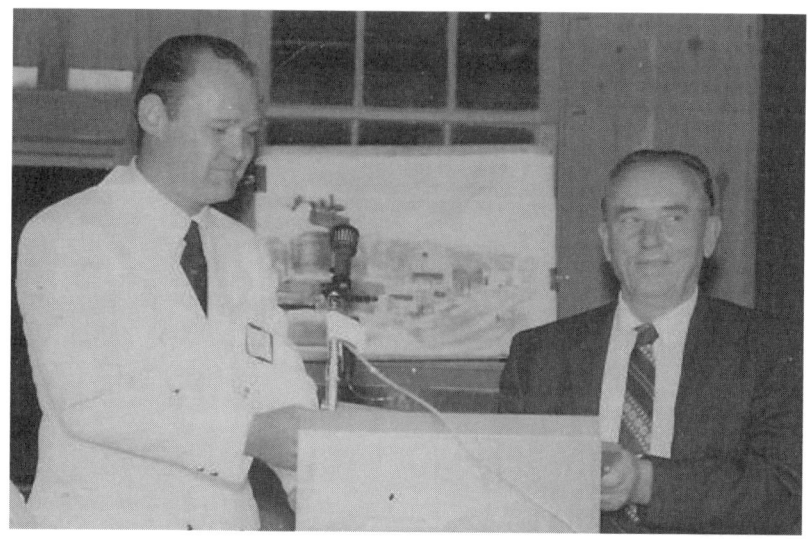

In 1969, Walter Taylor introduced Dr. Frank at the Finger Lakes Wine Museum. They respected each other despite the fact that Dr. Frank did not have a very high opinion of French-American hybrid wine.

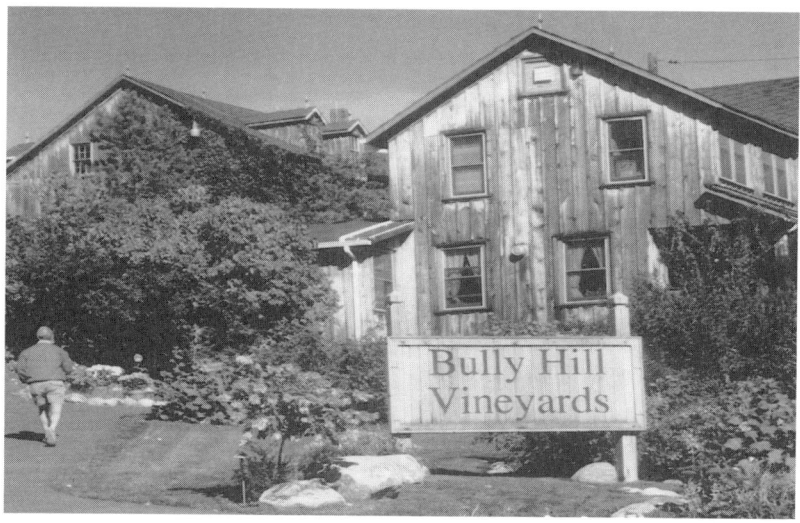

Bully Hill Vineyards has a fine restaurant with indoor and terrace dining, as well as a two-story gift shop and a wine retail store. Just up the hill from the winery is the Greyton H. Taylor Wine and Grape Museum and adjacent Art Museum.

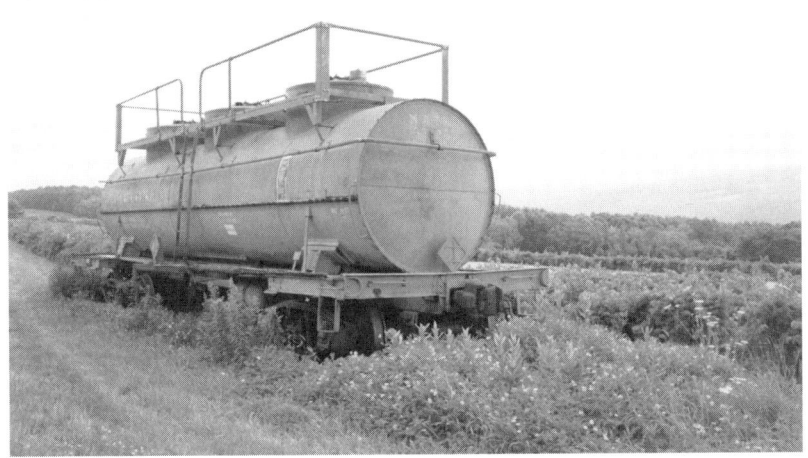

Walter did not agree with New York State wineries that blended with California wine. Legally, wine can be called New York State wine if has no more than 25 percent wine from out of State. Walter bought a railroad tank car for Bully Hill to make a point. He never used it.

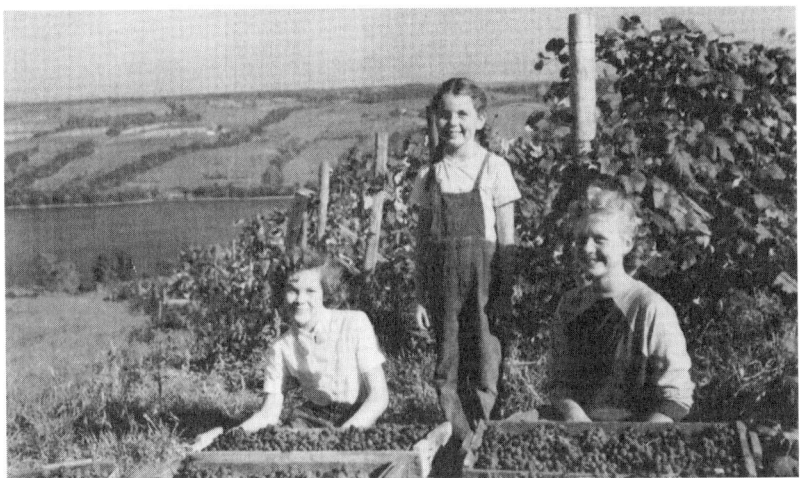

Betty, Edna May, and Sandra Ball have just finished picking grapes on Bully Hill. As you can see, picking grapes is not always viewed as hard labor; it can be fun as well. However, it is not a good idea to wear white while picking grapes, particularly red grapes.

79

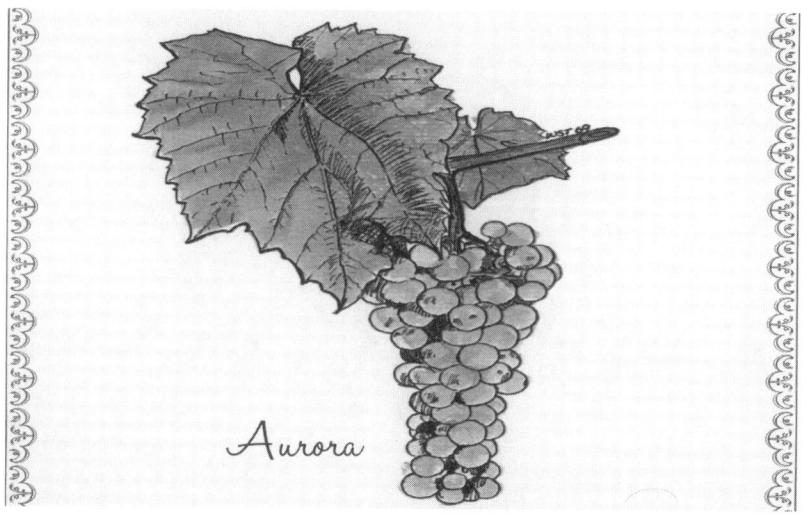

Aurora is a white French-American hybrid variety. It does well in cool climates and is suitable in regions with a short growing season. The wine has a delicate, fruity flavor with a recognizable aroma and some residual sugar. It has moderate alcohol, is well balanced, and is frequently used for blending.

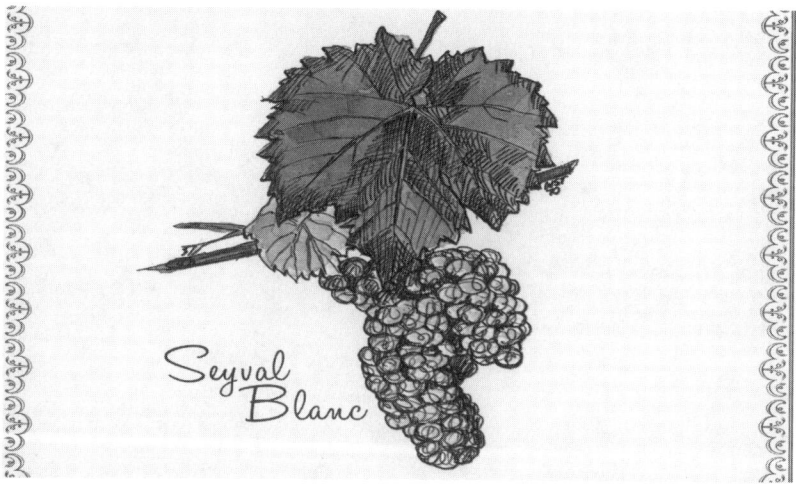

Seyval Blanc is a white French-American hybrid variety. Initially, the wine was dry, flinty, and made in the Chablis style. A wider range of styles is used today. The wine is delicate with a notable bouquet, an excellent sugar-acid balance, and an apple, citrus, or melon flavor.

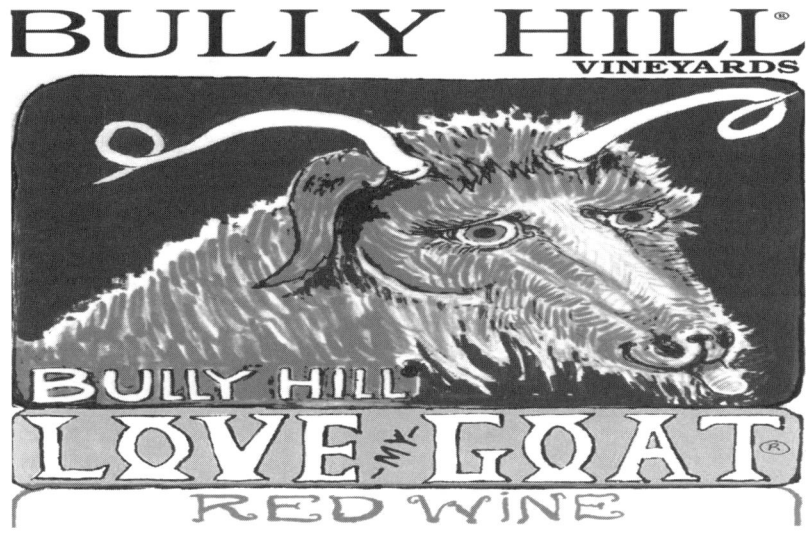

In 1976, when Coca-Cola sued Walter to prevent him from using the name "Taylor" on his Bully Hill bottle labels, Taylor drew his Love My Goat Red Wine label after buying a goat. He said, "They can take my name and my heritage, but they can't get my goat."

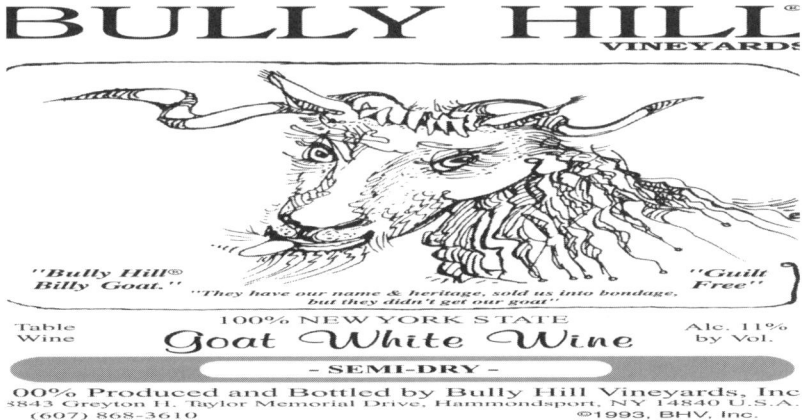

Walter wanted to get as much as out of his "They can take my name and my heritage but they can't get my goat" line as possible, so he designed a label for white wine as well, Great Goat White. He sketched the "Bully Hill Billy Goat." He also sketched bulldogs, frogs, and raccoons on his labels.

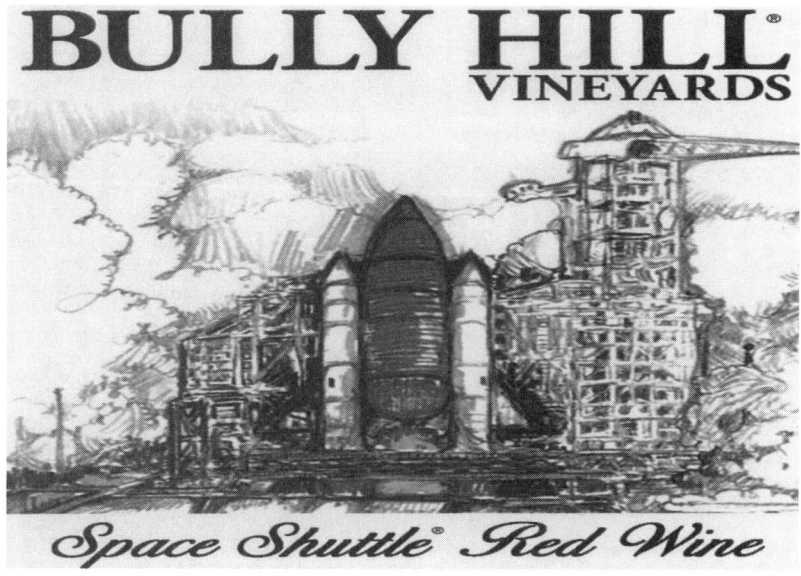

Taylor attended one of the rocket launches at Cape Canaveral, Florida, where he sketched the blast-off. For an artist known as a free spirit, this was one of his more traditional drawings.

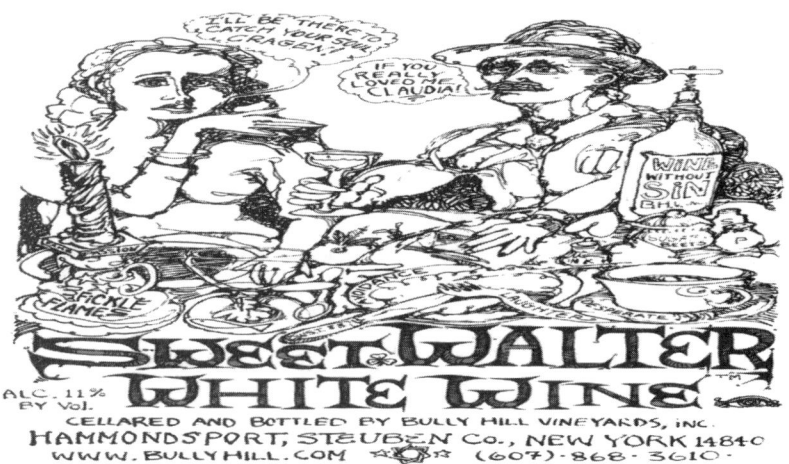

This label is an example of one of the more out of the ordinary of Walter's drawings, which includes a sketch of Wine Without Sin and conversational balloons. The range of his art was wide, from the truly unusual to many outdoor scenes.

CHAPTER 8 DR. KONSTANTIN FRANK, PIONEER

Dr. Konstantin Frank was born on July 4, 1899, in the Ukraine, the fourth of 10 children born to German parents. His father was a farmer and vineyardist. Dr. Frank studied agriculture at the Polytechnic Institute of Odessa. He managed a 20,000-acre estate for one of the royal families and later organized farms in southern Ukraine for the Communist government. When he completed his studies, including viticulture and agronomy, he taught and conducted research at the Institute of Viticulture and Enology in the Ukraine. During the German occupation in World War II, Dr. Frank was the director of the Institute of Viticulture and Enology. When the war ended, he went to Austria to manage farm properties for the allied occupational forces.

Dr. Frank emigrated to the United States with his wife and three children in 1951. He spoke eight languages but not English. He worked at an Automat restaurant in New York City to earn fare to the nearest grape research station, the New York State Agricultural Experiment Station at Geneva. He worked there for two years.

When Dr. Frank asked why Finger Lakes Region grape growers were planting French-American hybrid grapes, he was told that the winters were too cold for the European varieties. He had grown vinifera varieties in the Ukraine along the Dneiper River, "Where the temperature goes to 40 below zero, where we had to bury the entire vine in the winter, and where when we spit, it froze before it hit the ground." He noted that vines didn't die from the cold, but from disease, such as mildew and fungus, as well as from vine pests; furthermore, modern technology knew how to control these problems.

Charles Fournier, president of Gold Seal Winery, agreed with Dr. Frank. He had seen Chardonnay and Pinot Noir varieties survive at Epernay and Rheims, France, which are seven degrees of latitude farther north than Hammondsport. Also, he had seen temperatures drop below zero in the Champagne district of France. In 1953, Fournier hired Dr. Frank as a consultant to Gold Seal.

Dr. Frank convinced Fournier that vinifera vines should be grafted onto winter-hardy rootstock obtained in Canada. Vinifera vines from the University of California ar Davis were grafted onto Canadian rootstock. During the winter of 1957, temperature dropped to 25 degrees below zero. Many native varieties, particularly Duchess and Isabella, suffered 100 percent bud damage. Grafted European vines experienced only 10 percent bud damage. Dr. Frank always asked, "Why not plant the best?" Then he proved it could be done.

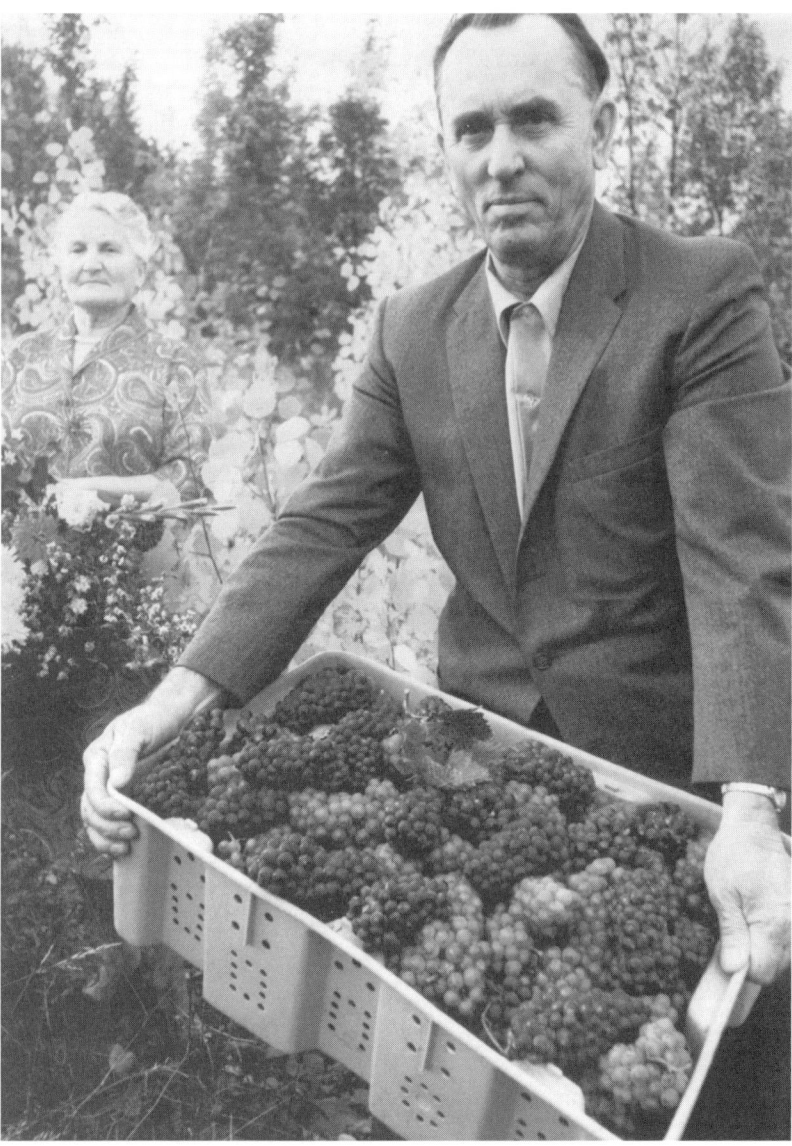

Dr. Frank and his wife, Eugenia, are shown in their vineyards. Initially, Dr. Frank planted Chardonnay, Riesling, Pinot Gris, Cabernet Sauvignon, and Pinot Noir in his vineyards in Pulteney, five and a half miles north of Hammondsport on the west side of Keuka Lake. Later, he planted Gewurztraminer, Rkatsiteli, and many other vinifera varieties.

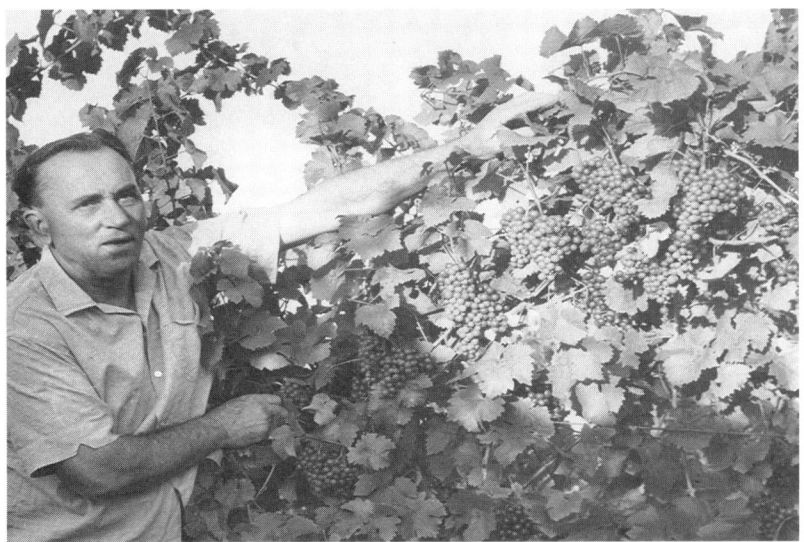

Dr. Frank is shown checking grapes in his vineyards. He was able to grow 10 tons of Chardonnay grapes per acre in his vineyards. In France, Chardonnay averaged three and half tons per acre.

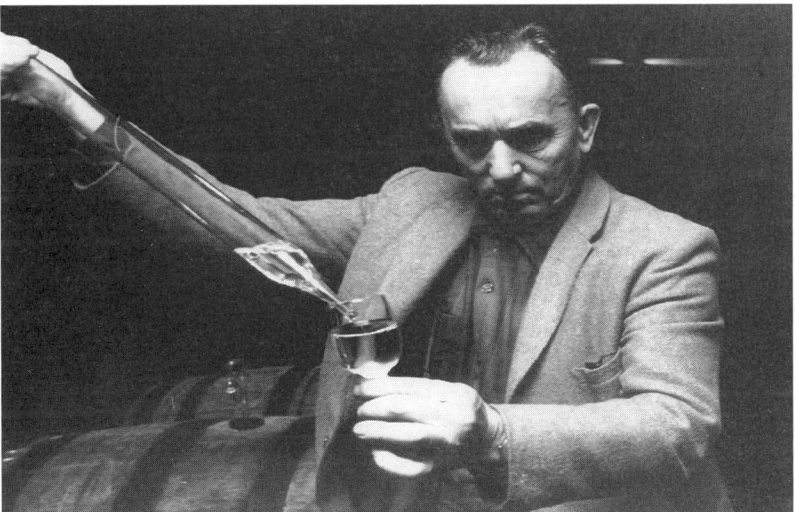

Dr. Frank is using a "wine thief," the glass tube used to draw a sample from a barrel. His main interest was research and development. He had a pilot vineyard next to his home with at least two vines each of 62 varieties / clones.

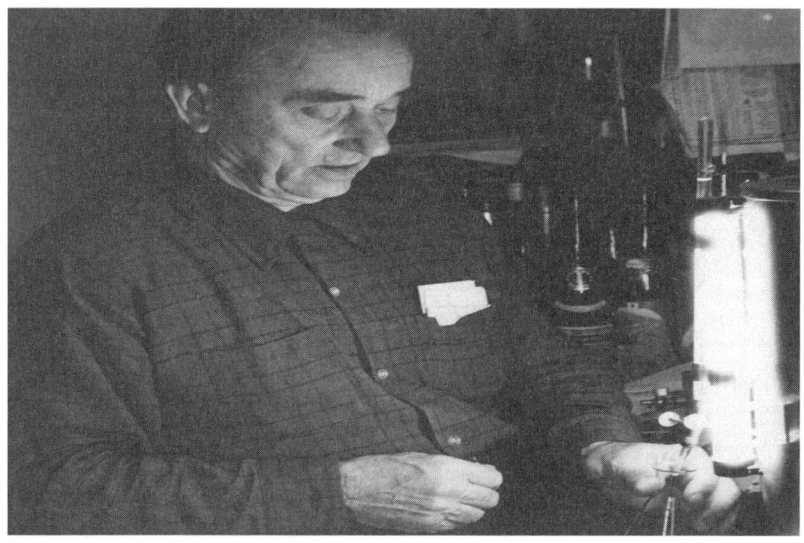

Dr. Frank is checking a wine sample in his office in the laboratory, Some of the little-grown grape varieties with which he experimented were Fetjaska from Hungary, Kara Burni from Bulgaria, and Sereksiya Tschornay from the Ukraine.

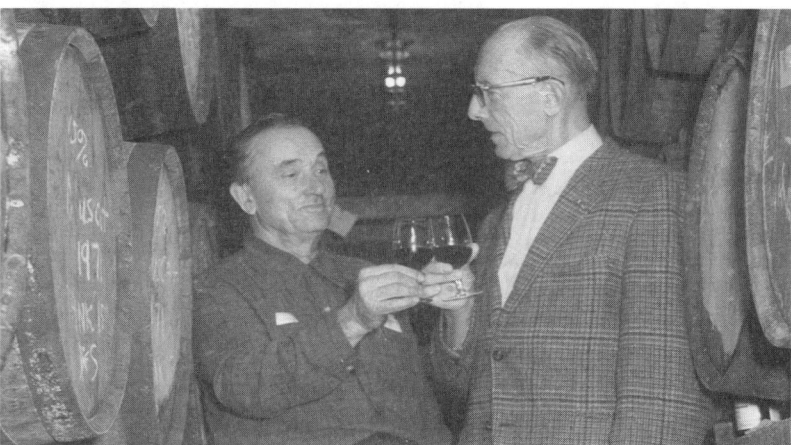

To grow vinifera vines in cool climates, Dr. Frank convinced Charles Fournier, who had hired him at Gold Seal Winery, that grafting vinifera vines onto native roots that would allow the ripening of the wood on the vine, the canes, before the first freeze of winter. Vinifera vines were grafted onto sturdy rootstock from Canada.

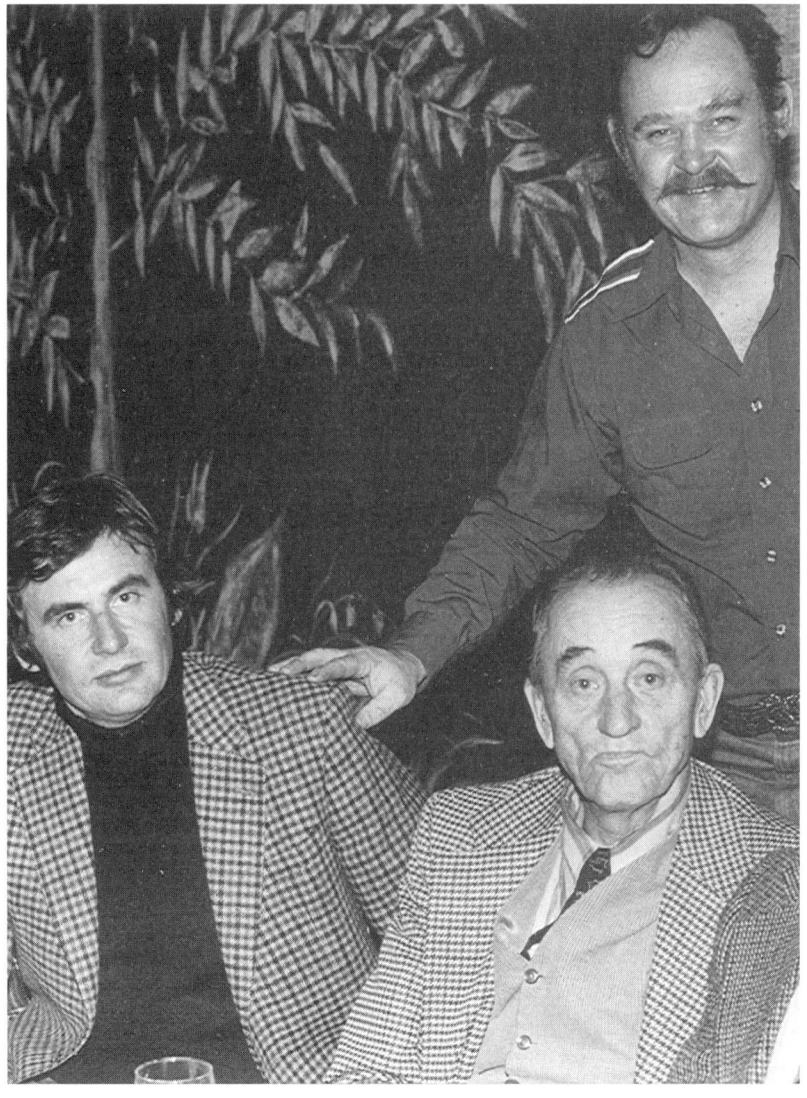

Dr. Frank is shown with Walter S. Taylor, who is standing, with his hand on the shoulder of Hermann Wiemer. Taylor was owner and manager of Bully Hill Vineyards. Wiemer managed the vineyards and the French-American hybrid nursery at Bully Hill from 1968 to 1980, when he founded his own award-winning winery on Seneca Lake, Hermann J. Wiemer Vineyard, specializing in vinifera varieties.

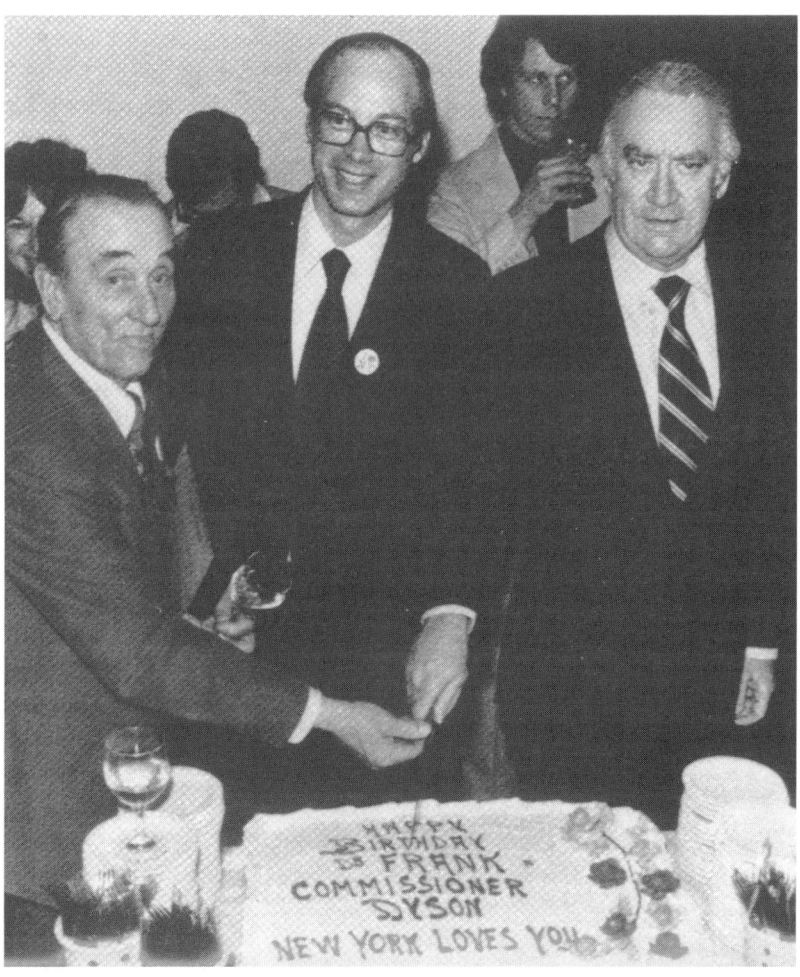

Governor Cary of New York State and Commissioner Dyson visited Dr. Frank at the winery to help celebrate his birthday. Dr. Frank's 1961 Trockenbeerenauslese ("dried-berry-selected" in German) was served in the executive mansion in Albany and at the White House. Dr. Frank became a U. S. citizen and vocal pro-American.

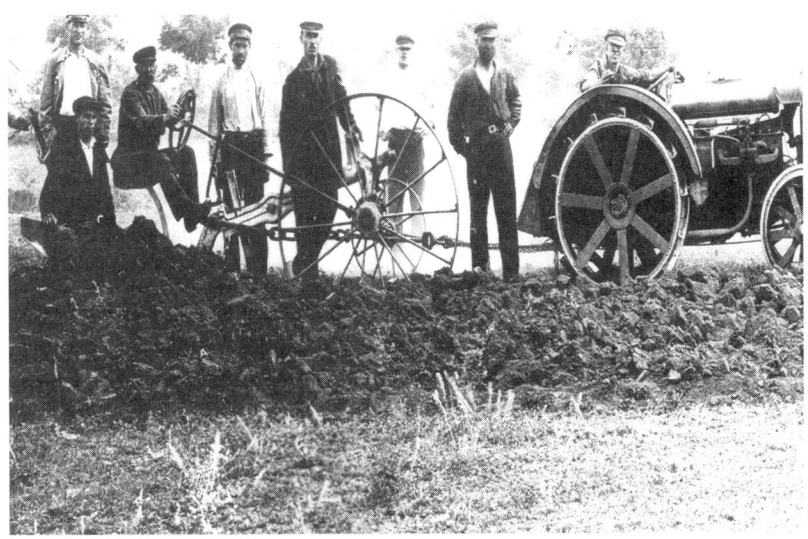

While living in the Ukraine, Dr. Frank designed several plows, one of which is shown here. His plow could do in one pass through the vineyard what it previously took 100 men to do. He was a believer in deep tilling of vineyards.

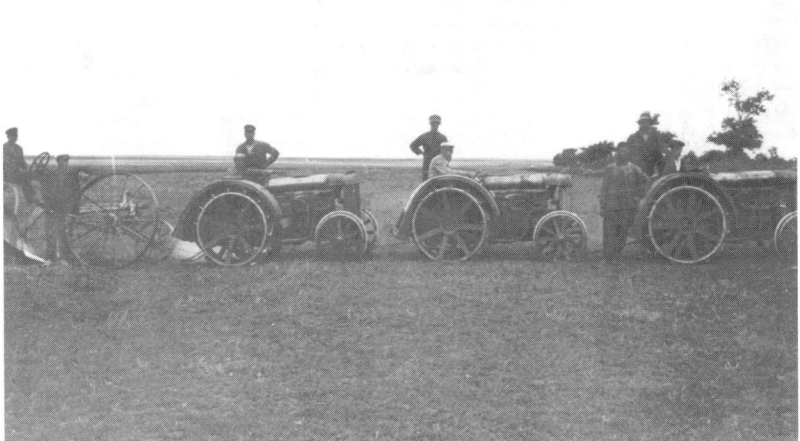

At the Institute of Viticulture and Enology in the Ukraine, Dr. Frank was responsible for the first three Ford tractors delivered to the Soviet Union. He hooked them up in tandem to pull a heavy load and destroyed one of the tractors. This happened during the reign of Josef Stalin. Fortunately, Dr. Frank was never reprimanded.

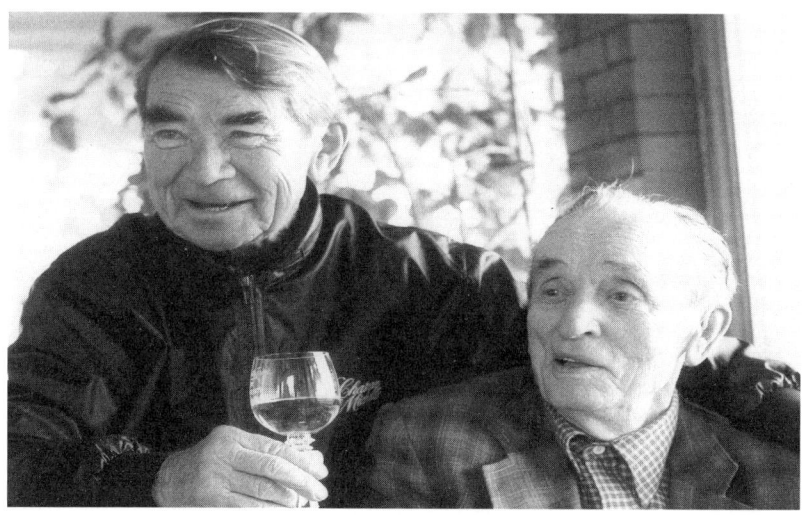

Andre Tchelistcheff, doyen of Napa Valley winemakers, is shown sharing a bottle of wine with Dr. Frank. Tchelistcheff, who trained in France, managed the vineyards and winery for Beaulieu Vineyards until he died in 1994. He also had his own enological laboratory and served as a consultant to other Napa and Sonoma Valley wineries.

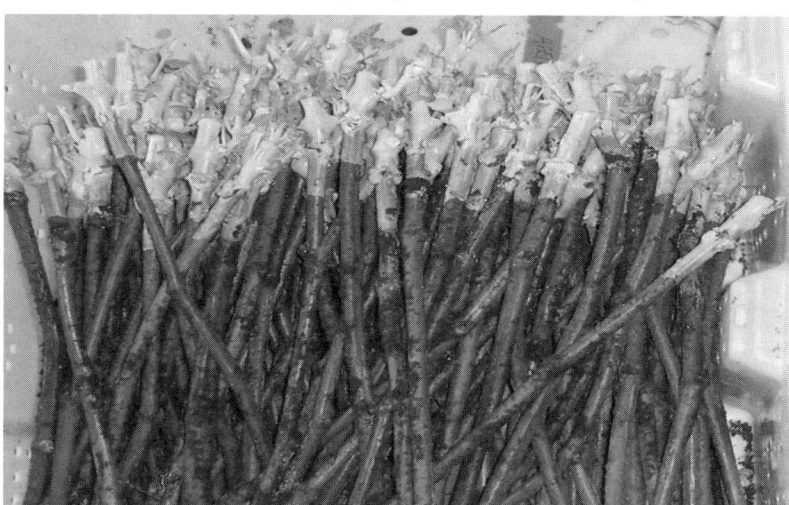

In growing vinifera vines in cool climates, Dr. Frank recommended grafting vinifera vines onto native roots that would allow the ripening of the wood on the vine, the canes, before the first freeze of winter. Vinifera vines were grafted onto sturdy rootstock from Canada.

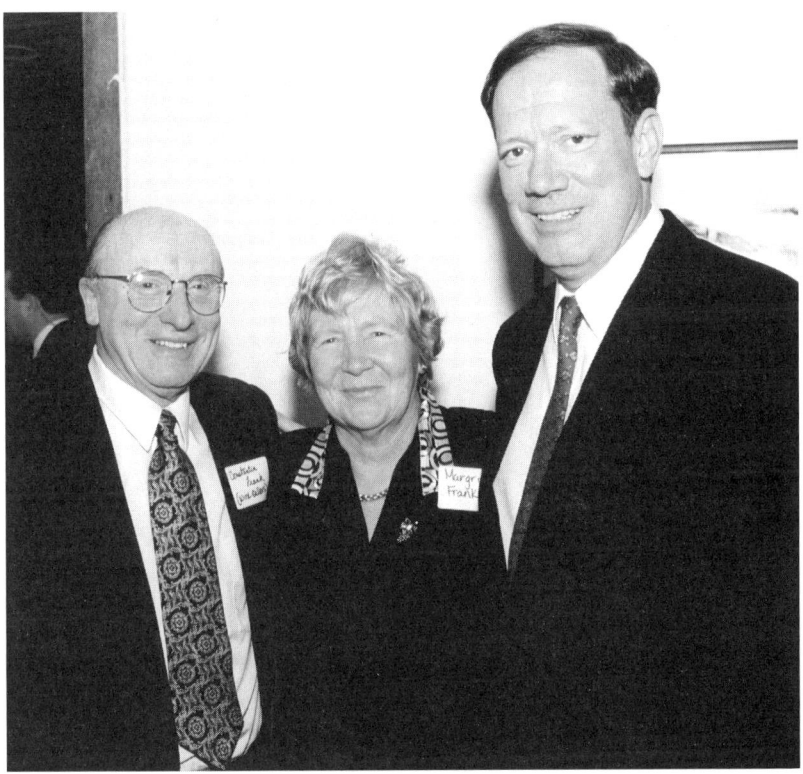

Willy Frank, Dr. Frank's son, and Willy's wife, Margrit, are shown with Governor George Pataki of New York State. After the winery began to win numerous awards, it became more than just of regional interest. Willy and Margrit sponsored the winery's entry into the champagne business with French-style Chateau Frank champagne.

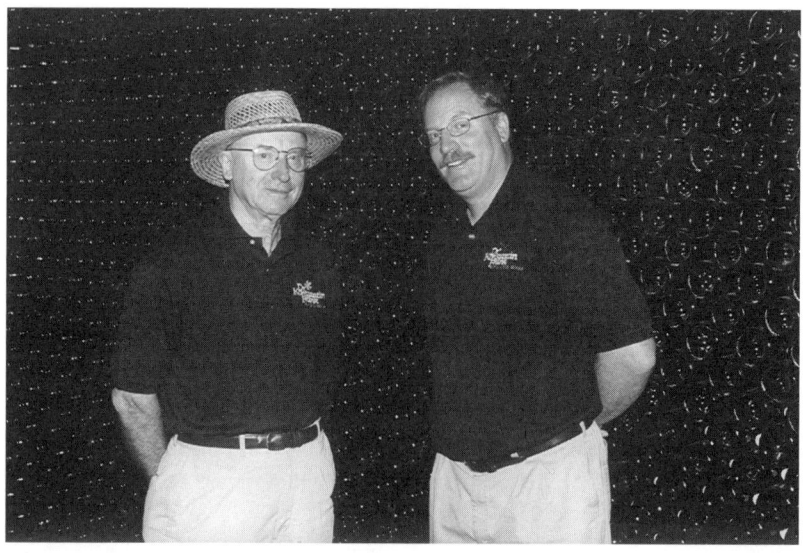

Willy Frank and his son, Fred Frank, are in the winery's wine cellars. Fred, a graduate of Cornell University, also attended Geisenheim University in Germany and worked in a management position at a Long Island winery before joining Willy at Vinifera Wine Cellars. Fred is the third generation to run the winery.

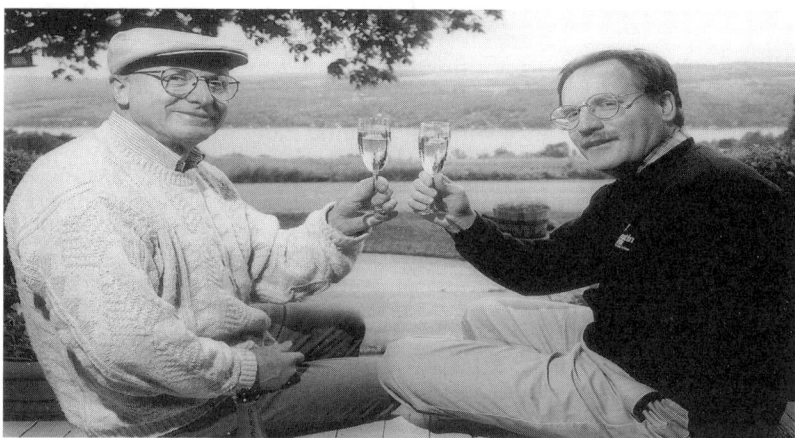

Willy Frank and his son, Fred, are enjoying a glass of wine at their winery overlooking Keuka Lake. Willy worked in the photographic business in New York City before moving to Hammondsport to join his father at the winery. Whereas Dr. Frank's main interest was research and development, Willy's was marketing and promotion.

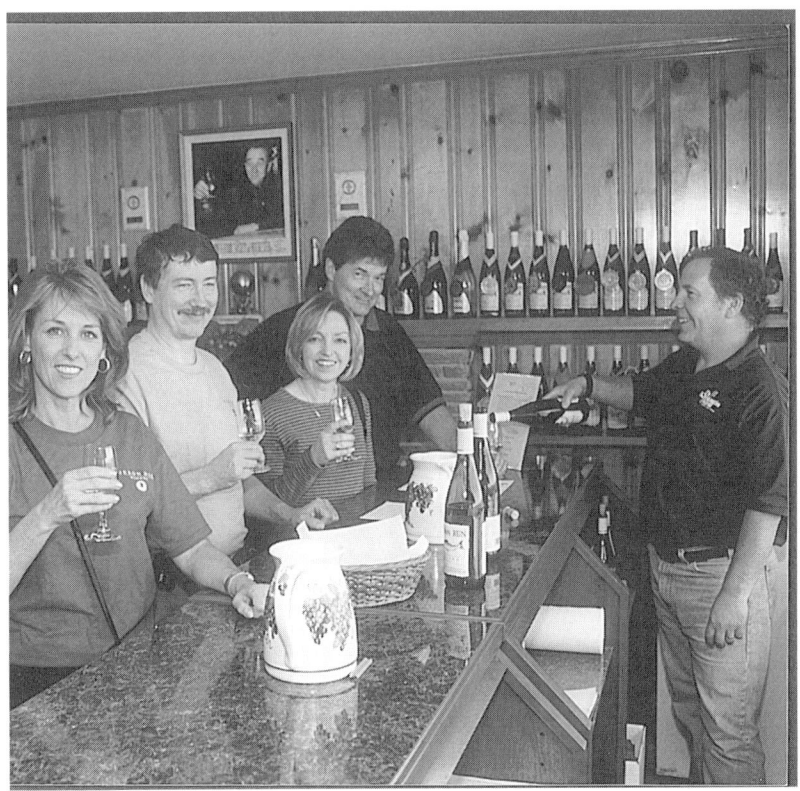

A wine tasting is shown at Vinifera Wine Cellars. Wine tasting is an enjoyable experience at Dr. Frank's, and visitors usually learn things about wine they didn't know. The winery is one of the few in the region producing wine from the Rkatsiteli variety that originated on the border of Armenia and Turkey over 5,000 years ago. It is similar to Riesling with a touch of spiciness.

Willy Frank passed away in 2006. His son, Fred, had been general manager and president of the winery since 1993. In addition to the Dr. Frank labels, the winery also produces a lower cost label, Salmon Run, which is made from grapes from younger vines and some contractor grapes.

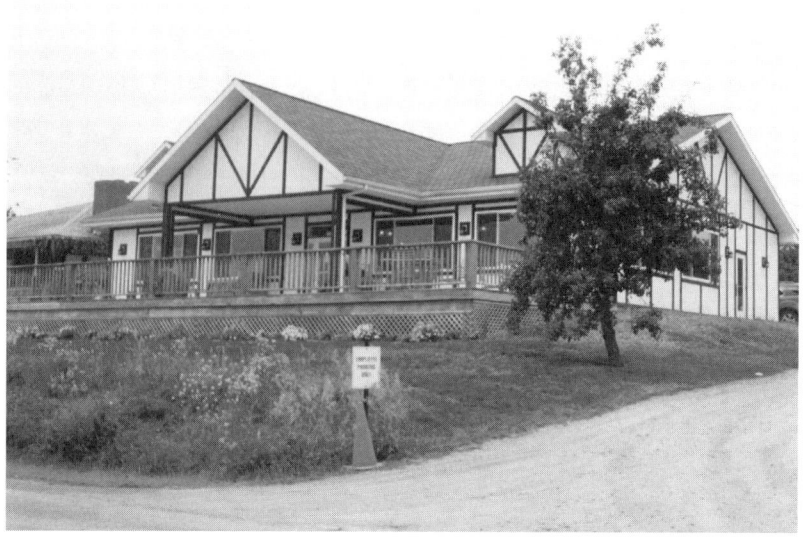

A large addition made to the winery is shown. The winery continues to make additional vinifera varietal wines beyond its original offerings, including Cabernet Franc, Lemberger, Rkatsiteli, Gruner Veltliner, and Sauvignon Blanc.

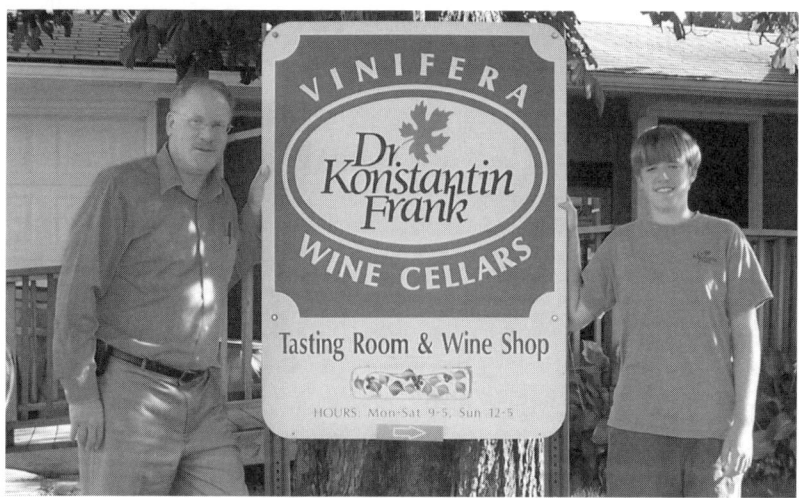

Fred Frank and his son, Kyle Konstantin Frank, are shown standing outside the winery, which used to be the home of Dr. Frank and his wife, Eugenia. Kyle is following his father to Cornell University. Might he eventually be the fourth generation to run the winery?

One of the most significant factors in the increase in the number of wineries in the United States and in the Finger Lakes Region, as well, was the passage of the State-by-State "limited winery" laws, also known as "farm winery" acts. One of the principal sponsors of Farm Winery Acts was Leon Adams of California, author of *The Wines of America*.

Adams urged grape growers to work with their State Legislators and Departments of Agriculture to allow wineries at their vineyards. He became known as the "father of farm wineries."

In the East, Pennsylvania, whose effort was spearheaded by Doug Moorhead of Presque Isle Winery north of Erie, was the first State to pass a limited winery law, in 1968. Limited wineries became known as farm wineries, and for the first time in the United States, a vineyardist didn't have to go through the formal, expensive process of becoming a bonded winery to produce and sell wine.

New York passed its farm winery bill in 1976. The annual fees to operate as a farm winery ranged from $125 to $300 instead of the $1,500 and upwards that commercial wineries had been paying. The license fee permitted a vineyardist to produce and sell up to 50,000 gallons per year.

One of the wineries that opened after the passage of the farm winery bill was Frontenac Point Vineyard, located 12 miles north of Ithaca on the west side of Cayuga Lake. Jim and Carol Doolittle planted their vineyard in 1978 and opened their winery in 1982. Jim had earned a degree in viticulture from Cornell University in 1975, and, as an employee of the New York State Department of Agriculture, helped draft the Farm Winery Bill of 1976.

As expected, the Farm Winery Act significantly stimulated the start-ups of wineries in the State. According to the New York Wine and Grape Foundation, by the end of 2011, New York State had 316 wineries, 118 of which were in the Finger Lake Region. The other major grape growing areas in the State are Lake Erie, Hudson Valley, and Long Island.

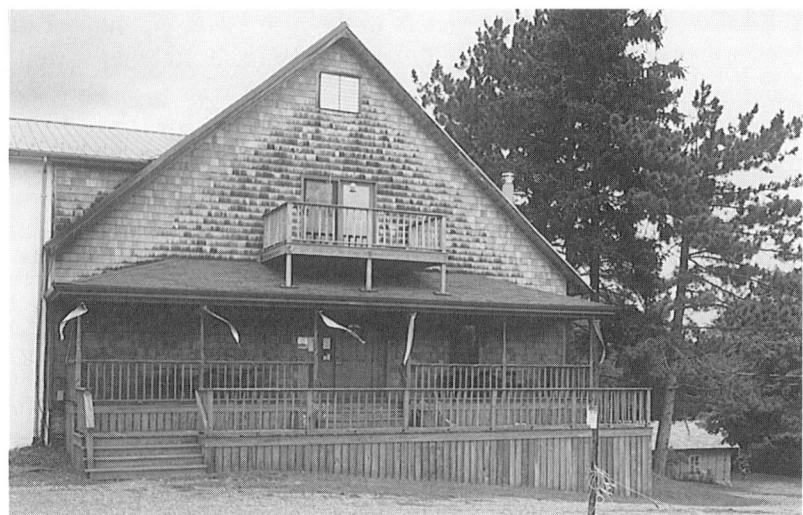

Eagle Crest Vineyards in Conesus was founded in 1872 by Bishop Bernard McQuaid, the first Catholic Bishop of Rochester, to supply his priests with wine for Masses. The winery, which closed during Prohibition, now produces O-Neh-Da sacramental wine as well as Eagle Crest popular wines.

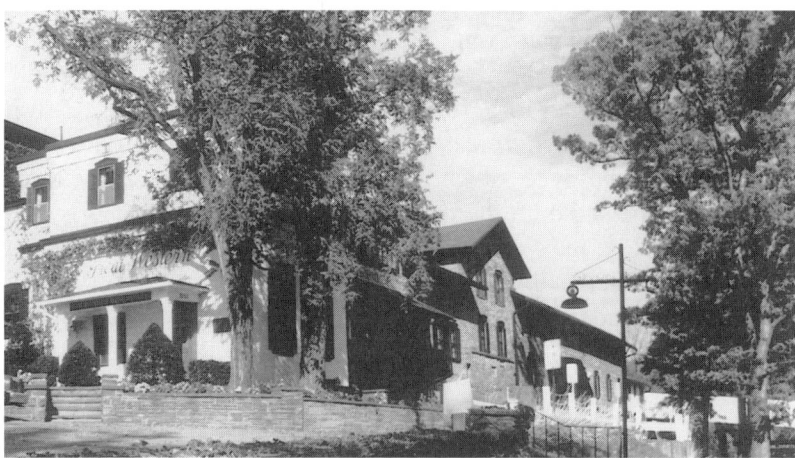

Pleasant Valley Wine Company on Pleasant Valley Road, south of Hammondsport, produces wine from native and vinifera grapes, fortified wine, such as Madeira, marsala, Port, and sherry, as well as Great Western Champagne. The winery provides a classic tour, and the visitor center has a comprehensive museum.

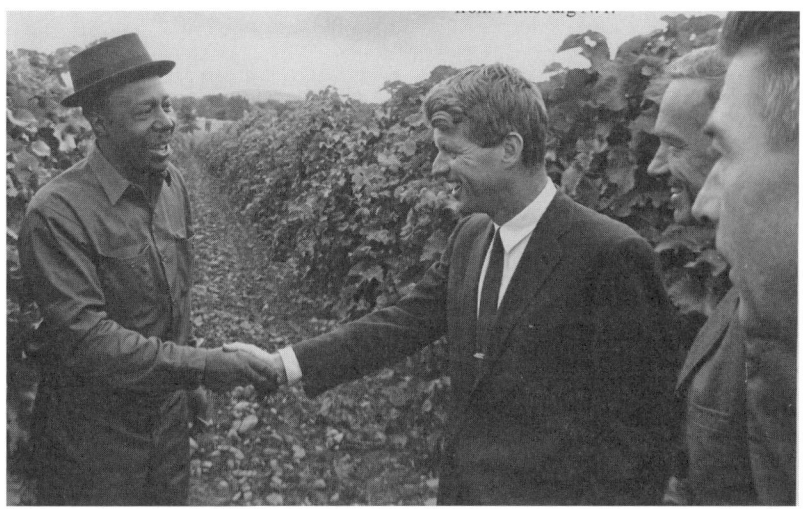

State Senator Robert Kennedy is shown greeting winery owner and winemaker Ray Fedderman of Prattsburgh in 1967. Fedderman moved to Prattsburgh from Virginia to work in an area muck farm. His work was so highly regarded that he was given the opportunity to buy 40 acres of the best farmland, on which he started a winery.

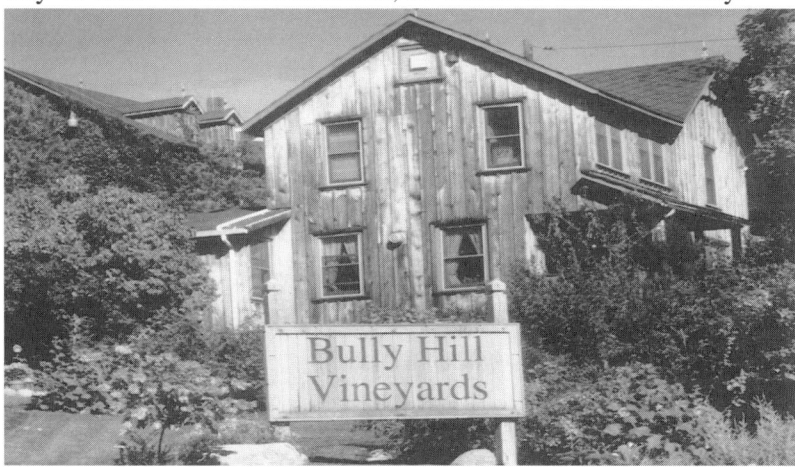

Bully Hill Vineyards specializes in French-American hybrid wine. Bully Hill has a popular restaurant with indoor and terrace dining, a two-story gift shop, a wine retail store, and wine and art museums. Winery and vineyard tours are offered, followed by an informative and entertaining wine-tasting.

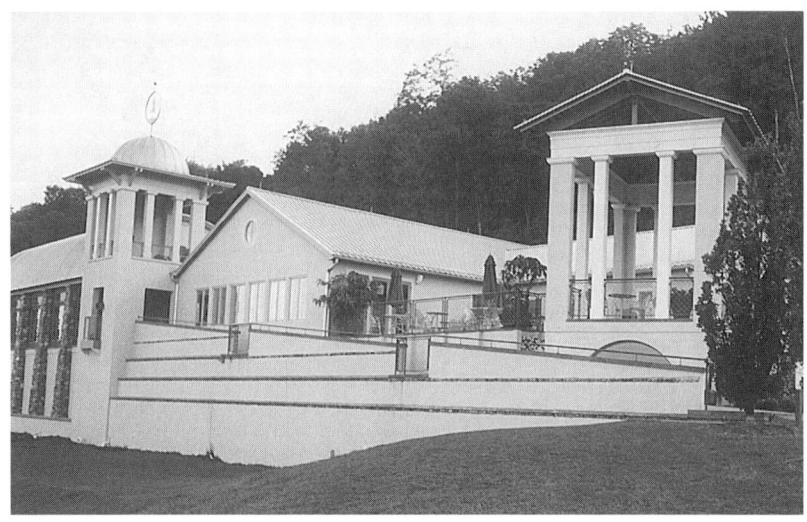

John and Jo Ingle of Naples established Heron Hill Winery, located three miles north of Hammondsport, in 1972. The winery, which has a spectacular view of southern Keuka Lake, produces wine from vinifera, French-American hybrid, and native grapes, and ice wine. Heron Hill has an active event and concert calendar.

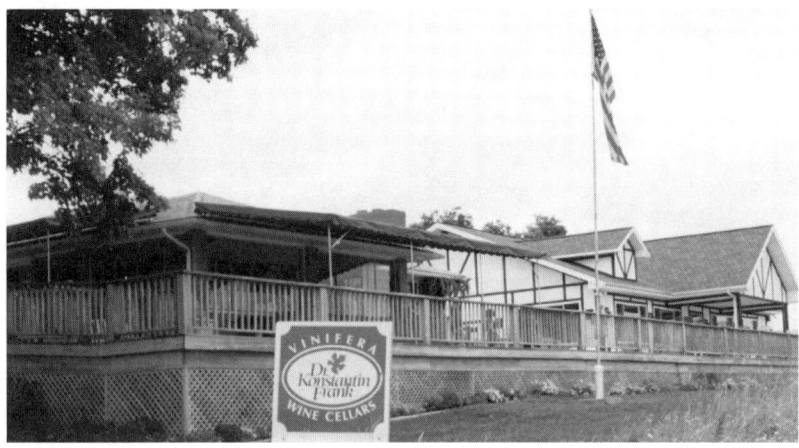

Dr. Frank Vinifera Wine Cellars, located on Middle Road five and a half miles north of Hammondsport, is known for its many award-winning wines and its Chateau Frank Champagne. The champagne is made from Chardonnay, Pinot Blanc, Pinot Meunier, and Pinot Noir, the grape varieties used to make Champagne in France.

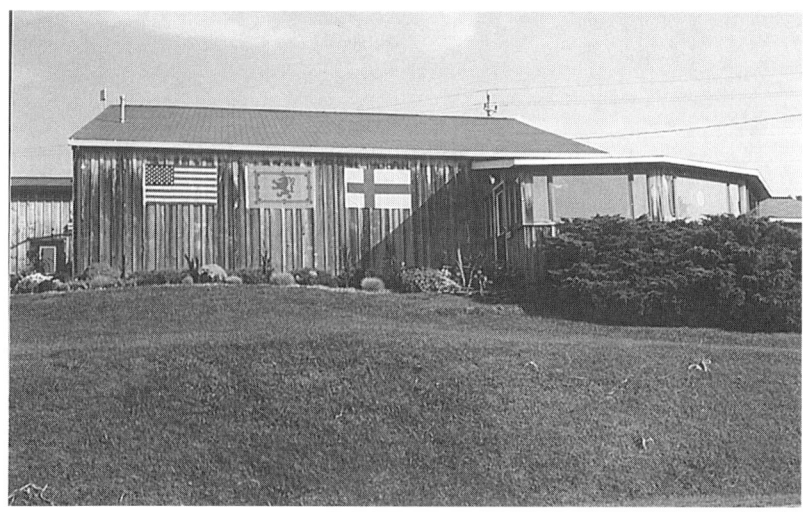

Bob and Marge McGregor founded McGregor Vineyard and Winery, located nine miles north of Hammondsport, off East Lake Road, in 1971. They produced their first commercial wine in 1980. The winery specializes in vinifera varietals and blends but also produces champagne and wine made from French-American hybrid grapes.

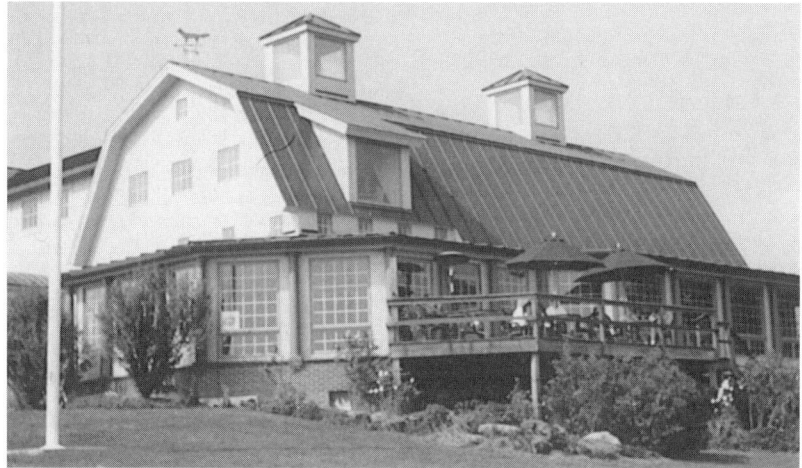

Fox Run Vineyards, located eight miles south of Geneva on the west side of Seneca Lake, is owned by Scott Osborn. The winery specializes in vinifera varietals and blends, as well as Port. Fox Run offers a comprehensive vineyard and winery tour, which includes the winery's state-of-the-art processing facility and a winetasting.

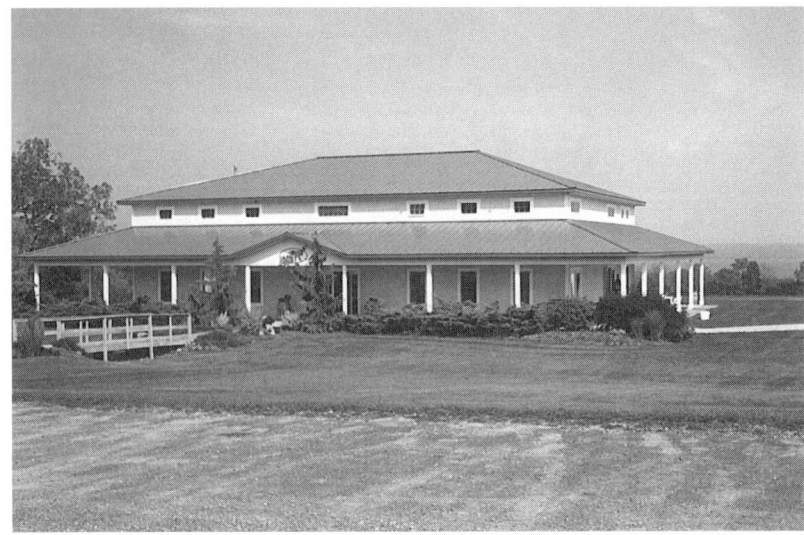

Anthony Road Wine Company, located 10 miles south of Geneva on the west side of Seneca Lake, was founded in 1989 by Ann and John Martini. It specializes in vinifera varietals and blends but also makes French-American hybrid wine, semi-sweet wine, and dessert wine.

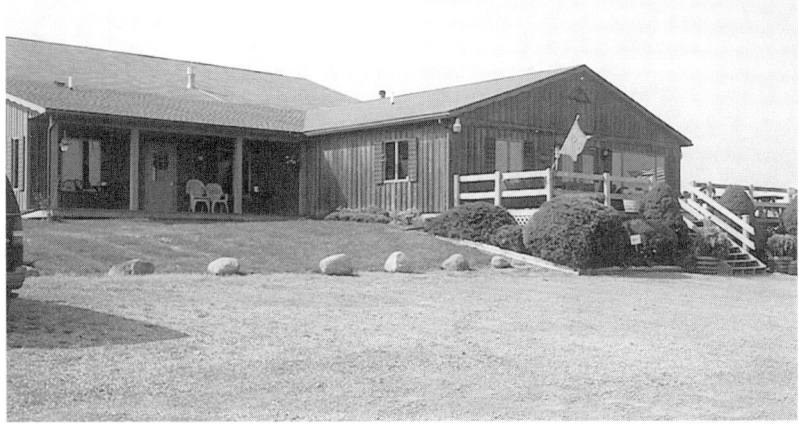

Prejean Winery, located south of Geneva on the west side of Seneca Lake, was established in 1985. It is managed by Elizabeth Prejean and her son, Tom. The winery, a 6,000-square-foot facility with over 36 acres of vineyards, specializes in vinifera varietals and blends but also makes French-American hybrid wine and Port.

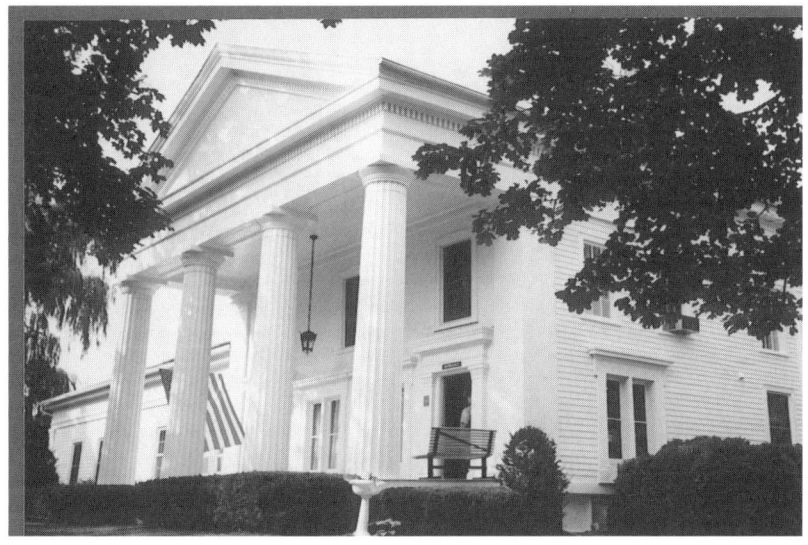

Miles Wine Cellars, located on the west side of Seneca Lake in a beautiful 1802 Greek Revival mansion, is owned and managed by Doug Miles and his wife, Suzy Hayes. The winery makes wine from vinifera, French-American hybrid, and native grapes. Because the mansion is rumored to be haunted, its speciality wine is Ghost.

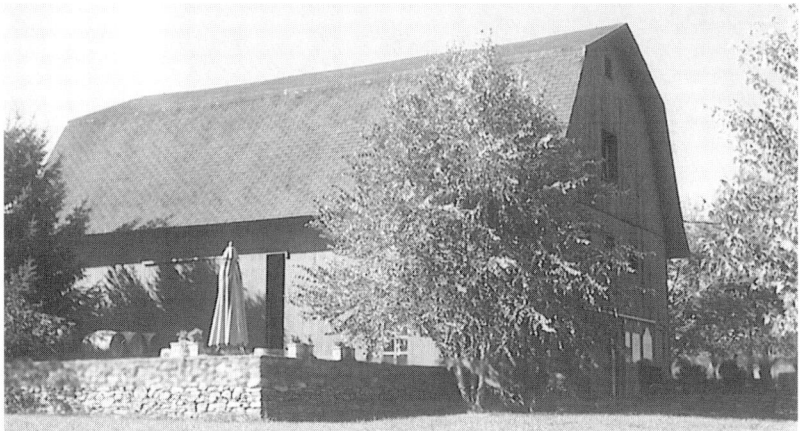

In 1973, Hermann J. Wiemer purchased vineyard land 14 miles north of Watkins Glen on the west side of Seneca Lake. Later, he estab-lished Hermann J. Wiemer Vineyard winery and, by 1992, had 50 acres of vinifera vines under cultivation. The winery is one of the most award-winning in the region.

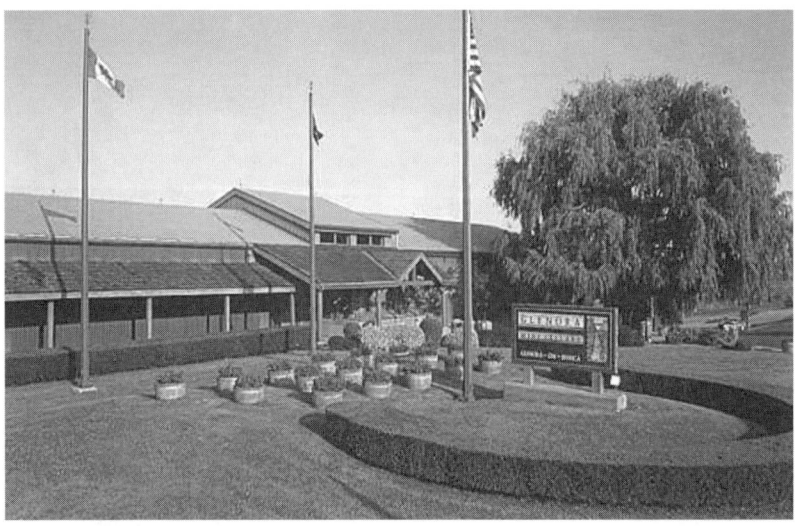

Glenora Wine Cellars, eight miles north of Watkins Glen on the west side of Seneca Lake, was established in 1977. The winery, managed by Gene Pierce, produces wine from vinifera, French-American hybrid, and native grapes, as well as sparkling wine, Port, spumante, and fruit wines. Glenora sponsors live music on the grounds.

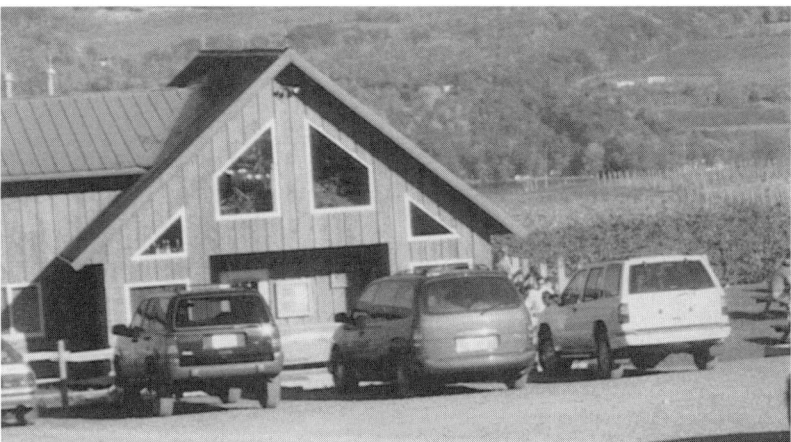

Lakewood Vineyards, located four and a half miles north of Watkins Glen on the west side of Seneca Lake, was established in 1988 by the Stamp family, who have grown quality wine grapes for generations. Lakewood produces wine from vinifera, French-American hybrid, and native grapes, as well as Port, mead, and ice wines.

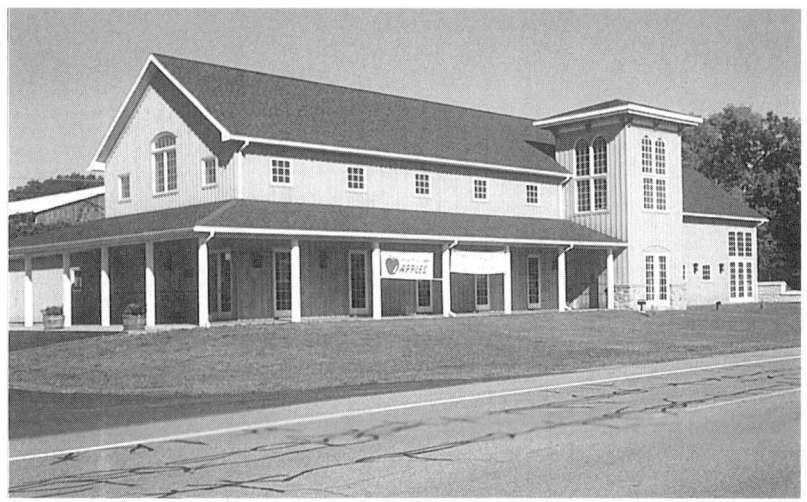

Fulkerson Winery and Juice Plant, owned by Sayre and Nancy Fulkerson, is located eight miles north of Watkins Glen on the west side of Seneca Lake.The juice plant offers over 30 varieties of grapes and juice. The winery, which opened in 1989, produces wine from vinifera, French-American hybrid, and native grape varieties.

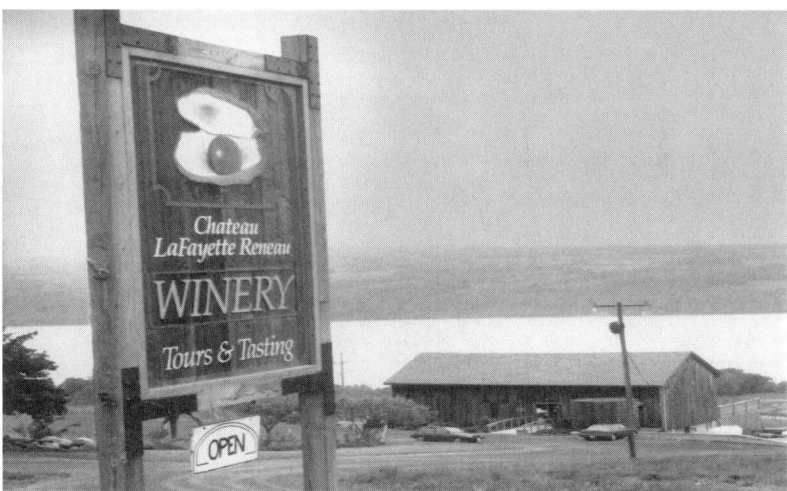

Chateau Lafayette Reneau, on the lower east side of Seneca Lake, was established in 1985 by Dick and Bette Reno. The winery makes wine from vinifera, French-American hybrid, and native grapes. The Renos have a 10-bedroom bed and breakfast inn on a 140-acre site.

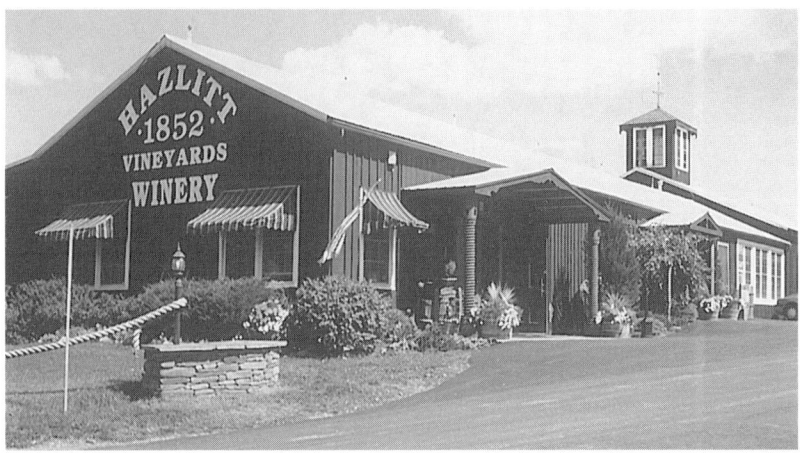

Hazlitt 1852 Vineyards was established by Elaine and Jerry Hazlitt on the east side of Seneca Lake in 1984. The winery makes wine from vinifera, French-American hybrid, and native grape varieties and fruit wines and has a friendly family atmosphere and a compact museum of local history. Production of its Red Cat series of wine moved to Hazlitt Red Cat Cellars in Naples.

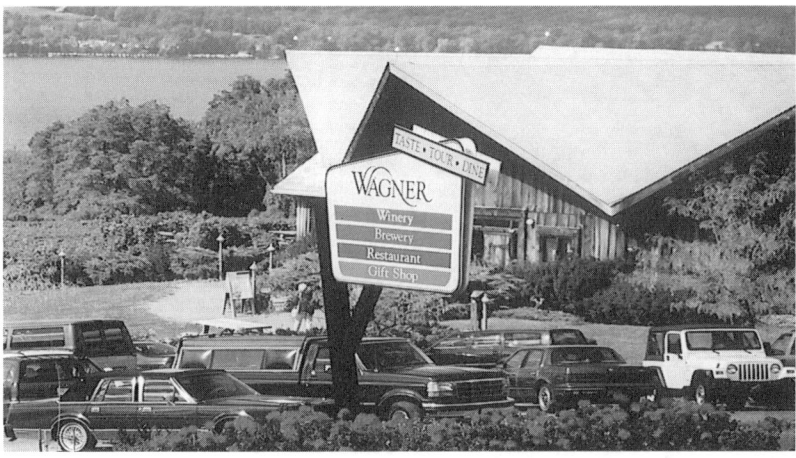

The octagonal Wagner Vineyards winery was established by Bill Wagner in 1978. The winery produces wine from vinifera, French-American hybrid, and native grapes, as well as sparkling wine, dessert wine, and ice wine. Its popular Ginny Lee Cafe opened in 1983 and its microbrewery in 1998. Tours are provided.

104

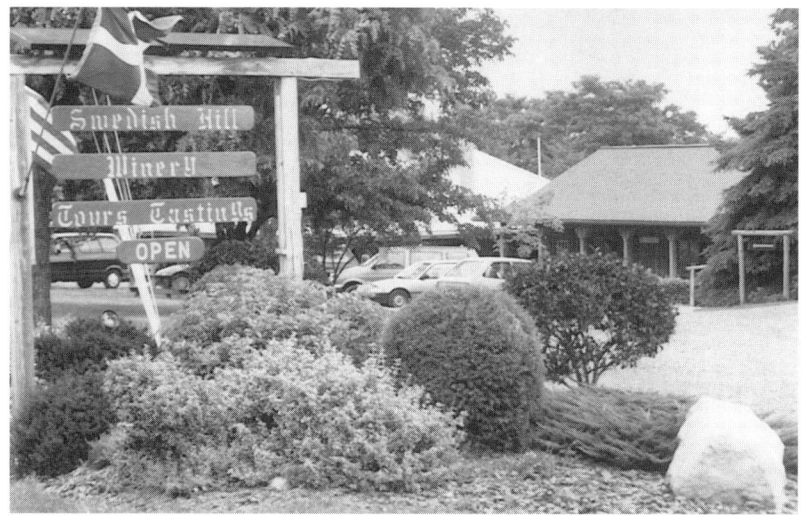

Swedish Hill Winery, located eight miles south of Seneca Falls on the west side of Cayuga Lake, was founded in 1985 by Dick and Cindy Peterson. It produces wine from vinifera, French-American hybrid, and native grapes, as well as champagne, spumante, Port, glogg, dessert wine, and fruit wine. Tours are offered.

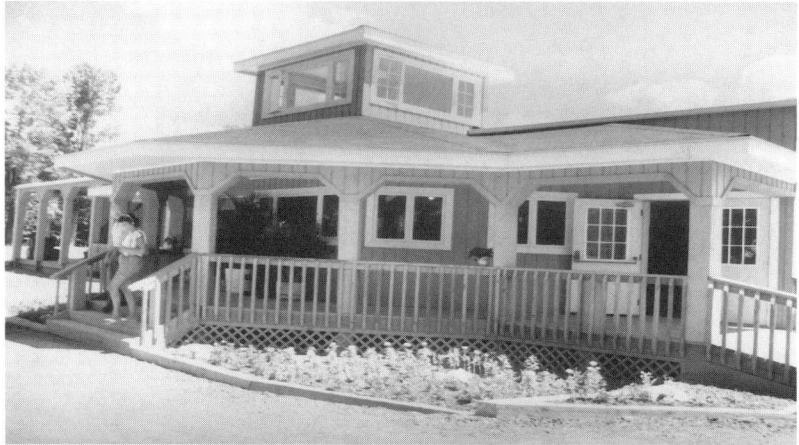

Knapp Winery and Restaurant, located on the west side of Cayuga Lake, was established in 1972 and is now owned by Glenora Wine Cellars. The winery produces wine from vinifera, French-American hybrid and native grapes, as well as sparkling wine, brandy, Port, cordials, grappa, and fruit wine.

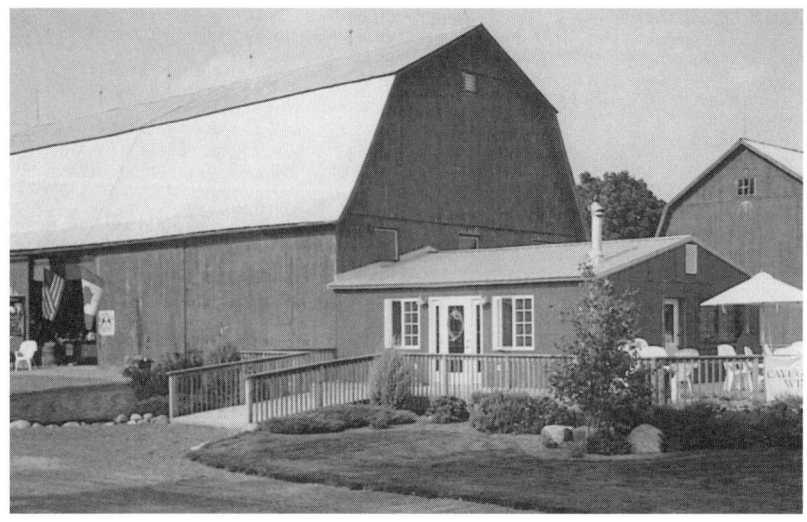

Cayuga Ridge Estate Winery, founded by Tom and Suzie Challen, is on the west side of Cayuga Lake. The winery produces wine from vinifera and French-American hybrid grapes and fruit wine blends. The winery has a vigneron (rent-a-grapevine) program. Participants lease, tend, and harvest grapes from 10, 20, or 30 grapevines.

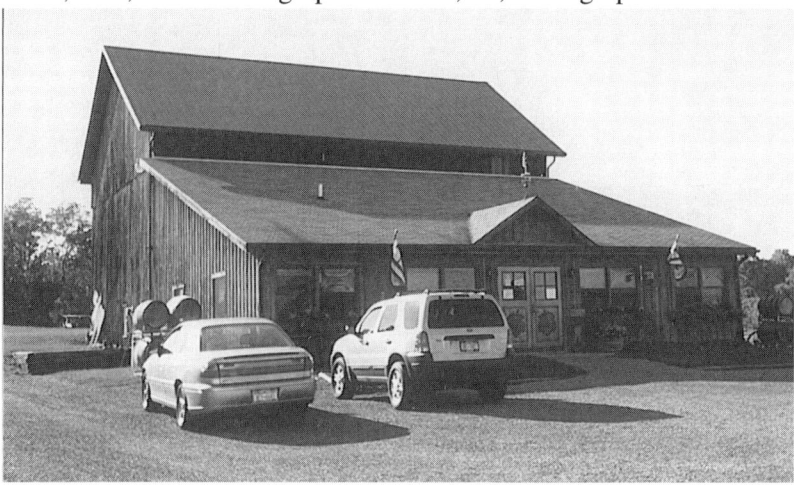

Hosmer Winery, founded by Cameron and Maren Hosmer, is located on the west side of Cayuga Lake. The winery produces wine from vinifera, French-American hybrid, and native grapes, as well as champagne, sangria, dessert wine, and fruit wine blends.

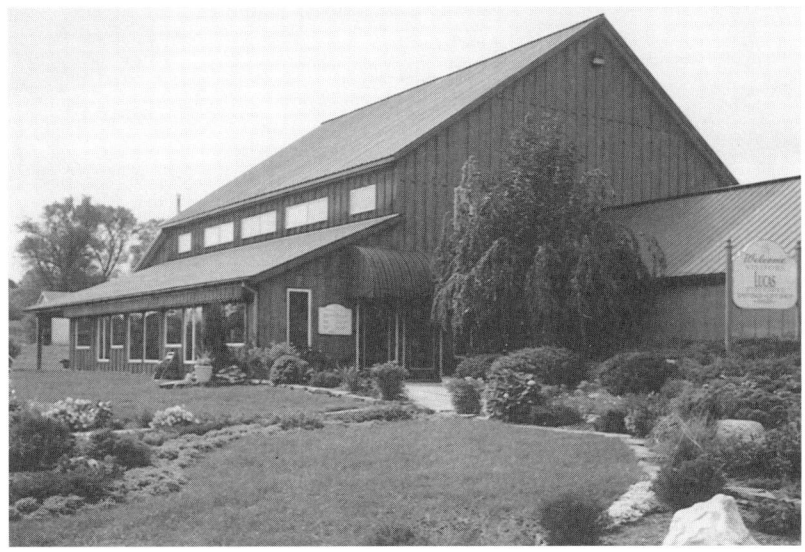

Lucas Vineyards, located 18 miles north of Ithaca on the west side of Cayuga Lake, was founded by Ruth and Bill Lucas, a retired tugboat captain. It produces wine from vinifera and French-American hybrid grapes, as well as champagne and fruit-flavored wine.

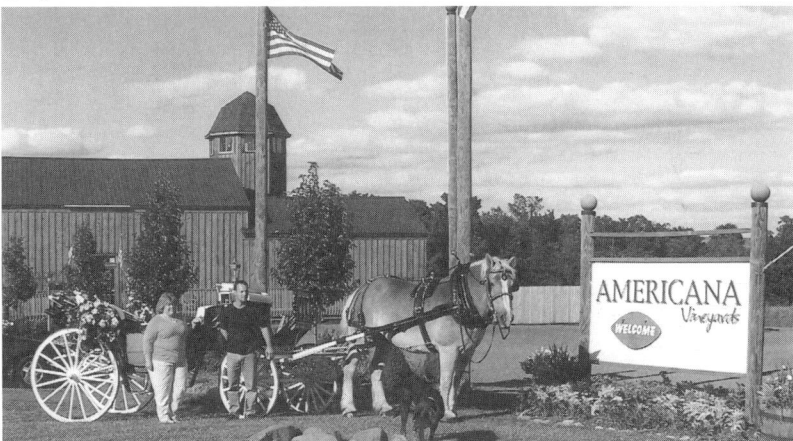

Americana Vineyards, located 14 miles north of Ithaca on the west side of Cayuga Lake, was founded by Joe Gober in the early 1980s. The winery produces wine from vinifera, French-American hybrid, and native grapes and dessert wine. Crystal Lake Cafe serves light fare, and the winery has a large outdoor pavilion.

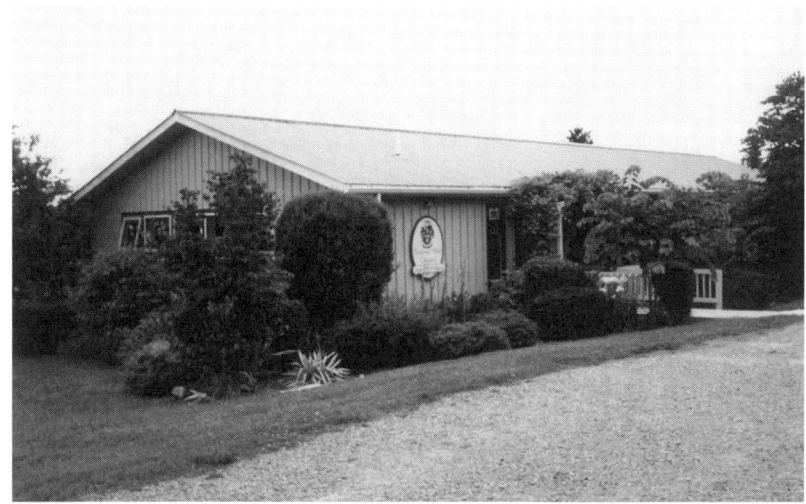

Frontenac Point Vineyard, located 12 miles north of Ithaca on the west side of Cayuga Lake, was established by Jim and Carol Doolittle in 1982. Their vineyard was planted in 1978. The winery produces wine from vinifera and French-American hybrid grapes, as well as champagne and dessert wine.

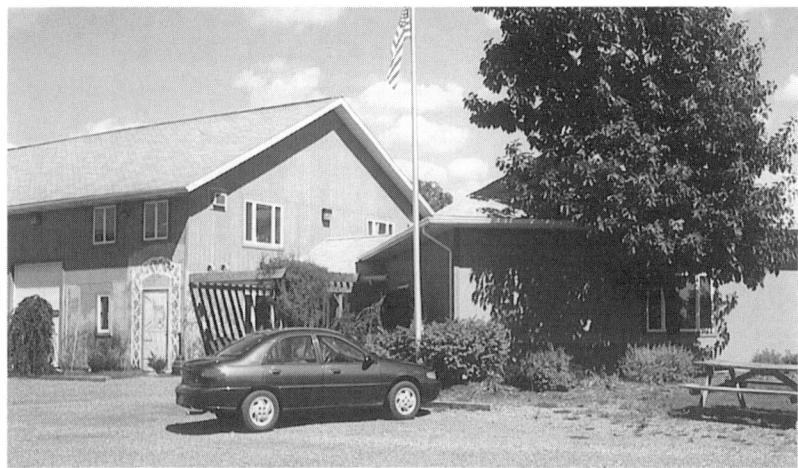

King Ferry Winery, on the east side of Cayuga Lake in the town of King Ferry, is owned and managed by Peter and Tacie Saltonstall. The winery produces wine from vinifera and French-American grapes, as well as fruit wine. The winery labels its wine "Treleaven," because the property was purchased from the Treleaven family.

CHAPTER 10 FROM THE 1980s TO THE PRESENT

The new wineries in New York State triggered by the Farm Winery Act of 1976 drove the total to 316. Of those, 198 wineries had opened between 2001 and 2011, more than had opened from 1829 to 2000. According to the New York Wine & Grape Foundation, the 152 wineries that have opened since 2005 represent a four-fold increase over the previous 20 years.

Jim Trezise, director of the foundation, observes that, initially, vineyard owners, such as the owners of Anthony Road, Lakewood, and Hunt Country, decided to go into the wine business. Some recent winery owners tend not to grow their own grapes but buy them from neighbors. New owners are usually entrepreneurs with a vision and know where they want to be in five to 10 years. They have a good business plan, and, if they are not knowledgeable in grape growing and winemaking, are astute enough to hire people who are.

There is a widening realization that the Finger Lakes Region is a very desirable place in which to grow grapes, to make wine, and to live. More individuals from outside the region are establishing vineyards and wineries in the region. In 2001, grape grower Robert Young of California's Alexander Valley purchased 105 acres of land north of Dresden. Young partnered with Anthony Road Wine Company and planted four vinifera varieties.

In 2004, Nancy Irelan and her husband, Mike Schnelle, purchased 32 acres of land south of Geneva. Mike came from California to clear the land and start a vineyard of 20 acres, which is now a model vineyard. Nancy, who had been vice president of Viticulture and Enology Research and Development for a large winery in California, moved east in 2006. In 2007, they established Red Tail Ridge Winery.

Another change in the region was the establishment of wine trails, beginning with the Cayuga Lake Wine Trail in 1982, the first in the Finger Lakes Region and the first in New York State. It was followed by the Seneca Lake Wine Trail (the largest), the Keuka Lake Wine Trail, and the Canandaigua Wine Trail. Each trail winery sponsors its own special events during the year, and members work together on same-weekend combined activities to promote area wine.

New York State's vineyard survey of 2011 indicated 31,000 acres of vineyards, 9,390 acres (30% of the total) in the Finger Lakes Region. The most commonly grown grapes in the Finger Lakes Region are Riesling, Chardonnay, and Merlot. Increasing acreage of Cabernet Franc, a popular red vinifera, is being planted in the region.

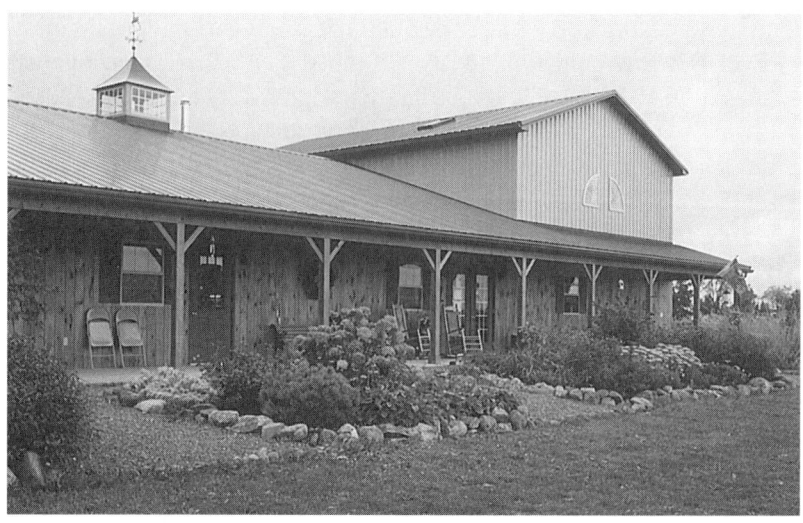

Deer Run Winery, founded by George and Susan Kuyon in 2002, is located on the west side of Conesus Lake. The winery produces wine from vinifera, French-American hybrid, and native grapes. The winery is committed to producing quality New York State wine at reasonable prices. The wine shop has locally produced food.

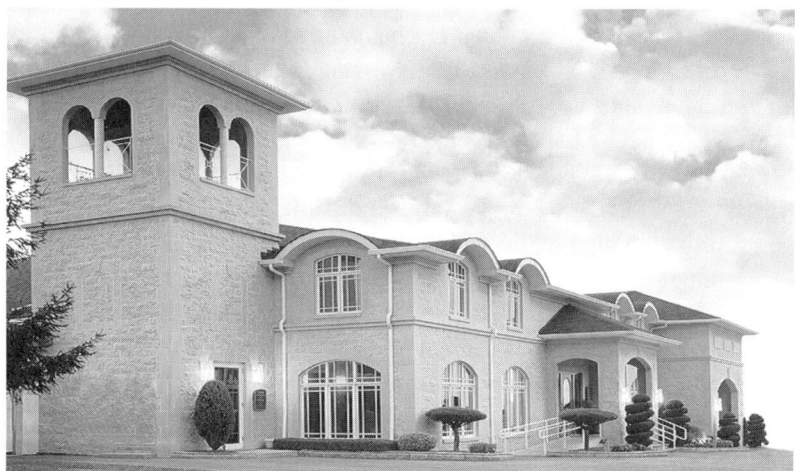

Casa Larga Vineyards is located on Turk Hill, 15 miles south of Rochester. Ann and Andrew Colaruotolo, and their son, John, planted their first vines in 1974. The winery specializes in wine from vinifera grapes but also makes wine from French-American hybrid grapes. The winery is known for its award-wining ice wines.

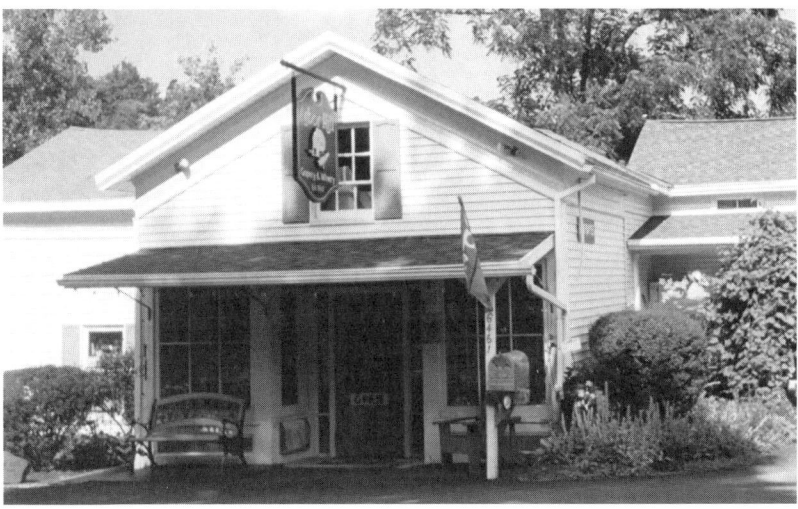

Arbor Hill Grapery and Winery, located six miles north of Naples, is owned and managed by John and Katie Brahm. The winery produces wine from vinifera, French-American hybrid, and native grapes, as well as champagne, dessert wine, and fruit wine. The winery offers the largest selection of grape products in the Finger Lakes Region.

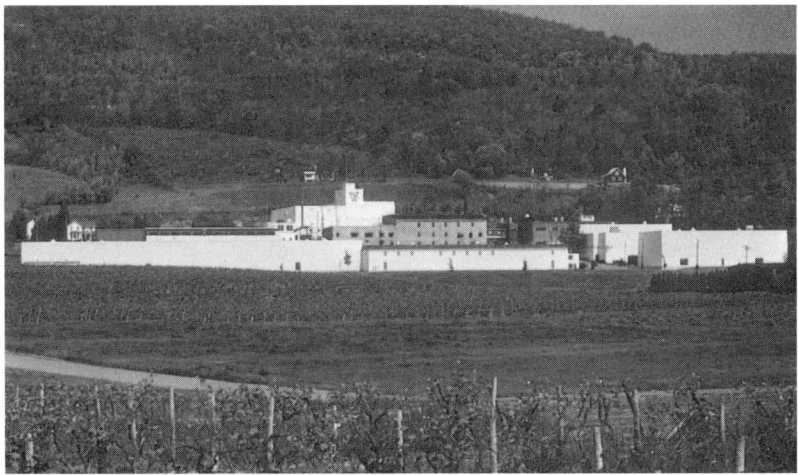

Hazlitt 1852 Vineyards on Seneca Lake purchased the closed Widmer Wine Cellars facilities in Naples and established Hazlitt Red Cat Winery to produce its popular semi-sweet wines: Red Cat, White Cat, Cabin Fever, and Sparkling Lame Duck, as well as fruit wine.

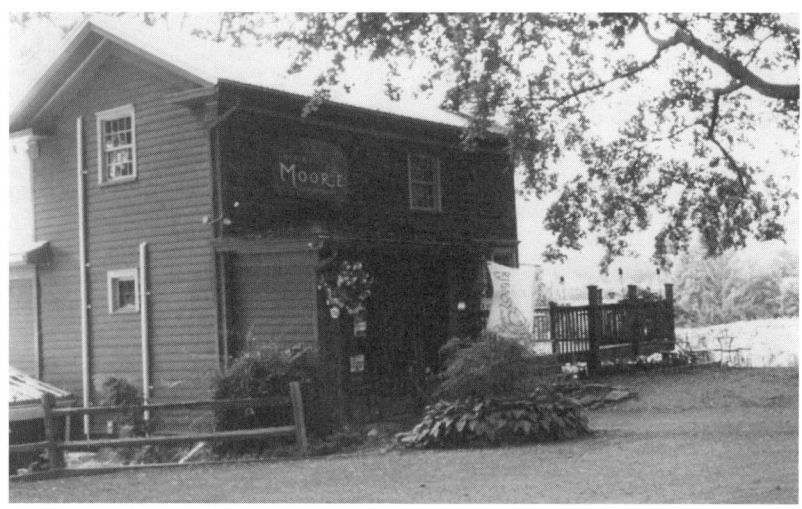

Imagine Moore Winery, owned and managed by Timothy and Diane Moore, is located in the Village of Naples. The winery, which has a 1865 stone cellar, produces semi-dry and semi-sweet wine from vinifera and French-American hybrid grapes. Imagine Moore's specialty is matching wine and food.

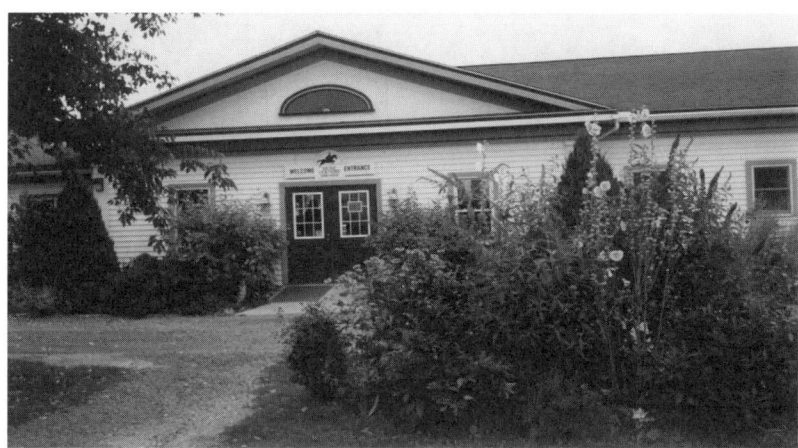

Hunt Country Vineyards, established by Art and Joyce Hunt in 1988, is located one mile west of Branchport. They are the sixth generation of the Hunt family to live on the property. The winery produces wine from vinifera, French-American hybrid, and native grapes, as well as champagne, ice wine, dessert wine, Port, and sherry.

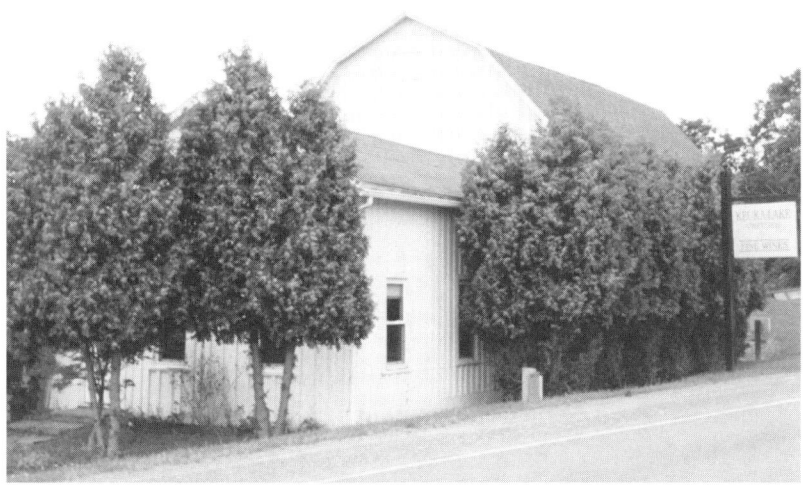

Keuka Lake Vineyards, two miles north of Hammondsport, is owned and run by Mel and Dorothee Goldman, who purchased the site and moved there in 1997 from Washington, D.C., and planted their first vines in 1998. The first vintage was 2005. The winery produces wine from vinifera, French-American hybrid, and native grapes.

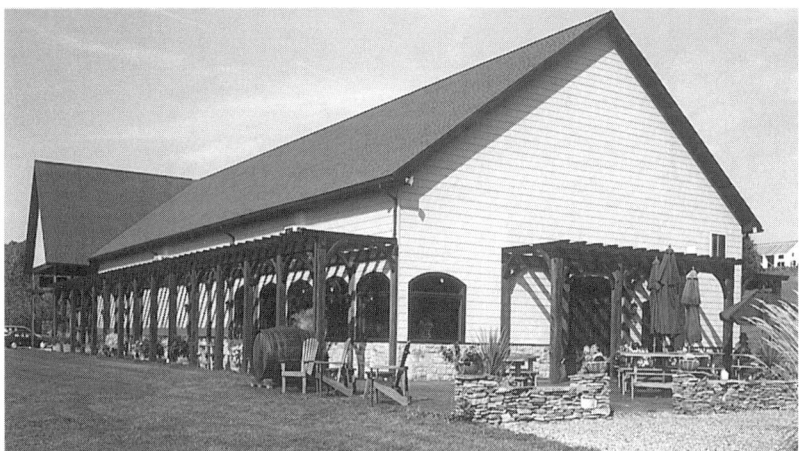

Keuka Spring Vineyards, located three miles south of Penn Yan on the east side of Keuka Lake, is owned by Judy and Len Wiltberger, who produced their first wine in 1985. The winery makes wine from vinifera and French-American hybrid grapes. Keuka Spring is known for its award-winning Riesling.

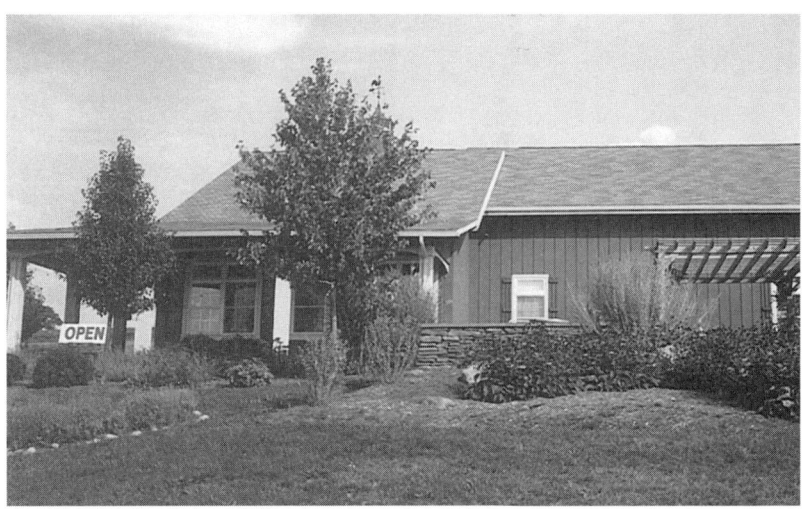

Rooster Hill Vineyards, located five miles south of Penn Yan on the east side of Keuka Lake, was opened by David and Amy Hoffman in 2003. Their motto is "Wine is the beacon we follow to discover nature, art, history, and people." The winery produces wine from vinifera and French-American hybrid grapes.

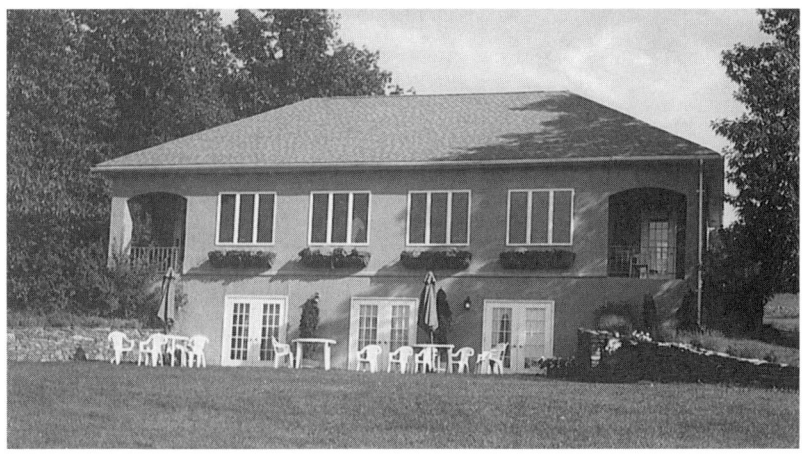

Ravines Wine Cellars, on the east side of Keuka Lake, was established in 2003 by Lisa and Morten Hallgren. Morten has a degree in enology from L'Ecole Agronomie Superior and worked in his family's winery in France. The winery produces wine from vinifera and hybrid grapes. Lisa specializes in matching wine and food.

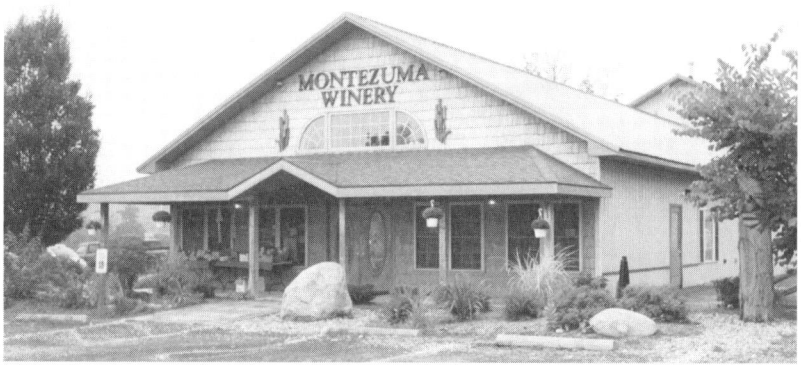

Montezuma Winery, located just east of Seneca Falls, is owned and managed by the Bill Martin family. The winery produces wine from vinifera and hybrid grapes, as well as honey wine (mead) and rhubarb wine. The winery's specialty is a wide variety of fruit wines.

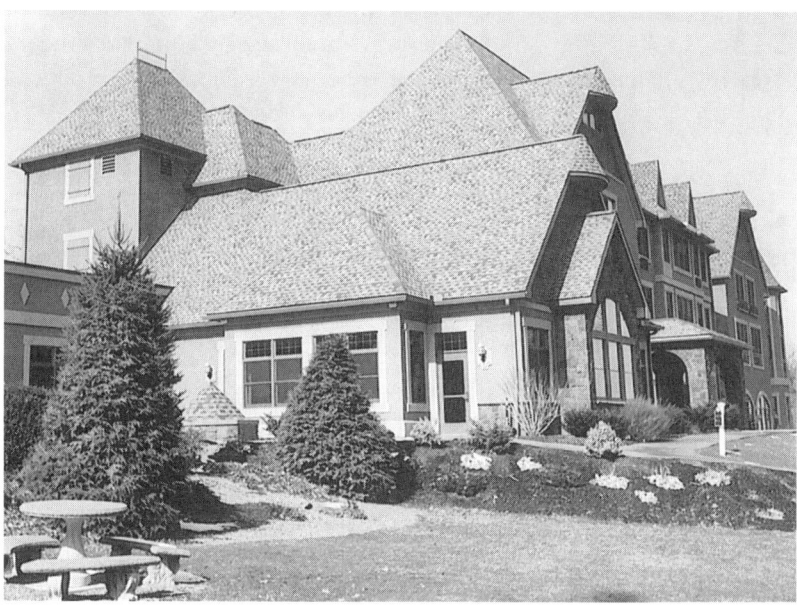

Belhurst Winery is located on the site of Belhurst Castle and Vinifera Inn, south of Geneva. The winery produces wine from vinifera and French-American hybrid grapes. Belhurst Castle, which was constructed from 1885 to 1889 in Richardson Romanesque style mainly from material imported from Europe, has two restaurants.

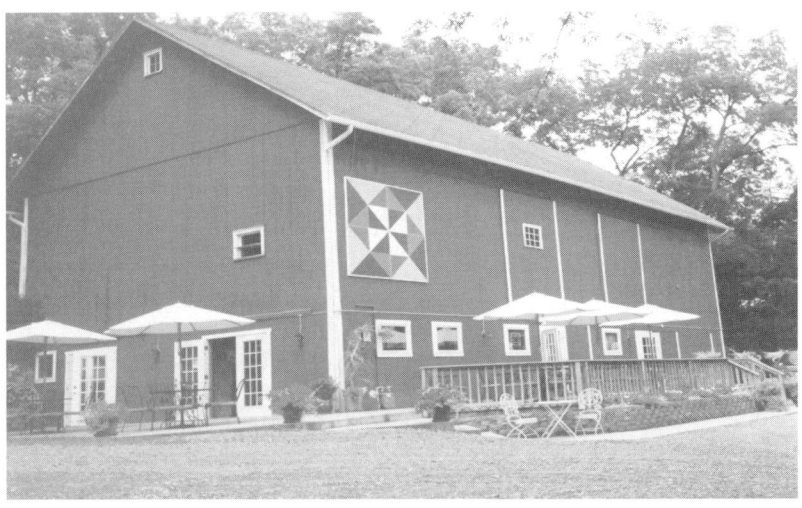

Billsboro Winery, located five miles south of Geneva, was founded in 2000 by Dr. Robert Pool of the Agricultural Experiment Station at Geneva. In 2006, the 20-acre site was purchased by Kim and Vincent Aliperti. Vincent Aliperti is also the winemaker. The winery produces wine from vinifera and French-American hybrid grapes.

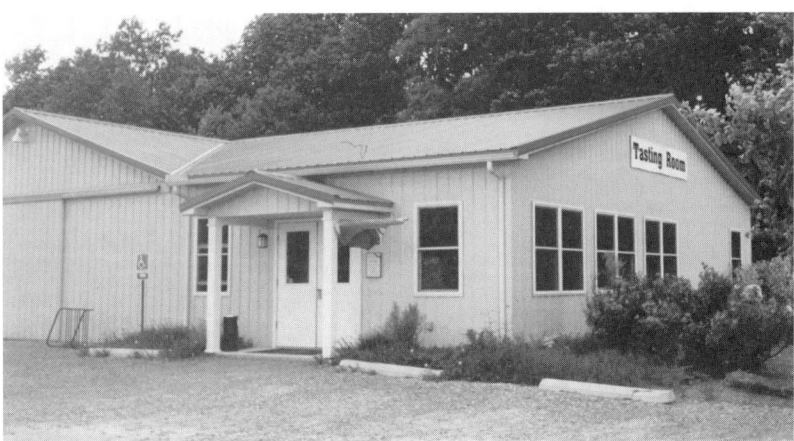

Red Tail Ridge Winery, located on the west side of Seneca Lake, was established in 2007, when Nancy Irlan and her husband, Mike Schnelle, moved east from California. Nancy is an adjunct professor at the Agricultural Experiment Station in Geneva. The winery specializes in wine from vinifera grapes from their model vineyard.

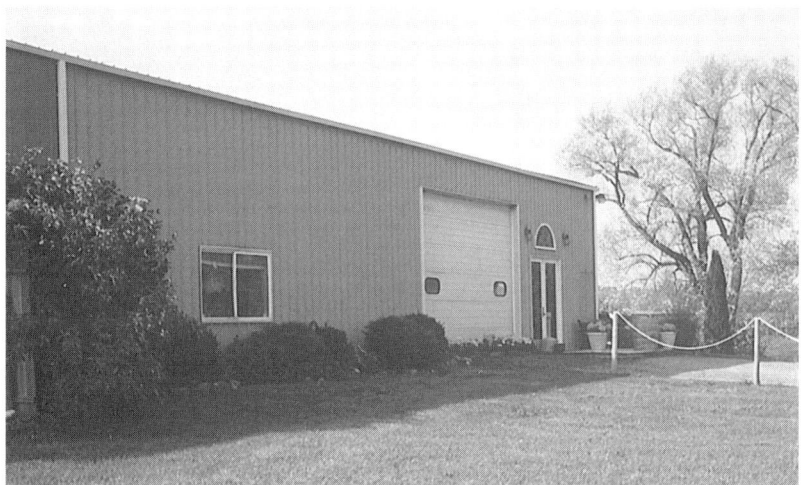

Seneca Shore Wine Cellars, owned and managed by David DeMarco, is located south of Geneva on the west side of Seneca Lake. The winery specializes in vinifera varietals and blends but also makes French-American hybrid wine, Port, sherry, and sweet blueberry wine. The motif of the winetasting room is a medieval castle.

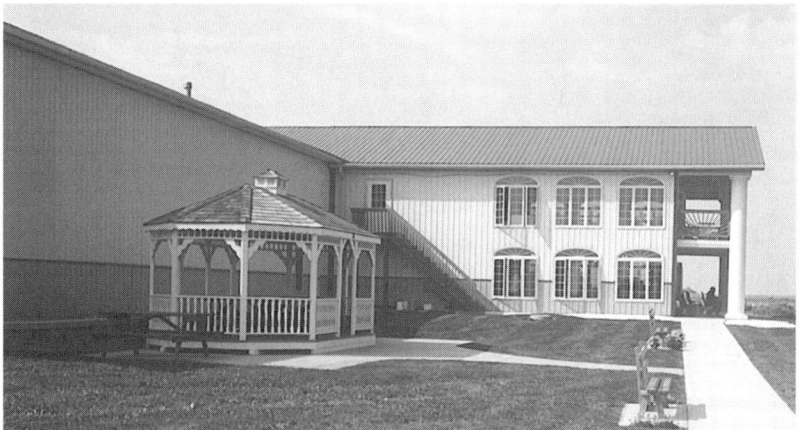

Torrey Ridge Winery and Earle Estates Meadery, located on the west side of Seneca Lake, were founded in 1999 by John and Esther Earle. The winery produces wine from vinifera, French-American hybrid, and native grapes, as well as fruit wines. The meadery produces 39 honey wines (meads) and blends.

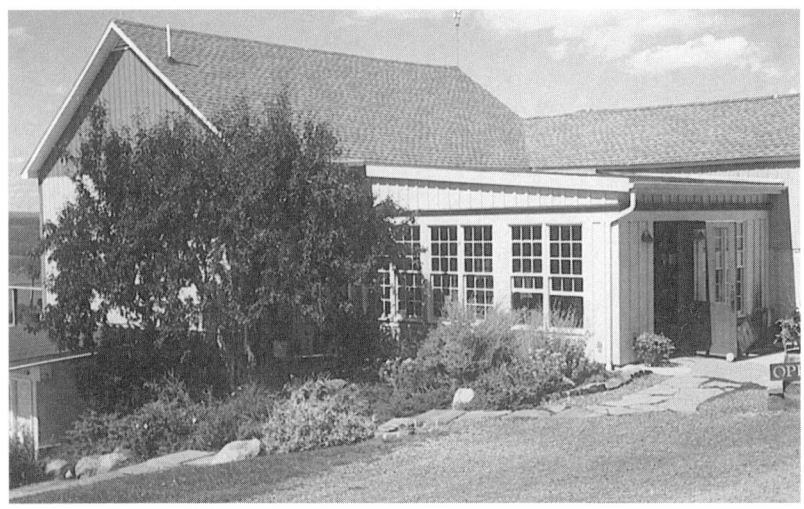

Atwater Estate Vineyards, located on the east side of Seneca Lake, is owned and managed by Ted Marks. The winery produces wine from vinifera, French-American hybrid, and native grapes, as well as sparkling wine. Its Chardonnay is made from grapes from over-30-year-old vines.

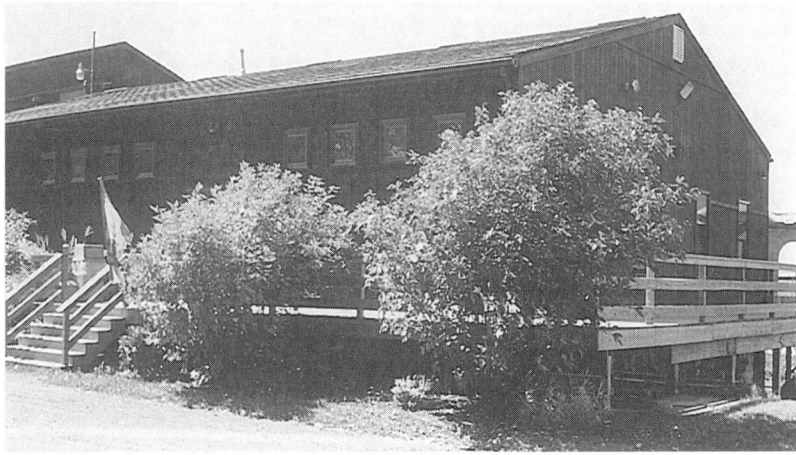

Red Newt Cellars, located on the east side of Seneca Lake, was founded by Debra Whiting and David Whiting. David Whiting is the winemaker. The first vintage was 1998. The winery produces wine from vinifera and French-American hybrid grapes, and Port. Red Newt's Bistro, an upscale restaurant, seats 50.

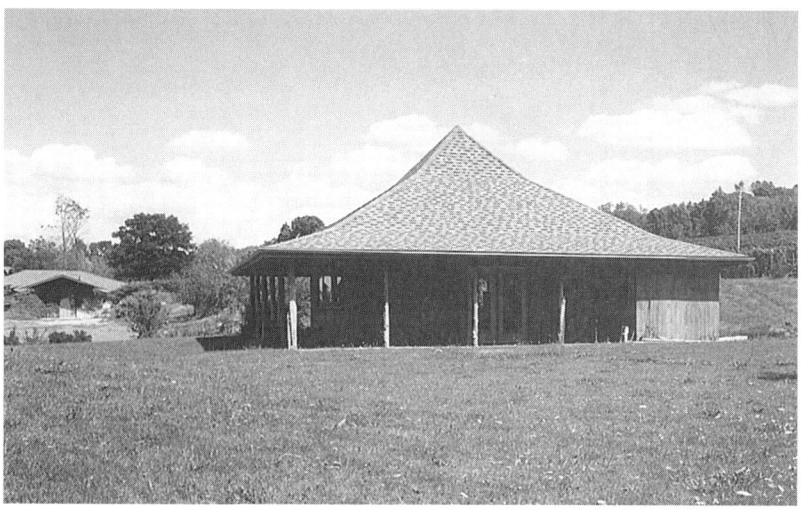

Shalestone Vineyards, on the east side of Seneca Lake, specializes in dry red vinifera wine. Its slogan is "Red is all we do." The owners and managers are Kate Thomas and winemaker Rob Thomas. In 2002, Shalestone added a 2,5000-square-foot-production facility built into the ground to take advantage of stable ambient temperature.

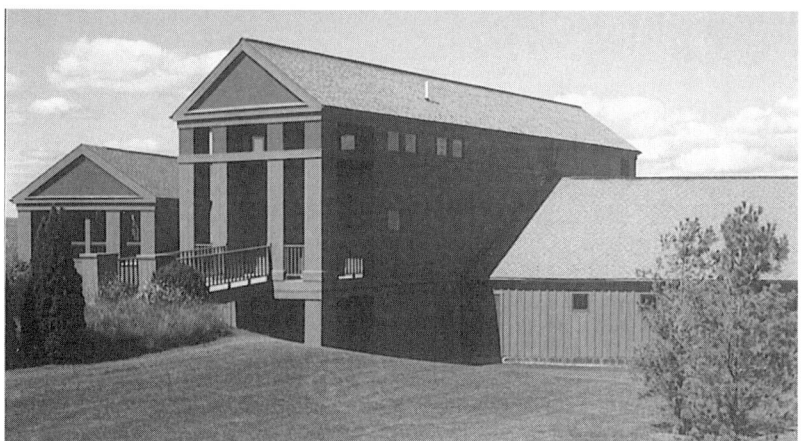

Lamoreaux Landing Wine Cellars, located on the east side of Seneca Lake, was established in 1990 by Mark Wagner, whose family have been vineyardists for decades. The winery produces wine from vinifera grapes as well as sparkling wine and ice wine. The winery was built in 1992, and two additions have been made.

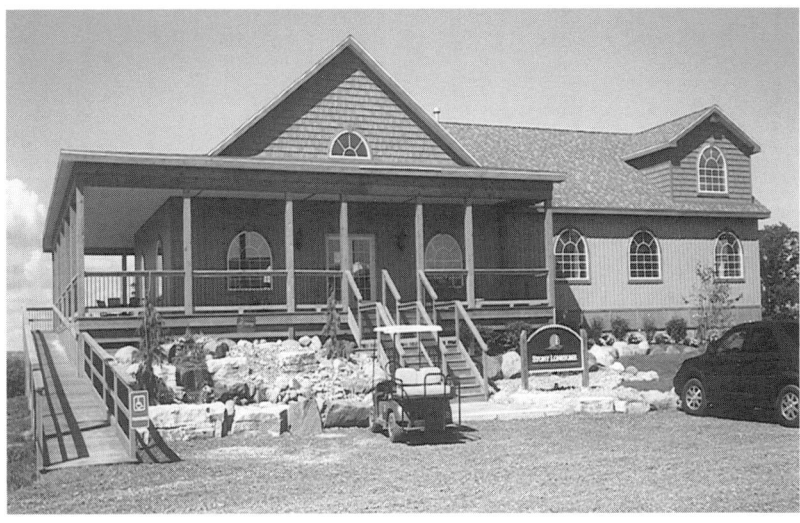

Stoney Lonesome Wine Cellars is located south of Geneva on the east side of Seneca Lake. The winery, which produces wine from vinifera grapes, is owned by Dave Mansfield and his two brothers. The 3,000-square-foot winetasting room's covered deck overlooks the lake and the vineyards.

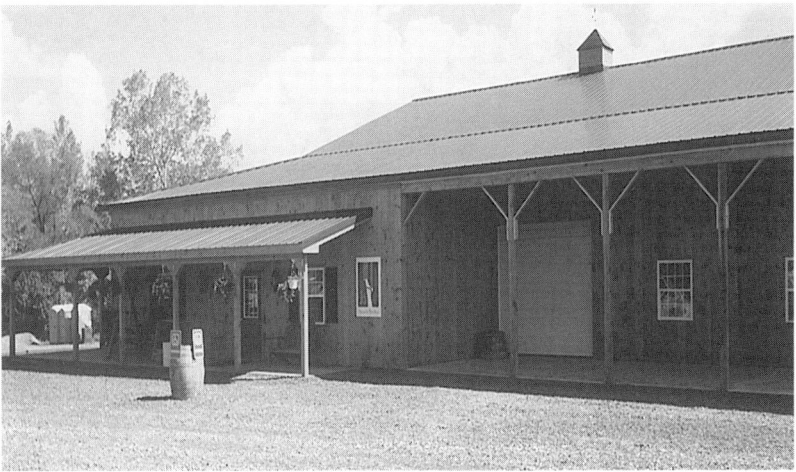

Passion Feet Vineyard & Wine Barn, on the east side of Seneca Lake, south of Geneva, is owned by Dave Mansfield and his two brothers. The winery specializes in semi-sweet and sweet blends made from vinifera and French-American hybrid grapes and fruit blends.

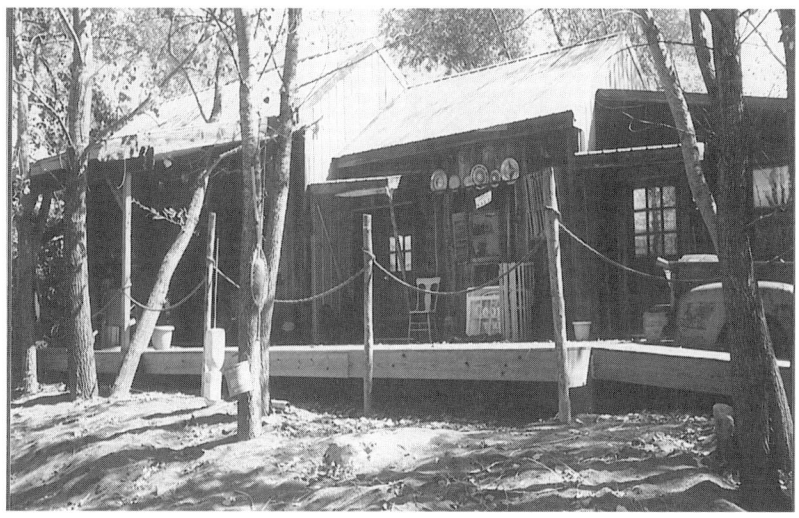

Rogue's Hollow Winery is located on the east side of Seneca Lake south of Geneva. It is owned by Dave Mansfield and his two brothers. The winery produces semi-sweet and sweet blends from vinifera, French-American hybrid, and native grapes. The winetasting room is based on a 1930s Louisiana Bayou roadhouse.

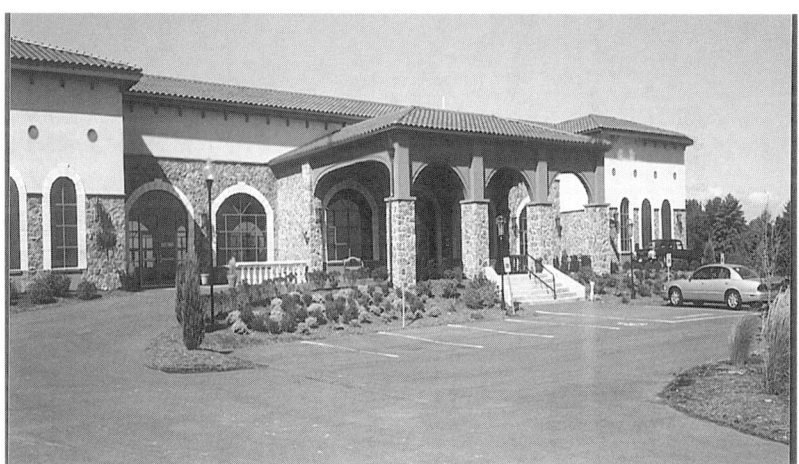

Ventosa Vineyards, located on the east side of Seneca Lake south of Geneva, is owned by Lenny and Meg Cevere. The winery specializes in wine made from vinifera grapes. Cafe Toscana serves lunch and seats 60 people. Ventosa's expansive terrace provides alfresco dining overlooking the lake and the vineyards.

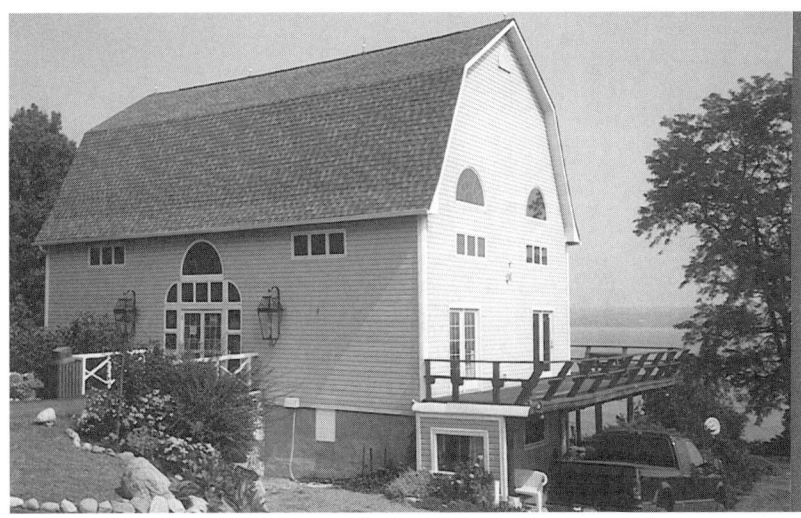

Goose Watch Winery, located 15 miles south of Seneca Falls on the west side of Cayuga Lake, is owned by Dick and Cindy Peterson, who also own Swedish Hill Winery. The winery produces wine from vinifera, French-American hybrid, and native grapes, as well as champagne, Port, spumante, sherry, and fruit wines.

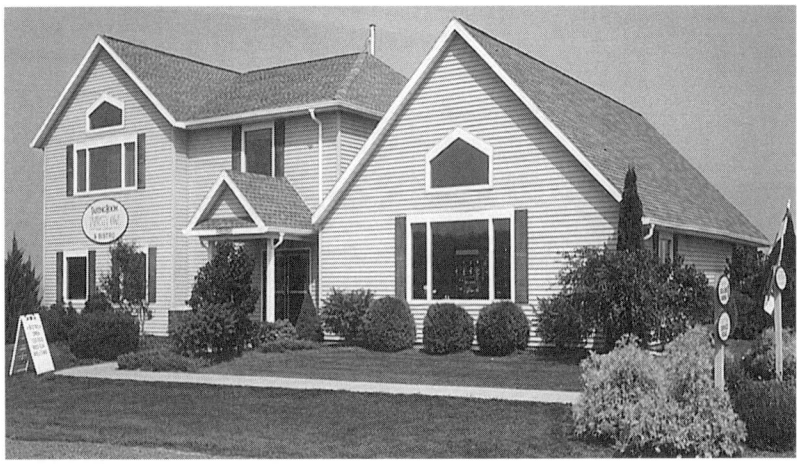

Thirsty Owl Wine Company, on the west side of Cayuga Lake, is owned by Ted Cupp of Utica. The winery opened in 2002 on a 150-acre site with lakefront and a dock. The winery produces wine from vinifera, French-American hybrid, and native grapes. Thirsty Owl has a bistro that seats 60 and a walkway along the waterfront.

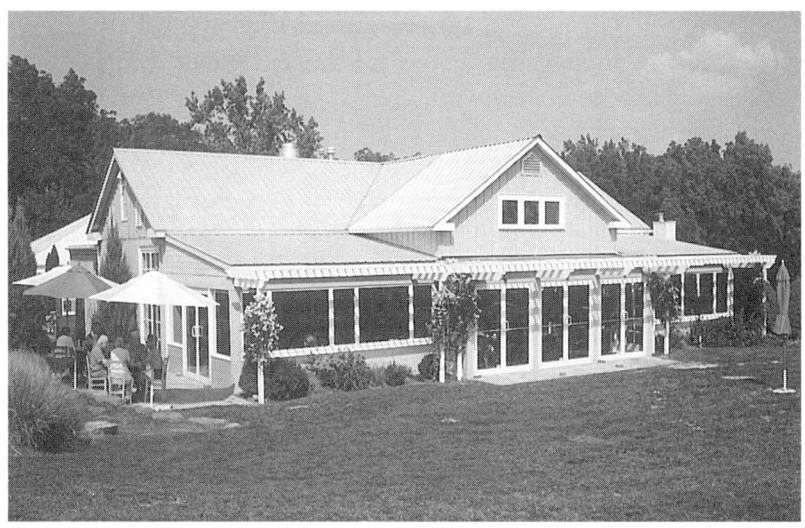

Sheldrake Point Vineyards is located on the west side of Cayuga Lake on the lakefront. The 1999 vintage was the first from estate vineyards. The winery produces wine from vinifera and French-American hybrid grapes, as well as ice wine and fruit wines. Simply Red Bistro offers lunch and dinner.

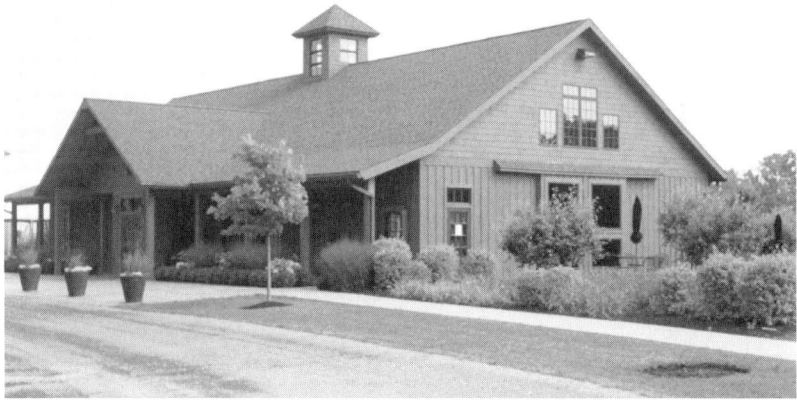

Anyela's Vineyards, the first winery on a major Finger Lake east of Cayuga Lake, is south of the Village of Skaneateles on the west side of Skaneateles Lake. It is owned by Jim Nowak. The winery, an attractive, modern facility with indoor and deck snack areas, produces wine from vinifera and French-American hybrid grapes.

EPILOGUE

"More and more producers have become familiar with which grape variety grows where and are increasingly trying out new combinations of grapes, grape varieties new to a particular area, or deliberately searching out old vines, capable of producing top quality juice, of grape types that may be obscure or archaic, but may be worth cherishing. They can choose from the scores of new grape varieties that have been deliberately developed by grape breeders during the last 100 years, designed for special purposes and conditions."

Jancis Robinson, *Guide to Wine Grapes*

Ongoing wine industry trends in the Finger Lakes Region include:
- Additional offerings of red wine, reflected by more plantings of Cabernet Franc, Pinot Noir, Merlot, and Cabernet Sauvignon vines.
- An increased willingness to grow varieties new to the region, such as Sangiovese from Italy, Viognier from France, and Gruner Veltliner from Austria.
- Increased awareness of the importance to viticulture of the mesoclimate, the environment within the vineyard, including elevation, angle of slope, and distance from the nearest large body of water, as well as the importance of terroir—the French word that literally means soil or earth but for vintners connotes the influence of the soil on the wine produced from grapes grown on it.

Local author Joy Underhill has noted:
:

The lower elevation lakes—Seneca and Cayuga—are surrounded by chalky, high-lime soil. Such soil is well suited for the vinifera grapes used in European winemaking. In the higher altitude Finger Lakes—Keuka and Canandaigua—the soil is more acidic, Native American varieties—Concord, Catawba, and Niagara—prefer acid soil, which may explain why the earliest vineyards developed around the smaller lakes.

Regardless of the predominate soil type, Finger Lakes wineries are now home to all type of grapes. Nearly every winery makes wines to suit your taste, from very dry to very sweet.

In Germany, it is said that the better vineyards overlook water. This is certainly true in the Finger Lakes. And it is the lakes themselves that provide the other two elements needed to create outstanding grapes: drainage and moderate temperatures.

Cornell University's College of Agriculture and Life Sciences has a cool-climate Viticulture and Enology Program with two concentrations: a viticulture concentration on grape growing to gain a firm foundation in biology, and chemistry, plant and agricultural sciences, and an enology concentration focusing on winemaking with a curriculum of biology, chemistry, and food and agricultural sciences. Both concentrations also offer specialized courses.

Cornell's Viticulture and Enology major addresses the region's unique challenges: the climate, soils, grape varieties, pests and markets—while also providing a grounding in other regions' climates, grape varieties, and winemaking techniques.

Fred Frank, president of Dr. Frank's Vinifera Wine Cellars and member of the Cornell University Agricultural and Life Science Advisory Council, has observed:

> The marketing of the Finger Lakes Region has improved with more cooperation between the tourism and winery organizations. In the past, Finger Lakes wineries marketed their wines primarily through the individual lake wine trails. These wine trails continue to market events and print brochures targeting a 100-mile radius around the Finger Lakes. A larger umbrella group has been formed called the Finger Lakes Wine Alliance to promote and market Finger Lakes wines beyond the region. In addition, the New York Wine & Grape Foundation promotes Finger Lakes wine along with that of other wine-producing regions of New York State.
>
> Two Finger Lakes tourist groups also promote Finger Lakes wineries because they are an important visitor attraction to the region: Finger Lakes Wine Country and the Finger Lakes Tourism Alliance both promote the many wonderful attractions of the Finger Lakes Region.

In 2009, Finger Lakes Community College in Canandaigua instituted a viticulture and enology program. FLCC established a vineyard at the Anthony Road Winery on Seneca Lake. In late 2014, the Community College will open a $3.25 million Viticulture and Wine Technology Center adjacent to the New York State Agricultural Experiment Station in Geneva. It will contain a winery, a laboratory, and a reception area with a wine-tasting room.

State Senator Mike Nozzolio, who secured $8 million for the center and 21,000 square feet of greenhouses at the Experiment Station, is optimistic: "As the home of the most innovative agricultural research in the nation, and in close approximation to over 100 wineries, the new Finger Lakes Viticultural Center will allow future winemakers to obtain the knowledge and skills necessary to develop New York's wine and grape industry as one of our area's fastest growing economic engines."

Awareness of the attractions of the Finger Lakes Region is increasing, but the number of tourists grows by only a few percent a year. Considering the fact that over 100 million people live within an eight-hour drive of the region, more can be done to promote the region, including increasing the radius of marketing and promotion.

BIBLIOGRAPHY

Adams, Leon D. *The Wines of America*. Boston: Houghton Mifflin, 1973.

Allen, H. Warner. *A History of Wine*. London: Faber and Faber, 1961.

Amerine, M. A., and A. J. Winkler. *California Wine Grapes*. Bulletin 794. Agricultural Experiment Station, University of California at Davis, 1963.

Amerine, M.A. and V. L. Singleton. *Wine, an Introduction*. Berkeley: University of California Press, 1977.

Behr, Edward. *Prohibition: Thirteen Years That Changed America*. New York: Arcade Publishing, 1996.

Garrett, Paul. *Reminiscences*. Self-published, 1940.

Champlin, Charles. *Back There Where the Past Was*. Syracuse, New York: Syracuse University Press, 1989.

Gohdes, Clarence. *Scuppernong: North Carolina's Grape and Its Wines*. Durham, North Carolina: Duke University Press, 1982.

Hedrick, U. P. *The Grapes of New York*. Albany: State of New York, 1908.

Jackisch, Philip. *Modern Winemaking*. Ithaca: Cornell University Press, 1985.

Johnson, Hugh. *Pocket Encyclopedia of Wine*. New York: Simon & Schuster, 1998.

Klees, Emerson. *Persons, Places, and Things Of the Finger Lakes Region: The Heart of New York State*. Rochester, New York: Friends of the Finger Lakes Publishing, 2009.

—. *Paul Garrett: Dean of American Winemakers*. Rochester, New York: Friends of the Finger Lakes Publishing, 2010.

—. *Wineries of the Finger Lakes Region—100 Wineries*. Rochester, New York: Friends of the Finger Lakes Publishing, 2008.

Lichine, Alexis, et. al. *New Encyclopedia of Wines and Spirits*. New York: Alfred A. Knopf, 1974.

Merrill, Arch. *Slim Fingers Beckon*. New York: American Book-Stratford Press, 1951.

Morton, Lucie T. *Winegrowing in Eastern America: An Illustrated Guide to Viticulture East of the Rockies*. Ithaca: Cornell University Press, 1985.

Pinney, Thomas. *A History of Wine in America, vol 2*. Berkeley: University of California Press, 2005.

BIBLIOGRAPHY

Robinson, Jancis. *Guide to Wine Grapes*. New York:
Oxford University Press, 1996.

Scherer, Richard. *Crooked Lake and the Grape*. N.p., N.d.

Schoonmaker, Frank. *Encyclopedia of Wine*. New York:
Hastings House, 1973.

Taylor, Walter S., and Richard P. Vine. *Home Winemaker's
Handbook*. New York: Harper & Row, 1968.

Underhill, Joy. "From Grapes to Wine." *Life In the Finger Lakes*
magazine. Geneva: Fahey-Williams Publishing.
Fall/Holiday 2001: 36.

Vine, Richard P. *Commercial Winemaking: Processing and
Controls*. Westport, Connecticut: AVI, 1981.

Wagner, Philip M. *Grapes Into Wine: The Art of Winemaking
In America*. New York: Alfred A. Knopf, 1976.

—. *A Wine-Grower's Guide*. New York: Alfred A. Knopf,
1973.

Winkler, A. J. *General Viticulture*. Berkeley: California
University Press, 1962.

APPENDIX

Species of Grapes

Vitis aestivalis — wild grape varieties occasionally used for making wine. The best-known *Vitis aestivalis* varieties are Cynthiana, Herbemont, Lenoir, and Norton. It is grown in most states bordering upon or east of the Mississippi River.

Vitis amurensis — A specie grown in Asia that can tolerate extremely low temperatures but is vulnerable to powdery mildew.

Vitis labrusca — hardy grape varieties known for their foxy or grapy taste. *Vitis labrusca* varieties include Catawba, Concord, Delaware, Elvira, and Niagara. The specie is grown in most states east of the Mississippi River.

Vitis riparia — herbaceous grape varieties that can be used to make high-acid wine. *Vitis riparia*, which has sturdy rootstock suitable for grafting, grows in the wild in Canada and in the Eastern United States, north of the Gulf states and the South Atlantic states. Baco Noir is probably the best-known *Vitis riparia* hybrid.

Vitis rotundifolia — popular grape varieties for wine and grape jelly in the South. *Vitis rotundifolia*, which is also known as Muscadine, varieties include Carlos, Magnolia, Noble, and Scuppernong. This specie is grown in all Gulf states and South Atlantic states.

Vitis rupestris — grows in Appalachia and in hilly soil west of the Mississippi River. This specie grows on rocky and hilly locations but does not like moist sites. The vines are vigorous and bushy, have deep roots, and are tolerant of alkaline soil.

Vitis vinifera — the classic "European" varieties of grapes considered to be the best in the world for winemaking, such as Cabernet Sauvignon, Chardonnay, Gewürztraminer, Pinot Noir, and Riesling. *Vitis vinifera* is widely grown in Europe and the United states, including the States of California, New York, Oregon, and Washington.

Vitis Vinifera Varieties for Red Wine

Alicante Bouschet—also known as Alicante and is occasionally used as a synonym for Grenache. Alicante Bouschet has intense color and is popular as a teinturier. It is an early ripening variety used mainly for blending.

Barbera—makes a heavy bodied wine with a distinct aroma that develops character with age. Barbera, a productive variety with a high level of natural acidity but good balance, is widely grown in Italy, particularly in the Piedmont.

Cabernet Franc—a French variety frequently blended with the later maturing Cabernet Sauvignon. Cabernet Franc is aromatic and tends to be lighter in color, body, and tannin than Cabernet Sauvignon, and it ripens in a cooler environment. Cabernet Franc usually makes a light-bodied or medium-bodied wine. Its vines are vigorous and fairly productive.

Cabernet Sauvignon—the world's most prestigious grape variety for the production of fine wine that ages well. It is the principal grape variety in Bordeaux wine in which it is blended with other varieties such as Merlot, Malbec, and Cabernet Franc to make a mellower wine. Cabernet Sauvignon, which is known for its deep color, high tannin, and flavor of black currants or eucalyptus, ages well in French oak. Its vines are vigorous but not particularly productive. It is a late ripening variety.

Carignane—an extremely productive grape variety that originated in Spain but is not widely grown there today. Because it ripens late, Carignane is suited only to relatively hot climates. Wine made from Carignane grapes has deep color, good body, and a clean flavor; it usually is high in acidity and tannin. Its vines are vigorous but not very disease resistant.

Carmine—in 1976, Dr. H. P. Olmo, plant geneticist emeritus of the University of California at Davis, developed this Cabernet Sauvignon-Carignane-Merlot cross attempting to combine the distinctive Cabernet taste and the productivity of Carignane with the mellowness of Merlot. Vines from an early planting in Georgia produced grapes from which a quality wine reminiscent of a Cabernet-Merlot blend was made.

Dornfelder—a red wine crossing from Germany, bred initially for its color but which inherited many good qualities, including desirable acidity, fruity aroma, and the benefits of oak aging. It is a high yield variety that is easier to grow than Pinot Noir.

Gamay—the grape of the Beaujolais region of France is one of numerous Gamay clones, many of which have been used as teinturiers. Gamay vines have a tendency to overbear; the grapes ripen early. The juice, which is relatively high in acidity, is usually vinified quickly and marketed as Beaujolais Nouveau. Beaujolais wine is meant to be drunk young; storing in a wine cellar for more than two or three years is not recommended. Two California variations are Napa Gamay and Gamay Beaujolais, a Pinot Noir clone.

Grenache—originated in Spain and is widely planted in Spain and southern France. The variety ripens early and is able to withstand heat and drought. Grenache, which is frequently blended with varieties higher in color and tannin, is popular with rosé producers, including those in the Tavel district of France. Its vines are vigorous and productive.

Lambrusco—a robust vine grown mainly in the three central provinces of Italy. Wine made from this variety, which is extremely productive, is fruity and meant to be drunk young. Lambrusco wine made in the United States is usually slightly sweet.

Lemberger—a German grape also known as Limberger and Blauer Limberger that is called Blauerfränkisch in Austria. Lemberger, which has notable color and acidity, is usually blended with Trollinger to produce a light-bodied red wine intended to be consumed young. Washington has sizable plantings of Lemberger.

Malbec—a variety rich in tannin and color that is blended with Cabernet Sauvignon in Bordeaux wine. It is declining in popularity in France because it has many of the disadvantages of Merlot, such as not being very disease resistant. Also, Malbec doesn't have Merlot's high level of fruit quality. Most Malbec grown in California is blended into Meritage wines to simulate Bordeaux wine. Its vines are moderately productive.

Merlot—known for years as a blending variety, along with Cabernet Franc and, decreasingly, Malbec, in Bordeaux wine to complement the late-maturing and less mellow Cabernet Sauvignon. Merlot has become a popular variety on its own merit. It is widely planted in the cool, damp soils of St. Emilion and Pomerol; Cabernet Sauvignon prefers the well-drained soils of Médoc. Merlot is fruitier, less tannic, and more full-bodied than its sophisticated and long-lived blending partner. The wine usually has a strawberry or raspberry aroma. It is a vigorous, productive variety that ripens in midseason.

Meunier—also known as Pinot Meunier, it is thought to be an early mutation of Pinot Noir. It was called Meunier (French for miller) because the underside of its leaves look like they have been dusted with flour. In Germany, it is known as Müllerrebe and Schwarzriesling. The variety is productive and winter hardy. Meunier, along with Chardonnay and Pinot Noir, is a component of the classic champagne blend. Pinot Blanc occasionally is the fourth variety in the cuvée. Chardonnay provides complexity to the blend, Pinot Noir the heaviness, and Meunier the fruity flavor.

Nebbiolo—grown principally in the Piedmont region of Italy, the variety is a late ripener that is very dependent upon the soil in which it is grown. When growing conditions are favorable, Nebbiolo wine is among the world's finest and long-lived; it tends to be high in color, tannin, and acidity while young, maturing into a wine with a notable bouquet. Wines made in Barbaresco and Barolo are the best-known Nebbiolo wines. Its quality has motivated winemakers around the world to experiment with the variety.

Petite Sirah—a variety principally grown in California and Argentina that is probably not related to the true Syrah or a sub-variety of Syrah called Petite Syrah in France. Petite Sirah is occasionally blended with lighter red wines such as Zinfandel in California, where it has been grown since the 1880s. The wine is deep colored and robust with a touch of spicy, sometimes peppery, flavor. It is astringent with a pronounced aroma. High tannin makes the variety potentially suitable for aging.

Petit Verdot—one of Bordeaux's classic black grape varieties. The vine ripens later than Cabernet Sauvignon and is equally resistant to rot. It is capable of yielding concentrated, tannic wines, rich in color with an extra spicy nose when it ripens fully.

Pinot Noir—the classic grape of Burgundy. Unlike Bordeaux wine, which is a blend, Burgundy is made from Pinot Noir grapes. Pinot Noir is difficult to grow, has low yield, and is very dependent on the type of soil in which it is grown. In *Guide to Wine Grapes,* Jancis Robinson observes: "If Cabernet wines appeal to the head, Pinot's charms are decidedly more sensual and more transparent." Pinot Noir is more fruity and has less tannin and pigment than Cabernet Sauvignon. When young, Pinot Noir has a taste of strawberries or cherries. Aged Pinot Noir usually has a velvety finish. It ripens early and is best grown in cool climates. Pinot Noir is widely grown in California; Oregon also has favorable growing conditions for it.

Ruby Cabernet—a cross of Carignane and Cabernet Sauvignon that reached the peak of its popularity in California in the 1960s. In 1949, Dr. H. P. Olmo of the University of California at Davis attempted to combine the high yield and heat tolerance of Carignane with the quality of Cabernet Sauvignon with this hybrid. Although it was meant to be a claret-type wine made from grapes grown in hot growing regions, it has done well in cooler growing climates. South Central San Joaquin Valley is one of the regions of California in which it is grown. It is a heavy bearer in South Africa and is grown in limited quantities in Australia.

Sangiovese—is heavily planted in central Italy and is the principal grape for red wine in Tuscany. The variety tends to be high in tannin and acid but not color; it varies widely, depending upon vineyard location. Brunello di Montalcino wine is made from Sangiovese; it is one of the grape varieties used in making Chianti. Literally translated, Sangiovese is "blood of Jove." The variety grows well in a range of soils, but it is particularly suited to limestone soil. It blends well with Cabernet Sauvignon. Sangiovese ripens late; it tends to be relatively high in alcohol and to be long-lived in hot growing seasons. In cool growing seasons, high tannin is a problem along with high acidity.

Saperavi—a Russian grape variety notable for its color and acidity. It is usually used in blends. As a varietal wine, it requires bottle aging. Saperavi is productive, ripens late, and is well suited to the cold winters of Russia and the former USSR republics. It has a relatively high sugar level.

Syrah—one of the noblest black grapes, particularly if longevity is considered. This great grape of the northern Rhone has questionable origins. The vines are productive and disease resistant. The dark, dense qualities of the wine have highlights of black pepper. A small-berried, superior version of Syrah is called Petit Syrah in the Rhone to distinguish it from the larger-berried Grosse Syrah. There is no relation between Petite Syrah in France and the variety called Petite Sirah in North and South America. In Australia, Syrah is known as Shiraz. A blend of Cabernet Sauvignon and Shiraz is a popular Australian export.

Teroldego Rotaliano, or just *Teroldego*—a variety from northeastern Italy capable of producing deep-colored, lively, light-bodied, fruity wines with moderate tannin for early drinking. Wines made from this variety have been compared to Zinfandel.

Zinfandel—grown primarily in California, the variety has been cultivated there since the 1850s. Zinfandel was grown in North Coast vineyards and was popular with gold miners in California in the mid-1800s. Although it is grown in hot climates, Zinfandel improves when grown in a cool climate that ensures a long growing season, and when productivity is limited. Zinfandel is not considered a noble grape; however, it makes a red wine with rich body, good flavor, and a sweet bouquet. The wine has a life of four to eight years. Occasionally, it is blended with Petite Sirah. In the late 1980s, surplus Zinfandel grapes were used to make White Zinfandel, which became a marketing success. The crisp, fruity wine is made by leaving the fermenting juice in contact with the skins for only a short period of time.

Vitis Vinifera Varieties for White Wine

Aligoté—a productive grape principally grown in Burgundy where Chardonnay predominates. Aligoté makes a tart wine not suitable for oak-aging that is characteristically high in acid, low in tannin, and is best consumed young. The variety's vines are vigorous, but yields vary widely. Aligoté is widely grown in Bulgaria and Rumania, as well as Russia, Ukraine, Georgia, and Moldova.

Chardonnay—the variety of White Burgundy. With the increased use of varietal names, Chardonnay has become a universally known grape variety. It produces high yields in a wide variety of vineyard locations; in fact, its productivity must be limited to ensure quality. Chardonnay is a fairly vigorous variety that matures early. It is suitable for climates with a short to medium growing season; it is moderately winter hardy. The variety is popular for its wide range of tastes, usually the fruity flavor of apples, melons, or pears. A wide range of winemaking techniques is used to produce Chardonnay. It can be bottled early after a long, cool fermentation process as with Moselle and Vouvray or aged in oak. It may have a nutty or buttery flavor. The variety is widely used in making champagne; its varietal taste is not lost when blended.

Chenin Blanc—widely grown in the cool Loire region of France. It is considered a quality wine in Anjou-Touraine, where its yield is limited, and the climate and soil are ideal. In California, it is predominately grown in the hot Central Valley where it loses some of its honey flavor. It is a versatile, productive grape with considerable bouquet and relatively high acidity. Chenin Blanc makes a fresh, light, fruity wine with a wide range of sweetness; it is frequently blended, usually with Colombard, sometimes with Sémillon. The variety is also used in producing sparkling wine.

Colombard—also known as French Colombard. Its popularity has waned in recent years, and Colombard vines are being pulled from vineyards in France and in California's Central Valley. The variety was frequently used as a clean, pleasant but neutral component of blends. Originally, Colombard was used in France, along with Ugni Blanc and Folle Blanche, in making Cognac. In California, it was also

135

used to make brandy. Most of the Colombard in France is north and west of the Bordeaux region in Bourg and Blaye.

Gewürztraminer—a light-bodied to medium-bodied white wine known for its notable aroma. The German word "gewürz," meaning spiced, is the usual way of describing the wine. It tends to be crisp with a bouquet of tropical fruit. Gewürztraminer wine has higher than average alcohol content and can be cellared for medium-term aging. It is a difficult variety to grow and with its small bunches is not considered a high-yield grape. It is a particularly suitable grape for the soil and growing season of Alsace, and it is very popular there. The variety grows well in rich, clay soils, such as those in the Haut-Rhine départmente. It ripens in early midseason. Washington and Oregon also provide a favorable growing climate for Gewürztraminer.

Grüner Veltliner—Austria's most important grape variety, grown in one-third of the country's vineyards, particularly in Lower Austria and around Vienna. The variety is productive and relatively hardy but is a late ripener. The wine is similar to Alsace in style and is usually drunk young. Wine from the Wachau has some characteristics of white Burgundy. It is also grown in Slovakia and Hungary.

Malvasia Bianca—Malvasia is a collection of grape varieties of Greek origin that is widely grown in Italy, the Iberian peninsula, and elsewhere in Europe. Malvasia Bianca produces tangy off-dry whites with substance and character. It is also grown in the southern Central Valley in California.

Muscat—scores of Muscat varieties are grown around the world, ranging in color from from pale yellow to blue-black, in quality from poor to excellent, and in yield from light to heavy. All of them are aromatic with a distinctive "spicy" taste. Muscat of Alexandria grown in California is known principally as a raisin and table grape. Wine made from Muscat grapes is usually low in alcohol and somewhat sweet; if made dry, it tends to be bitter.

Muscat Ottonel—the palest of the Muscat varieties has a less grapy aroma than other Muscat grapes. This low-yield grape ripens early and grows well in deep, damp soils in a cool climate. Little Muscat other than Muscat Ottonel is grown in Alsace, where it is made into a dry wine. Muscat Ottonel is grown in Austria, Hungary, Rumania, Russia, and the Ukraine. Small quantities of the variety are grown in the Finger Lakes Region. Occasionally it is used to make sparkling wine.

Pinot Blanc—widely planted in France, it is a mutation of Pinot Gris, which is a relative of Pinot Noir. The variety is not particularly productive, but new clones have higher yields than early Pinot Blancs. It is widely cultivated in Alsace and in Germany. Pinot Blanc is relatively full-bodied but is not known for its aroma or for being long-lived.

Pinot Gris—called Pinot Grigio in Italy, it is a widely planted grape that makes soft wine with body and color and a mildly perfumed bouquet. Pinot Gris is one of the best-known mutations of Pinot Noir. Its leaves are identical to Pinot Noir leaves, and the appearance of the berries is similar to Pinot Noir berries late in the growing season. Pinot Gris wine is made with a wide range of sweetness. It is a popular wine in Alsace, where it is a dry wine that is not overpowered by hearty food. It is called Tokay D'Alsace in Alsace. In some growing regions, it is low in acidity.

Riesling—one of the world's premier wine grapes because of its longevity and its ability to retain its style wherever it is grown. Riesling wine, which has a desirable level of acidity, is made with a wide range of sweetness. Riesling made with higher levels of sweetness has probably lessened the variety's reputation compared with other varieties, such as Chardonnay. The taste of Riesling is sometimes described as steely with an aroma of flowers, honey, or tropical fruit. The wine is light-bodied or medium-bodied. Riesling vines are winter hardy, making it a suitable *Vitis vinifera* variety for growing in cool regions. It is moderately vigorous and ripens in late midseason. Riesling is also used in making ice wine pressed from frozen grapes. The variety is grown in Alsace where Riesling is a prime example of its specialty, dry wine from aromatic grapes.

Rkatsiteli—a little-known grape considered to be a Russian variety but whose origins were probably on the border between Armenia and Turkey near Mt. Ararat. It is widely grown in the countries of the former Soviet Union, particularly Georgia, Ukraine, and Moldova. It is also grown in Bulgaria and Rumania. Rkatsiteli is known for having a touch of spiciness, similar to but different from Gewürztraminer. It is relatively high in acid with high sugar levels; its vines are winter hardy, making it a desirable variety for cool or cold regions. Small quantities of Rkatsiteli are grown in the Finger Lakes Region.

Sauvignon Blanc—the white-wine grape of Bordeaux that is the source for well-known dry white wines such as Pouilly-Fumé and Sancerre from France and Fumé-Blanc produced in California. It makes a crisp and aromatic wine with a herbaceous taste. It is frequently blended with Sémillon. This zesty wine is intended to be drunk young except when aged in oak, which requires an additional year or two of cellaring. The variety, which is known for vigorous vine growth, is widely grown in the regions of Entre-Deux-Mers, Graves, and Sauternes in France. The vine is particularly suitable to the limestone vineyards of the Loire. Robert Mondavi named California wine made with Sauvignon Blanc grapes "Fumé-Blanc." It ripens in midseason. The variety is popular in South Africa and is also grown in the State of Washington.

Sémillon—its reputation is based upon the dry and sweet wines of Bordeaux, particularly in Sauternes and Graves, where it is frequently blended with Sauvignon Blanc and occasionally with Muscadelle. Sémillon, known for its body and lack of aroma, complements Sauvignon Blanc, which tends to have light body, high acid levels, and a strong aroma. Sémillon has been blended with Chardonnay in response to a demand for Chardonnay that exceeded the supply. Sémillon vines are vigorous, producing high grape yields. It is less winter hardy than Riesling and Chardonnay. The variety is widely grown in South America and Australia.

Siegfried—a Riesling cross from Germany that makes a quality late harvest wine similar to late harvest Riesling.

Tocai Fruilano—the most popular and widely grown Fruili grape in northeast Italy. It is not related to either Tokay D'Alsace, which is what Pinot Grigio is called in Alsace, or to the Hungarian dessert wine Tokay. This productive, late-budding variety produces a wine that is light in body and color. It is intended to be drunk young.

Ugni Blanc—known as Trebbiano in Italy and St. Émilion in the Cognac region of France, is vigorous and is the most widely planted grape variety in France. It is known for high yields, high levels of acidity, and relatively low alcohol content. Wine made from Ugni Blanc grapes is light and crisp but unfortunately neutral. Ugni Blanc is the staple of the French and Spanish brandy industries and is the principal ingredient of Armagnac. Ugni Blanc is widely planted in Italy and South America.

Viognier—the grape variety whose reputation is based on the highly regarded wine, Condrieu, that is high in color, acid, and aroma. Its flavor is reminiscent of apricots and peaches. However, the wine is low in acid and is usually drunk young. Viognier vines can be cultivated in dry growing conditions. The variety is increasingly being planted in California and in Australia.

French-American Hybrid Varieties for Red Wine

Baco Noir—a hybrid of Folle Blanche and a *Vitis riparia* variety, it is medium-bodied to full-bodied and is relatively high in acidity. Baco Noir has deep color and benefits from aging. When young, it has strong character reminiscent of Cabernet Sauvignon; however, it is frequently described as having a smokey taste and a fruity, black pepper aroma. The variety, which ripens early, is vigorous, disease resistant, and moderately winter hardy. It is widely grown in the United States in the East and Midwest and in Canada.

Cascade—a winter-hardy, early ripening grape usually used for rosé or in blends because of its neutral taste. It has no foxy flavor. Birds love Cascade grapes.

Chambourcin—of uncertain parentage, it is popular in the Loire Valley and the Touraine Region of France, probably because it has some of the characteristics of Cabernet Franc. It can be made into quality red wine as well as pleasant rosé wine. Chambourcin vines are vigorous and disease resistant. The variety ripens in late midseason and therefore is suited to regions with long growing seasons. It is rich in color and body but has little aroma.

Chancellor—initially called Seibel 7053 for the hybridizer, it was widely grown in France. In recent years, many French-American hybrid vines, including Chancellor, have been pulled out and replaced in French vineyards. It is a productive variety that makes well-balanced wine with deep color and is suitable for blending and for wood-aging. It is susceptible to downy mildew. Chancellor grows well in cool climates and is well represented in vineyards in the Finger Lakes Region.

Chelois—another Seibel hybrid, it makes a Burgundy-style hearty red wine with good balance that ages well and is a desirable ingredient of a full-bodied blend. It is lightly flavored and has a mild bouquet. In deep, well-drained soil, its vines are vigorous and provide a high yield. It is disease resistant and moderately winter hardy. Substantial plantings of Chelois have been made in the Eastern United States, when early midseason ripening is required.

Colobel—a teinturier, it is not usually made as a varietal wine. It has three to five times (up to 10 times) the color intensity of average red wine. It blends well; however, in France, where authorized, the legal limit of Colobel addition is five percent. The variety is fairly vigorous and productive. It ripens in midseason. The vines are moderately winter hardy.

Corot Noir—the eighth hybrid variety developed by the New York State Agricultural Experiment Station at Geneva has a deep red color and berry and cherry aromas. This superior red hybrid variety is a cross of Seyve-Villard 18-307 and Steuben. It is moderately winter hardy.

DeChaunac—a Seibel hybrid, the variety is vigorous, productive, disease resistant, and winter hardy. It ripens early. In the early 1970s, thousands of acres of DeChaunac were planted to fill the demand for a basic red-wine grape. However, overplanting occurred; the real demand was for white grapes. Many DeChaunac vines producing low quality fruit were pulled out and replaced with other varieties. Canadian viticulturalist Adhemar DeChaunac, for whom the variety is named, preferred Chelois.

Landot—Landot 4511, a cross of Landot 244 (Landal) x Villard Blanc, is designed to combine the excellent red-wine qualities of Landal with the vigor and high yield of Villard Blanc. Landot is vigorous, productive, and disease resistant. It has an agreeable aroma; however, its wine quality is slightly inferior to Landal, which gives only moderate yields but produces a Beaujolais-type wine with deep color.

Léon Millot—a cousin of Maréchal Foch, it is more vigorous, more productive, and the wine has a deeper color than its relative. It ripens early and is a good choice for growing in regions with short growing seasons. The variety is disease resistant and winter hardy. It produces a good varietal wine, and it is suitable for blending.

Maréchal Foch—named for the World War I French general, it was originally called Kuhlmann 188-2. The variety is an Alsatian cross of Pinot Noir x Gamay x *Vitis riparia* that produces a Burgundy-type wine without the complexity. Maréchal Foch has a strong, somewhat herbaceous flavor and a deep color. It develops a fruity bouquet reminiscent of claret. The vines are vigorous, disease resistant, and winter hardy. The variety ripens early, is suitable for cool climates, and therefore grows well where the growing season is short. The strong Maréchal Foch character can be moderated by nouveau-style carbonic maceration.

Noiret—the seventh hybrid variety developed by the New York State Agricultural Experiment Station at Geneva has hints of green and black pepper with raspberry and mint aromas. This excellent red hybrid variety is a cross of NY65.0467.08 (NY 33277 x Chancellor) and Steuben. It is moderately winter hardy.

Rosette—known initially as Seibel 1000, it was one of the first French-American hybrids grown in New York State. Its vines are winter hardy and vigorous, but yield is moderate. Rosette makes a neutral wine of good quality; however, it lacks the deep color of some of the other hybrids and is usually used to make rosé wine. Its popularity has declined, and it is being replaced by other varieties.

Rougeon—used primarily as a teinturier and in blends because of its high color; however, it is not as intense a teinturier as Colobel. It is grown in the Finger Lakes Region where occasionally it is made as a varietal wine. Rougeon is an early midseason grape with erratic production—a large quantity of fruit one year, very little the next. Its vines are vigorous.

Note: Maurice Baco, Georges Couderc, M. Louis Seibel, and Seyve-Villard were among the early hybridizers in France. Later hybridizers included Kuhlmann, Landot, Johannes-Seyve, and Vidal.

French-American Hybrid Varieties for White Wine

Aurora—ripens early and is usually picked the first week of September in the Finger Lakes Region. The variety does well in cool climates and is suitable for regions with short growing seasons. The vines are vigorous and winter hardy. The wine has a delicate, fruity flavor with a recognizable aroma and some residual sugar. It has moderate alcohol, is well balanced, and is frequently blended.

Cayuga White—a New York State Agricultural Experiment Station cross of Seyval Blanc x Schuyler, which is a hybrid of Zinfandel and Ontario. Ontario is a cross of Winchell x Diamond. The vine is vigorous, moderately hardy, and disease resistant. The wine has a pleasant, apple-like fruity flavor and is well-balanced with a delicate aroma. It is medium-bodied with a pleasant aftertaste. It resembles Riesling.

Chardonel—a New York State Agricultural Experiment Station cross of Seyval Blanc x Chardonnay. Chardonel, which requires a longer than average growing season, is moderately winter hardy—more hardy than its Chardonnay parent. The variety ripens late, has a high yield, and retains good acid balance during ripening that makes it suitable for sparkling wine production. The wine is clean and crisp with a Chardonnay character. It is usually described as pleasant with a delicate, fruity flavor.

Horizon—a New York State Agricultural Experiment Station sister seedling of Cayuga White, a cross of Seyval Blanc x Schuyler. The variety, which is suitable for cool growing climates, outperforms Aurora and Cayuga White in the vineyard. The grapes have low acidity and a neutral flavor; the wine, which is suitable for blending, is rated above Aurora but below Cayuga White in quality.

Melody—a New York State Agricultural Experiment Station cross of Seyval Blanc x Geneva White 5, which is a cross of Pinot Blanc x Ontario. The vines are vigorous, productive, and moderately winter hardy, similar to Seyval Blanc. Melody grapes ripen in late midseason and produce wine with varietal character that has a neutral, fruity flavor with a hint of herbs and a flowery aroma.

Ravat 6 (Ravat Blanc)—a Chardonnay cross that is early ripening, disease sensitive, and difficult to grow. It has only moderate vigor, is not fully hardy, but is a heavy producer. It produces a high quality white Burgundy-type wine. Ravat 51 is Vignoles.

Rayon d'Or—a Seibel hybrid with a spicy, fruity taste that makes a pleasant still wine or sparkling wine. It is also used in blends. The variety ripens in early midseason and is capable of high sugar content in cool growing regions. Rayon d'Or wine has a notable aroma and a raspberry taste. The variety is disease resistant and moderately winter hardy. It is widely grown in France.

Seyval Blanc—has fairly vigorous, productive vines that are moderately winter hardy. Initially, the wine was dry, flinty, and made in the Chablis style. A wider range of styles is used today, including wine with a touch of sweetness. The wine is delicate with a notable bouquet and an excellent sugar-acid balance. It has an apple, citrus, or melon flavor. The wine is light-bodied to medium-bodied.

Traminette—a cross of Seyve 23.416 hybrid x Gewürztraminer. This productive variety ripens in late midseason and is moderately winter hardy—more hardy than its Gewürztraminer parent. Traminette has an average-length growing season. It produces wine of good body, superior quality, and excellent sugar-acid balance with the distinct bouquet and spicy character of Gewürztraminer. Wines are finished dry or semi-dry depending on preference.

Valvin Muscat—the ninth hybrid variety developed by the New York State Agricultural Experiment Station at Geneva is noted for its strong aroma. Wine made from it has the distinctive Muscat flavor and bouquet. This mid-season white wine grape is a cross of Couderc 299-35 (Muscat du Moulin) and Muscat Ottonel. It is moderately winter hardy.

Verdelet—has healthy vines of average vigor. The grapes are delicate and ripen in early midseason. The wine has a light aroma similar to Gewürztraminer, is well-balanced, and has good flavor. The variety has a pronounced, delicate bouquet and low acidity. It is sometimes aged in oak, after which it develops its own character imparted by the type of soil and climate. Verdelet is not widely planted in the Finger Lakes Region.

Vidal Blanc — a hybrid of the grape called St. Émilion in the Cognac district of France, Ugni Blanc in southern France, and Trebbiano in Tuscany in Italy, with Rayon d'Or, which is grown widely in the Loire Valley of France. The vines are vigorous, productive, disease resistant, and winter hardy. It is a late-ripening variety that grows well in cool climates. The wine has the pleasant character of the St. Émilion grape and a touch of spiciness and high alcohol content similar to Rayon d'Or. When fermented with German yeast, it resembles Riesling. It is high in acid, causing some residual sugar to be necessary to produce a balanced wine. It is suitable for producing late harvest wine and ice wine. The wine has a delicate flavor and bouquet with a fine aroma.

Vignoles — a cross of Seibel 6905 hybrid x Pinot Noir. It is also called Ravat 51. The vines are vigorous and moderately hardy but yield is low because the bunches are small. The grapes ripen in early midseason. The variety produces a clean, crisp, well-balanced wine capable of a subtle fineness with a distinct bouquet. Vignoles makes wine of high quality similar to Chablis; it is suitable for making champagne.

Villard Blanc — a late-ripening Seyve-Villard cross. The vine is vigorous, productive, and winter hardy but suitable for warm climates and long growing seasons. It was widely planted in southern France in the 1950s and 1960s because of its high yield. Villard Blanc produces a neutral, soft wine with good body that is meant to be consumed young. It is considered a good variety for blending.

Native-American Varieties (Vitis Labrusca)

Alexander—a native-American grape grown in colonial times in Lieutenant Governor John Penn's garden near Philadelphia. This red grape, later miscalled the Cape grape, was subsequently grown in Ohio and Indiana. It was winter hardy and withstood vine pests.

Catawba—was the foremost wine grape in the United States in the 1800s. The vine is vigorous and productive but not particularly hardy or disease resistant. This white variety ripens in midseason and is frequently used as a blend in champagne. Catawba wine is made in a wide diversity of styles. The variety has a high sugar content and high acidity. It has a clean taste and a spicy aroma. Its slightly tart flavor occurs occasionally as an aftertaste.

Clinton—a productive native-American red grape with a pronounced foxy taste that yields wines suitable for blending. The vine is usually cultivated for its rootstock. The vine was planted on the Italian border of Switzerland and across the border in Italy in response to the Phylloxera epidemic of the late 1800s.

Concord—the most widely grown variety in New York State. This red-grape variety is principally grown for juice and jelly. Its dominant foxy, grapy taste makes it unsuitable for wine, and its powerful aroma makes it undesirable for blending. The vine is hardy, vigorous, productive, and disease resistant. Concord ripens in midseason. It is occasionally used in making port and sherry.

Cynthiana—makes wine with intense color and a distinctive, pleasant aroma. It usually acquires bouquet with aging.

Delaware—is a highly regarded native white-wine grape with high sugar and only a moderate *Vitis labrusca* flavor. The vine is winter hardy but not particularly vigorous. Delaware grows in a wide range of soils. The variety produces a light, flowery-fruity, dry or semi-sweet wine with a delicious aroma. It is used in champagne blends. Delaware is widely planted in Japan, probably because its early ripening quality is suited to Japan's damp autumns.

Diamond—a white variety also known as Moore's Diamond. In 1873, Jacob Moore of Brighton, New York, crossed Concord with Iona to create Diamond. It make a fruity, piquant, high-quality wine.

Duchess—the vines are not vigorous and are only moderately productive. It is grown in well-drained, moderately fertile soils. This white-grape variety ripens in early mid season. Duchess is known for low acid and low sugar levels and therefore makes a low-alcohol wine. It is suitable for oak-aging and is one of the few whites to improve with age, for at least 10 years. It makes quality wine with a pleasant, delicate flavor with little *Vitis labrusca* in its aroma or character.

Elvira—the vine is healthy, vigorous, winter hardy, and moderately productive. This white-grape variety ripens early. The juice tends to be low sugar and high in acid, giving the resulting wine a sharp aroma and hard flavor. It is frequently used for blending.

Iona—an Eastern red-purple grape used for making white wine. It used to be widely grown in the Finger Lakes Region but is now uncommon. It was named for Iona Iasland in the Hudson River near Peekskill, where it was first grown.

Ives—is hardy, vigorous, productive, and disease resistant. The variety has deep red color and ripens in midseason. The wine has a strong foxy flavor that makes it too highly flavored and heavy for producing a varietal wine. It is used mainly for blending.

Isabella—the vine is healthy and vigorous with above average yield. It ripens in early midseason. It is rarely made into a varietal wine; it is usually blended. Occasionally, it is fermented on the skins to produce pink wine. The wine has a foxy, grapey flavor with a musky aroma. When pressed and fermented in white-wine style, the foxiness is reduced, and the resulting wine is pale, growing paler with age.

Niagara—the vine is very vigorous with extremely high production when grown in deep, rich soil. This white-grape variety ripens in early midseason. The wine is noticeably foxy and is usually made semi-sweet. Niagara is usually served very cold.

Native-American Varieties (Vitis Labrusca)

Norton—considered to be one of the better native-American wine grapes. It is sometimes blended with Ives.

Scuppernong—oldest and best-known variety of the Muscadine family grown widely in the Carolinas. A *Vitis rotundiflora* variety that produces intensely flavorful, distinctive sweet wines—red, white, or rosé. Wine has been made from its bronze-colored grapes since colonial times. Some well-structured, sweet dark golden wines are made from it.

Steuben—was developed at the New York State Agricultural Experiment Station and released in 1947. The blue-black grape produces a popular rosé. The wine is light, almost pink in color, and pleasant on the palate. It has a *Vitis labrusca* taste with a spicy fruitiness similar to Muscat.

Vergennes—a native-American grape variety, probably a *Vitis labrusca* seedling whose origin dates from Revolutionary War days that makes a slightly fruity, crisp, dry white wine. This grape was discovered in 1874 in the garden of William E. Green in Vergennes, Vermont, which was named for the Foreign Minister of France, Comte Charles de Vergennes, who, like Lafayette, was a staunch champion of the cause of American Independence.

Vincent—was developed by the Horticultural Research Institute of Ontario, Canada. The vines are vigorous, productive, and moderately winter hardy. The dark-blue grape produces deep-red-colored wine of high quality. It is widely used in blends in the Finger Lakes Region.

Glossary of Grape and Wine Terms

Acid—The natural fruit acid in grapes, e.g. tartaric acid.

Aftertaste—The sensation produced in the mouth and nasal passages after the wine has been swallowed.

Aging—The process by which wine develops character, mellowness, and smoothness.

Alcohol—Sugar is converted into alcohol and carbon dioxide by the fermentation process. Alcohol usually ranges from nine to 14 percent of the total volume in naturally fermented wine.

Amelioration—Adding water to grape juice to lower acid level.

Appellation Contrôlee—Short for Appellation d'Origine Controlee, France's prototype controlled appellation, a system of designating and controlling geographically based names of wine, selected spirits, and certain foodstuffs.

Aroma—The component of the fragrance of wine that originates from the grapes used.

Astringency—The quality in wine that causes the mouth to pucker. The level of astringency is dependent upon the amount of tannin absorbed into the juice from seeds and skins. Astringency usually lessens with age.

Auslese—From the German "selection." A sweet, usually more expensive white wine made by selecting, at the time of harvest, the especially ripe and perfect bunches, particularly those affected by the noble mold, botrytis.

Avinac—A fruit-flavored cordial.

Balance—A state in which acid, alcohol, fruit, sugar, and tannins are in harmony; none dominate the finished product.

Balling—A scale graduation for a hydrometer, or saccarometer, used to read the the specific gravity of liquids or their sugar content. Used interchangeably with *Brix*.

Barrel fermented—Fermentation in oak barrels instead of large stainless-steel tanks, imparting complex flavors and making the wine more full-bodied.

Berry—An individual grape.

Bloom—The blush on grapes that sometimes has the appearance of powder. It contains natural yeast.

Body—The feel of the wine in the mouth; described as light-bodied, medium-bodied, or full-bodied.

Bottle shock, previously called bottle sickness—The condition a wine finds itself in immediately after bottling, due to undergoing filtering and the bottling process. Wine should be "rested" for several weeks to several months after bottling to overcome this handling.

Botrytis cinerea—A mold known as "pourriture noble" ("noble rot") sucks moisture out of grapes on the vine, concentrates sugars, reduces acids, contributes flavor elements, and, depending on weather conditions, usually improves wine quality. Botrytised grapes are used to make French Sauternes.

Bouquet—The component of the fragrance of the wine that originates from the aging of the wine.

Breathe—Wine is allowed to breathe by uncorking it a period of time before it is served to allow any undesirable odors to escape.

Brix—A scale indicating the percentage of sugar in the grape juice before fermentation that is an indicator of the alcoholic content of the finished wine, also called *Balling*.

Brut—An indication of the dryness of champagne. From sweet to dry, champagne is categorized as extra dry, brut, or naturel.

Bulk process or *charmat process*—A method of producing inexpensive sparkling wine in vats or tanks instead of in the bottle.

Carbon dioxide—The gas generated during the fermentation process. It is also generated in making champagne by the fermentation-in-the-bottle process or *méthode champenoise*.

Carbonic maceration—The method of producing nouveau wines in Beaujolais that makes wine with a distinctive fragrance and taste. Whole grapes are placed in a container filled with carbon dioxide and allowed to stand for a week or more while the grapes are softened by natural enzymes. Fermentation begins from natural yeasts on the skins. The grapes are pressed, and the wine is fermented dry. Malolactic fermentation usually follows immediately.

Cassis—A dry pale gold wine made principally from the Ugni Blanc grape. Also, a syrup made from black currants, usually with 10-16% alcohol.

Chablis—The steely, dry white wine of the most northern vineyards of Burgundy in northeast France, named for the village—made from Chardonnay grapes like all fine white Burgundy. In North America and Australia, the name Chablis is used to describe a dry white wine made with no specific grape variety.

Chapitalization—Addition of sugar to sugar-deficient musts—never to the wine—to ensure that the wine's alcoholic content will be commensurate with its other qualities. Used discreetly, it may bring the alcohol into better balance with the other constituents of the wine.

Character—Used to describe a wine that possesses the bouquet, color, and taste of a quality wine.

Clos—French word for an enclosed vineyard.

Cluster-thinning—The process of trimming excess clusters from the vine to create fewer and larger grape clusters. It is also a technique used to prevent vines from overbearing.

Cold duck—a sparkling wine, usually with a *Vitis labrusca* taste, is made in the United States and Canada by blending red and white wines.

Cold stabilization—Chilling wine to 30° F to 40° F to precipitate out potassium bitartrate from the fermenting wine.

Corked or *Corky*—An unpleasant smell and taste caused by a bad cork.

Cream of tartar—The white crystalline deposit resulting from cold stabilization of fermenting wine. It is also called potassium bitartrate.

Cru—French word for growth. A type of classification that refers to specific vineyards of quality.
Cuvée—A blend of wine prepared for the production of champagne.

Decant—To pour wine carefully from a bottle in which sediment has been deposited into a decanter or carafe to prepare the wine for serving.

Delicate—Used to describe a wine, usually a white wine, with a light, subtle flavor. The fragile flavor can be overwhelmed by full-flavored food.

Demi-sec—"Half-dry," but when applied to Champagne and sparkling wines means "sweet."

Doux—"Sweet." Vin doux is wine possessing a sweetness from being only partially fermented. Another adjective, "liguoreux," is applied to naturally sweet wines, such as the great Sauternes, or the finer wines of Anjou.

Dry—The opposite of sweet; that is, lacking in sugar. A dry wine is one in which all of the fermentable sugars have been consumed by the fermentation process.

Enologist—Winemaker.

Enology—The science of winemaking from harvesting the grapes to bottling the wine.

Enophile—One who appreciates wine. A lover of wine.

Estate bottled—Indicates that the wine was produced and bottled on the property on which the grapes were grown.

Fermentation—The anaerobic (oxygen-free) process by which sugar in the presence of an active yeast is broken down into alcohol and carbon dioxide.

Fermentation lock—A device filled with water that allows the carbon dioxide generated during the fermentation process to escape while preventing air (and therefore oxygen) from entering the wine.

Filtering—The process of clarifying wine by using filters.

Fining—The process of clarifying wine with a fining agent, e.g. Bentonite, during the winemaking process.

Finish—Flavors that remain in the mouth after swallowing wine.

Flowery—A word used to describe a wine with a bouquet that smells of fruit blossoms.

Fortified wine—Wine to which brandy had been added to raise the alcohol content above 18 percent, e.g. Madeira, Marsala, Port, and Sherry.

Foxiness—The "grapy" aroma and taste of most native-American grapes, particularly Concord, but also to some extent Niagara, Catawba, Isabella, and others.

Free-run juice—Grape juice that flows from the press before pressure is applied. It is considered to be of higher quality than juice obtained after pressure is applied.

Fruit wine—Wine made from fruit other than grapes, e.g. apples, apricots, blackberries, boysenberries, cherries, cranberries, peaches, pears, raspberries, or strawberries.

Generic wine—A wine with definite type characteristics, frequently associated with a geographic area. Examples are Burgundy, Champagne, Port, Rhine Wine, and Sherry.

Grappa—A pomace brandy made in Italy. It is called Marc in France.

Grow Tubes—Pale blue plastic tubing placed over the bases of young vines to protect them from being eaten by small animals, such as groundhogs and racoons.

Herbaceous—Herb flavor in wine such as Sauvignon Blanc and Maréchal Foch as well as other varieties.

Hybrid—A grape variety created by crossing two or more species, such as French-American hybrids developed by crossing European *(Vitis vinifera)* varieties with native-American varieties, e.g. *Vitis labrusca* or *Vitis riparia.*

Hydrometer—A device used in measuring the density of liquids. It is used to determine the Brix or Balling, the percent of sugar, of juice or wine.

Kabinett—A German term, especially in the Reingau district, to designate a superior grade or special reserve of natural, that is, unsugared, wine that is usually estate-bottled. Kabinett wines were usually those put aside for the vineyard owner's own use.

Late harvest—Grapes picked very ripe or overripe when they have a high concentration of sugar.

Lees—Sediment generated by the fermentation process that precipitates to the bottom of the carboy or tank.

Legs—The rills or rivulets of wine that flow down the side of the wine glass after swirling the wine. Legs, a result of ethyl alcohol after sugar-alcohol fermentation, was once thought to be due to glycerin, or glycerol, which donates some of the sweetness and smoothness to a wine. Legs, particularly noticeable in Sauternes, are an indication of body.

Liquoreux—Used in French to describe a sweet, luscious with wine that has retained, without fortification, a good deal of natural grape sugar.

Malic acid—Malic acid contributes to the tartness of grapes and wine. It is second in importance to tartaric acid in the "total acidity" of must and wine.

Malolactic fermentation—A secondary fermentation that converts harsher malic acid into softer lactic acid in the finished wine. It usually increases wine complexity but reduces fruitiness. It can reduce the total acidity of the wine by as much as one third.

Mead—Honey wine, occasionally blended with fruit wine.

Mellow—A term used to describe a soft wine, e.g. Merlot.

Meritage wine—Wine made from grape varieties used in Bordeaux wine, e.g. Cabernet Sauvignon, Cabernet Franc, Merlot, Malbec.

Méthode champenoise—The process of making champagne in which the secondary fermentation that produces the bubbles occurs within the bottle.

Microclimate—The environment of the individual vine, influenced by pruning, shoot thinning, vine training, trellising, and leaf removal. Air circulation and exposure to sunlight are critical factors.

Mesoclimate—The environment within the vineyard: e.g. elevation, angle of the slope, distance from the nearest body of water.

Macroclimate—the environment of the region within which the vineyard is located, including the range of temperatures and the length of the growing season.

Must—Unfermented grape juice with pulp.

Nose—The way a wine smells. A term used to describe the aroma of the grape and the bouquet of the wine. Wine having a pleasant aroma and bouquet is said to have a good nose.

Oak aging—The quality of some wine, for example, full-bodied red wine and white wine such as Chardonnay, is improved by the extract and tannin added by aging in oak barrels. European oak is usually from France, Austria, or Yugoslavia. American oak, which imparts less extract and tannin than European oak, is grown in eastern U.S., and as far west as Texas.

Oidium—Also called powdery mildew, a fungus that attacks the leaves, shoots, and tendrils of the vine. Sulphur was an early spray material used to prevent powdery mildew during the growing season.

Oxidation—A change in wine, usually an undesirable change, due to contact with air. Oxidized white wine appears brownish.

Pedicels—Grapes are attached to the stem of their cluster by pedicels, through which they receive nourishment from the vine.

Perfume—The bouquet of wine.

Petioles—Thin stems between the grape leaves and the grapevine.

pH—The level of a wine's acidity. The desirable pH range for dry table wine is 3.2 to 3.6. If acidity is higher, the wine will taste harsh or green.

Phylloxera—An insect that attacks the soft, fleshy roots of the *Vitis vinifera* grape varieties. In the 19th century, thousands of European vineyards were destroyed by this root louse. By grafting European vines onto the hardy, resistant rootstock of native-American grapes, European vineyards were successfully replanted, reviving the wine economy.

Pomace—The residue, seeds and skins, from the pressing process.

Potassium bitartrate (cream of tartar)—a salt of tartaric acid that precipitates as crystals in the fermenter or bottle, lowering the wine's acidity.

Press—Equipment that applies pressure to harvested grapes to force out juice.

Primary fermentation—The initial, violent fermentation during which about two-thirds of the sugar in the must is converted into alcohol by the yeast.

Racking—Transferring the fermenting juice from one container to another. When using small containers, it is done with a syphon.

Reserve—Indicates wines that the winery considers special. Also called Private Reserve, Proprietor's Reserve, and Special Reserve. The term is not regulated.

Residual sugar—The sugar level in the wine after fermentation is complete.

Resveratrol—A antioxident that occurs naturally in grapes to protect them against fungal infections. Its high concentration in grape skin reduces the risk of cardiovascular disease.

Riddling—The process of rotating bottles of ferment-in-the-bottle champagne a one-fourth, one-sixth, or one-eighth turn to move the sediment into the neck of the bottle so that it will form into a plug that can be disgorged.

Secondary fermentation—The slower, anaerobic (oxygen-free) fermentation that reduces sugar left after primary fermentation to alcohol.

Sec—A French word for dry.

Sediment—The solid particles deposited in the bottom of a bottle during aging, particularly in red wine.

Sensory qualities of wine—Clarity, color, odor, and taste are determined by winemaking practices, such as racking, addition of sulfur dioxide, fining, cold stabilizing, filtering, etc.

Sommelier—French for "wine steward." The individual in charge of wine service from the cellar to the dining room.

Sorbic acid—Sorbic acid or its potassium salt is used in the fermentation of some sweet wines to deter yeast growth.

Spatlese—German wine term, which means "late harvest" or "late picking." Spatlese wine is full-bodied, riper, and a trace sweeter than other wines of the same vineyard and the same year,

Still wine—Non-sparkling table wine.

Sulfites—The presence of sulfur dioxide must be noted on the label; some people are allergic to it. Sulfites are used to preserve freshness in fruit and vegetables. Also, they are a natural by-product of the fermentation process.

Sur lies—Wine aged sur lies is kept in contact with the dead yeast cells and other sediment after fermentation has been completed. The practice has become common in making Chardonnay and is occasionally used for Sauvignon Blanc. The intent with sur lies aging is that a complex quality, a roasted-grain and toasty character, will be added to the wine.

Table wine—White, pink, or red still wine that is naturally fermented. It is usually consumed with food. It contains from seven to 14 percent alcohol.

Tannin—A substance present in grape stems, skins, and seeds. It promotes a clean, healthy fermentation, aids in stabilizing the color of red wine, and adds astringency to wine. Tannin contributes to the "body" of wine.

Tartaric acid—The major grape acid. Tartaric acid and its salts usually provide over half the total acidity of musts and wines.

Teinturier—A grape variety used in a blend to add color to the wine.

Terroir—A French word that literally means soil or earth but has connotations for vintners due to the influence of soil on the wine produced from grapes grown on it. In its extreme, certain wines produced on heavy soil have a characteristic earthy flavor, known in France as gout de terroir.

Toasty—Sometimes used to describe the bouquet and taste of wine aged in oak.

Total phenols—Phenols in wine include red pigments, tannins (the most important phenol), and similar substances.

Trockenbeerenauslese—Literally, "dried-berry-selected" in the German language, that is, wine made from a selection (auslese) of individually picked grapes (beeren) that have been left on the vine until so ripe as to be practically dry (trocken) or raisened. Because extremely small quantities of grapes are hand-selected, the wine is expensive.

Varietal wine—A wine named for the principal grape variety from which it is made. It has the characteristic flavor and aroma of the grape variety for which it is named.

Véraison—The French word for the turning point in the vine's growth in early August when the green bunches begin to change color and ripen. The grapes have attained almost full size and most of their natural fruit acidity.

Vertical—A bottle of wine for every year it was made at a winery.

Viticulture—The process of grape growing, winemaking, and marketing wine.

Vinification—The process of converting grapes into wine by fermentation.

Vintage—The year in which the grapes were harvested and fermentation was begun.

Vintner—A wine merchant. One who makes wine.

Viticulture—grape growing.

Wine Thief—A device used to obtain a wine sample for tasting or testing from a carboy, barrel, or vat. It is usually a glass tube open at both ends with a bulb at one end.